East Asia Modern

East Asia Modern

Shaping the Contemporary City

Peter G. Rowe

REAKTION BOOKS

To Lauretta, my travelling and other companion in life

Published by Reaktion Books Ltd
33 Great Sutton Street, London EC1V ODX, UK

www.reaktionbooks.co.uk

First published 2005
Transferred to digital printing 2007
Copyright © Peter G. Rowe 2005

Printed and bound by the University of Chicago Press

British Library Cataloguing in Publication Data
Rowe, Peter G.
    East Asia modern: shaping the contemporary city
    1. Cities and towns – East Asia – Growth 2. Cities and towns
    – East Asia – History – 20th century
    I. Title
    307.7'64'095'0904

ISBN 978 1 86189 249 2

Contents

1 Introduction 7
2 Relationships and Urbanizing Trajectories 11
3 Outside Influences and Urban Patterns 45
4 Urban Forms and Local Expressions 93
5 Urban Experience and Shaping the Space
  of a Time 158

References 201
Bibliography 212
Acknowledgements 217
Photo Acknowledgements 218
Index 219

one
Introduction

When one thinks of contemporary urbanism in East Asia, certain images leap to mind. Cities are big in both geographical coverage and numbers of inhabitants, and crowded and dense in their living patterns. In fact, of the top twenty cities in the world, by population size, eight are in East Asia, with Tokyo at the top with around 30 million inhabitants, and, of the top ten densest cities, six are in the region, headed by Hong Kong with 28,405 people per square kilometre and spot densities of 2,500 people per hectare.[1] Urban development is rapid and, in some places, explosive, with five of the top ten fastest growing cities located in East Asia. The pace of daily life is quick, with people scrambling to get ahead and caught up in the process of what is loosely described as globalization. Statistical estimates of economic growth, concentrated in urban areas over comparable recent periods, show rates equal to or close to double digits of Gross Domestic Product (GDP) in most places, well in excess of comparable rates in Europe or the United States, and working hours for many are both long and laborious.

Urban landscapes are often chaotic, suffused with a cacophony of sounds and blaring images. The shape of new buildings and other feats of engineering compete with each other for the tallest structure, the largest port, the biggest airport, the fastest railway and the longest bridge. Indeed, in all of these categories, achievements in East Asia are at or near the top, with the Taipei 101 building; the Jurong port in Singapore and emerging rivals in China; Chek Lap Kok airport in Hong Kong; the MAGLEV railway in Pudong, Shanghai, and the enormous spans reached in southern Japan. Then, too, there is the exotic otherness of the Orient, often regarded from within and without with a certain nostalgia for the past and for tradition. Amid the hurly burly of contemporary life and the towering structures that line major streets, it is remarkable how, within a few steps, one can enter the tranquillity of a rural village-like setting, via the lanes and alleys of such places as inner-city Beijing, or Tokyo. Juxtapositions of poverty and wealth confront local inhabitant and visitor alike, although Tokyo and Singapore have two of the world's highest GDPs per capita, while China remains poor, and sometimes the mind's eye may wander off towards matters of governance and authoritarian regimes, rampant corruption and outwardly murky political dealings.

All these images, though differently rendered in one place from another, or more or less present in one place over another, represent facets of modernization that either sprang up or evolved and, by now, have overtaken many, if not most, East Asian cities. Each city also has its own local history, different manners of progressing forward and different trajectories of modernization. Nevertheless, there is a suspicion that the shaping of urban space is dictated, as much as anything, by the time, era and intense period of its construction – a particular nexus in the flux of recognized demands coupled with available technical, material and informational flows, especially in a more fluid global environment.

Indeed, what prompted the writing of this book, after some fifteen years of working in, or on, the region in various educational, consulting and advisory capacities, was a growing realization that many aspects of contemporary East Asian urbanization seemed to cohere, despite substantial cross-national differences and distinct local identities, raising questions as to why. Moreover, when looked at from the perspective of Western experience with modernization and urbanization many aspects appeared to be the same, whereas others, especially those tied up with deeper cultural and core values, did not, raising the intriguing prospect of whether East Asian cities are on a different path.

Then, too, there was a fascination with the sheer scale, rate and bold newness of modernization and consequent changes to built environments, which appeared to be pushing and reshaping accepted understandings of modern urbanization. Partly this seemed to be due to the 'all at once' pattern of development compared to a sequential unfolding more common in the West, and partly to ready borrowing of international approaches to urbanization, usually originating in the West, but at a time when the potency of these borrowings was at an all-time high, at least with regard to their technological capacities for change. Certainly, the manner of borrowing varied from place to place in East Asia, ranging from episodic adoption, reaction and indigenization in Japan, to a more compressed adoption with local characteristics, now going on in China. However, overall, it appeared to lead inexorably in the same direction, towards thoroughgoing contemporary transformation of urban circumstances.

Furthermore, it seemed that there might be positive lessons to be learned from the region, despite some less than ideal living circumstances and unsightly results. For one, cities in East Asia offer potential models of workable density at new levels and scales of building. For another, old and new ways of making cities seem frequently to be blended together, often with unusual yet beguiling results. More theoretically, the influence of time, or timing, on urban space and how a history turns, or becomes written on an urban landscape, offers the potential for new insights into contemporary urban phenomena. Finally, at this time East Asian urbanism appears to be moving into, or through in some cases, a turning point in direction, raising questions about whether the current differences will persist, or whether recent developments are just a phase in modernization that will eventually become more reconcilable with other outcomes and experiences.

Indeed, underlying all these observations and conjectures, two broad questions emerge. First, how well, in fact, do cities in this region conform to concepts of modernization to be found elsewhere in the world and particularly in the developed West? Second, to what extent might they also collectively describe a regional urban modernity that is different in kind, as well as degree, from other modern cities? Responses to both questions seem likely to be a matter of perspective, the focal length of the lens being used. However, as elsewhere in the world, it is precisely where one cone of vision becomes blurred by another that is of importance. After all, people invariably see the same world differently from high altitude, in a helicopter, from a car, or on foot.

Throughout the text, East Asia, as a region, conforms to a standard scholarly and widely held definition: China, Hong Kong, Japan, Korea, Taiwan and Singapore. The underlying logic for this definition is the shared Confucian base of culture among these nations, quite apart from more recent manifestations of other kinds of beliefs and socio-political orientations. Although, more strictly speaking, located in South-East Asia, Singapore conforms to this logic and therefore is included in East Asia. Also of significance in grouping these nations together is the time of their contemporary modern emergence. Although this varies from Japan, well on its way to modernization by the 1930s, to China, which has only recently burst on to the modern scene, the so-called East Asian miracle, at least in economic terms, is usually associated with the later twentieth century up to and including the present. In the case of Korea, only the Republic of Korea (South Korea) will be discussed in any detail, precisely because of its recent modernization, in sharp contrast to the isolation and developmental backwardness of the North. Other countries in South-East Asia, like the Philippines, Indonesia, Malaysia, Vietnam and Thailand, have yet to emerge so strongly on the world scene, have substantially different historico-cultural backgrounds, and confront different sets of social and political issues, as well as stages in a modern development process.

Primarily, discussion will focus on seven major cities in East Asia: Tokyo, Seoul, Beijing, Shanghai, Hong Kong, Taipei and Singapore. More than others, these cities have come to epitomize the East Asian development phenomenon and contemporary urbanization, certainly from the standpoint of outside perceptions, as well as being seen at the forefront of modernization internally. They are all large cities within their national context; some, like Seoul, accounting for nearly one third of their nation's urban population. They dominate national thinking and agendas about urbanization. Certainly there are or have been other cities of note, some of which will be discussed in passing. For example, Guangzhou and Shenzhen probably leap to mind because of their early contributions to China's recent modernization. Osaka is another big city in Japan, but it is Tokyo that sets the pace, so much so that Osaka-based corporations generally have their titular headquarters there, and nowadays what happens in Beijing and in Shanghai has a similar impact on urbanization and urban-architectural expression in China.

Following the analogy of lenses with different focal lengths, the second chapter of this book looks down, as it were, from afar, scrutinizing the extent to which, in aggregate, East Asia cities appear to conform to broad socio-economic relationships that elsewhere have been used to define modernization. Trends in key areas are discussed, as well as qualities of life, which have primarily been improving, often at rapid rates. Consistent peculiarities of East Asia's urban landscapes are also identified, to be taken up principally in chapter Four. Returning to broad socio-economic and political dimensions, current and likely future dilemmas are discussed, together with several scenarios outlining what might transpire. Chapter Three essentially chronicles developments in urbanization among the seven primary cities, from pre-modern beginnings to the present, before taking a somewhat lower-altitude view – returning to the lens analogy – overlooking the layout of cities through characteristics of general plans, the spatial orthodoxies they seem to represent, and the guidance that was given, largely from those in power. Chapter Four is more of a vehicular and pedestrian tour of cities, focusing on those expressive forms of urbanization and, ultimately, architecture, that both singularly and collectively give immediate presence to East Asian cities. Finally, discussion in chapter Five spirals back out again, concentrating on a temporal view of East Asian urban experience, especially in contrast to the West, and how East Asian urbanization might well be regarded as different in kind, not just in degree. Future prospects are also outlined, with speculation on where the current drift in direction might be leading.

two

Relationships
and Urbanizing Trajectories

Modernization is commonly understood through an ensemble of interrelated characteristics. Chief among them is industrialization, or the conversion of raw materials into marketable manufactured products and sources of power and propulsion, along with tertiary functions to deal with the mass distribution and information transactions involved. Beginning in earnest during the early nineteenth century in Britain, this phenomenon quickly appeared in other Western nations, while also going through several phases of continued development and deployment. One seemingly inevitable outcome of industrialization was urbanization, as workers migrated and located close to centres of manufacturing, accompanied by other necessary and related functions. Over time, this process of settlement was transformed by increasing levels of access and personal mobility. However, in the beginning it resulted in relatively dense urban environments, frequent overcrowding and poor public health conditions.

Another seemingly inevitable outcome of modernization was the specialization of labour and other human activity, together with considerable diversification of occupational opportunities within society. By and large, people moved off the land, in search of new opportunities in urban areas. Consequently agriculture was superseded in importance as a source of employment by industry and, ultimately, by other service enterprises. Fortunately for many, at least over time, modernization also provided significant improvements in general education, health, wealth and relative standards of living. Fetid slums in places like New York, London and Paris, dating from the nineteenth and early twentieth centuries, were transformed into the relatively clean, well-functioning and modern urban environments of today. Social mobility also increased with a progressive erosion of class barriers and occupational distinctions in many places, and a steadily improving capacity for personal movement from one locale to another. Modernization, in short, became defined in a large part by the combined processes of industrialization, urbanization, labour diversification, social mobility and, as a result, substantially improved material standards of living.

Widely Accepted Relationships

Implicit in what has become a widely accepted and dominant version of modernization are several relationships between one social phenomenon and another. Often there appears to be a strong tie, for instance, between modernization and Western intellectual, social-economic and political practices.[1] After all, modernization, as we have understood it since the eighteenth century, has been a phenomenon closely associated with the West in two distinct forms, at least for about a 75-year period in the twentieth century, before the demise of the Soviet Union and its satellite bloc. Setting aside the Soviet model, although many modern traits still apply, modernization has typically brought with it the rule of law, social pluralism and a reliance on representative bodies for governance. There have been collective manifestations of constitutionalism and especially the protection of property and personal rights. Groups have emerged in society, not based upon blood relations or marriage, but frequently in the form of voluntary associations, professional classes and guilds of various kinds and, ultimately, as civil society. In many Western places, individualism, or the tradition of individual rights and liberties, has risen, at least since the fourteenth and fifteenth centuries and certainly since the Franco-American revolutions of the late eighteenth century. Consequently, the separation of spiritual and temporal authority in many places is almost absolute, in spite of a clear capacity for religious observance. If anything, in the interaction among different ideologies and preferences for representation and self-rule, liberal democracy and its institutional components, the Soviet model notwithstanding, emerged as a widespread and consistently emulated practice.

Moreover, the overwhelmingly instrumental quality of this form of social and political organization, especially the relatively diversified and specialized character of its institutional arrangements, has contributed considerably to the process of modernization. Markets and other economic devices, for example, have been allowed to form without much interference. In many instances, they have been mandated or actively promoted. Technological advancement has blossomed under widespread individual intellectual freedom and economically based competition for ideas, or under state initiative. In addition, human capital, regardless of prior background or social class, has been allowed and, again, even actively guided to form along meritocratic lines, thus maximizing the human effort societies can bring to bear on important issues and tasks. For all intents and purposes, post-Enlightenment modernization appear to have coincided. In order to modernize it appears that one must first Westernize or, more pointedly, by becoming modernized one also becomes more thoroughly Westernized.

Another persistent relationship is the close tie between modernization and urbanization, through industrialization in both its secondary and tertiary manifestations. As we have seen, in the past industrialization and modernization have been axiomatically linked. Without an increasing capacity to perform work efficiently, to produce excess goods and services and generally to increase the value added to production, material progress could not be made in society, or at anything like the same rate. In fact, what might be termed a technological orientation and imperative was implanted in society early on during several industrial revolutions, and has served as a guiding force for much of the modernization that has occurred since. The pervasive equation of technical progress equalling social progress, although coming under frequent attack on grounds of social injustice, alienation and despoiling of future social prospects, is by now a familiar trend and is largely synonymous with the congruence between modernization and continuing industrialization, characterized by shifts in the preponderance of employment, if not monetary value, from the secondary or manufacturing sector to the tertiary or service sector. In the United States, for instance, between 1950 and 2000 secondary production declined by about 33 per cent, while tertiary production rose by around 57 per cent.[2] Underlying this shift were higher degrees of modernization and labour productivity in secondary industry and a proliferation and expansion of needs and markets, especially for services, as incomes grew and as requirements for transactions in information increased substantially.

Certain patterns of spatial organization seemed to be required in order for industrialization to take place effectively and efficiently. Simply put, until radical improvements in transportation took place, industries needed to be located close to requisite raw materials and sources of power. The labour force, working largely in manufacturing industries, was in contrast generally regarded as footloose and attracted towards the industries as demands for production increased. Constrained by poor transportation, workers resided close to industries, frequently within walking distance. Other commercial trades, wholesaling and retail outlets located nearby, and cities, at least as they were understood in the nineteenth century, began to emerge and develop in a compact manner. Even with a shift from manufacturing to managerial and other service activities, strong centres were established in what is often referred to as the 'monocentric model' of the city, with a dominant industrial and commercial centre at its core and residential, commercial and other developments spreading out in more or less concentric rings of declining density. Variants of this urban pattern materialized, depending upon local geography, land-use regulation, specific historical circumstances, and so on. Public regulation tended to separate any tendency for uses to mix and aggregate together across broad functional lines, in order to eliminate the incidence of public nuisances like noise and air pollution, and generally to safeguard the public health, safety and welfare of society. Nevertheless, urbanization was strongly associated spatially with industrialization and, therefore, with modernization.

As transportation improved and horizontal mobility increased, adjustments were made in the proximity of industry and other forms of employment to their labour forces and sources of raw materials and power. Residential communities could now be developed further away from employment centres, taking advantage of cheaper land, abundant fresh air and other amenities. In many places suburbia blossomed, not as an inferior environment, as it was originally outside the medieval city wall, but as a desirable place to live. Further adjustments in transportation accessibility and the increasingly metropolitan scope of most urban activities produced a 'polycentric model' for the spatial distribution of urban functions, with several commercial and other employment centres, linked by a vastly improved roadway system, and with residential developments in between.[3]

Responding to increased competition for labour, employers now located their establishments closer to specific residential areas in the hopes of attracting the best talent and skill. Indeed, in a national context, particular regions began to compete with each other for population, as the quality of the physical work environment and the relative amenity of urban areas became increasingly important considerations. Nevertheless, aggregation and agglomeration of economic activities continued, now on a broad metropolitan basis. Today, even with vast improvements in telecommunications and transportation, the need for physical proximity in many sectors of economic production continues to be high.[4] Indeed, modernization, now propelled mainly by a service industry, also expanding in many parts of the developed world, can result in

1
Improved horizontal mobility: heavy rail in Singapore. 1994.

even higher degrees of urbanization. This is so much the case that varying degrees of development and, therefore, of modernization, are often equated not only with the proportion of a national population that is urban compared to that which remains rural, but to the sectoral shifts that have occurred between primary, secondary and tertiary forms of production. In the United States, for example, the proportion of people living in what are classified as urban areas stands at over 77 per cent, with 1.4 per cent, 21.9 per cent and 76.7

per cent respectively in the three sectors of production.[5] In Australia, another modern although more sparsely populated country, the proportion of urban population is as high as 87 per cent, with a 7.8 per cent, 20.4 per cent and 71.8 per cent distribution among the three sectors.[6]

A third relationship implicit in the dominant version of modernization, or so many believe, is the strong tendency towards a universalization of cultural norms and values. In short, communities become more similar as they modernize and acquire standardized practices of production and service delivery, as well as in their independence from local geography. Furthermore, with increased contact between towns and cities because of trade, other productive relations, and wholesale consumption of mass media, the assumption is that differences between one place and another tend to erode. Older reflections of inherently different regional circumstances, ethnicity and religious persuasion give way to the conduct of daily life with essentially the same activities, observances and rhythms, and a shape and appearance to communities that is much the same, regardless of where they are in the world. Although overstated, this is a widely expected outcome of modernization, and can certainly be observed in the extraordinary similarity between modern residential developments from, say, the 1960s and '70s in the outskirts of the historic cores of cities as otherwise disparate as Istanbul in Turkey, Lyon in France and Buenos Aires in Argentina.

One phenomenon, which has recently strongly reinforced the equating of modernization with the formation of universal cultural norms and practices, is the commonly referred to globalization of many aspects of daily life. Although in terms of world trade, if not origins and destinations, volumes are only now climbing back to levels comparable to those in the late nineteenth and early twentieth centuries, vastly increased and diversified capacities for communication, and widespread use of telematics, have begun to turn the world into a virtual global village.[7] At the flick of a switch you can be in Beijing or in Rome over the Internet, and in contact with strangers on the other side of the world. Just as pervasively, increasing levels of privatization – at least over the past twenty years – and correspondingly dramatic expansions in methods for investing capital, have also transgressed traditional state boundaries. Furthermore, competition for mobile global capital has become increasingly fierce, again if only in relatively recent times, allowing for a far freer and more widespread imposition of outside requirements and performance stipulations.

One seemingly obvious outcome is the sameness of commercial environments in many parts of the world. Merchandizing has become standardized, or so the argument goes, as transnational companies impose marketing strategies and 'branding', successful in one place, on another, often with only minor modifications.[8] Corporate office environments often exude a comfortable familiarity to the employees and clients of multinational companies, no matter where they are in the world. The similarities between them also assuage the fears of fickle investors, by conveying the appearance of something well known and predictable. Moreover, this common look seems to form an integral part of the global marketing of goods and especially services, requiring at least some modicum of consistency in the image being projected. Financial institutions in particular – among the recent stimulators of globalization – tend to adhere strongly to this type of projection of universal messages about state-of-the-art performance. One often accepted consequence of continuing modernization and globalization appears to be a levelling of the spatial distinctions between one place and another or, more properly, between one recently constructed environment and another.

In stricter urban-architectural terms, at the risk of caricature, one set of practices that has led to a substantial breakdown in the distinctions between places is 'modernism' – loosely framed as an aesthetic orthodoxy – and especially its inherent transcultural assertions. For one thing, there is the inherent correspondence between form and function; logically, if this function happens to be the same in one part of the world as another, the resulting architectural form will probably be similar. Small wonder, then, that office and other commercial environments in various parts of the world are alike, under the pressures of relatively intense use of well-equipped yet economical space and central locations requiring efficient deployment of that space. For another, an increasing reliance on internationally available building practices as an emerging industry standard tends to ensure similar results, quite apart from the needs of unified corporate expressions that may reach across the globe. Furthermore, the technological advancement of building materials and mechanical systems, another orientation of a modernist perspective, invariably brings with it an independence from local climate and other geographical circumstances, as well as from local building materials, all of which formerly shaped local architectural expressions quite strongly. In short, rising expectations with regard to building quality, material integrity and technological performance – all strongly endorsed by a modernist outlook – as well as similarities in building programmes that substantially transcend in both size and scope traditional ways of building, have led inexorably to a sameness in contemporary built environments throughout the world, save, perhaps, for the superficial decoration and adornment of structures to suit the tastes of patrons, or to conform to expressive norms of a local culture.

Broad Modernizing Trends

Until comparatively recently, modernization occurred mainly in Western nations and, to a lesser extent, in the states of what was once the Soviet Union. Japan was a conspicuous exception in East Asia, modernizing from the onset of the Meiji Restoration in 1868, and particularly before and after World War II. Indeed, if the development of an urban rail and subway system is any indication, Tokyo was well and truly on its way to modernization as early as the 1920s, in this respect alongside only a few cities in the well-developed West. By the 1970s, however, this global picture had begun to change dramatically. The so-called Asian Tigers of Singapore, Hong Kong, Korea and Taiwan suddenly emerged on the world scene, to be followed by China in the late 1980s and '90s, with relatively sustained annual economic growth rates at or near 10 per cent of GDP, and larger and larger market shares of manufactured goods and services.[9]

Historically, such was the fluctuation of fortunes that industrialization – the engine of modernization – in Western Europe, the United States and the British colonies of Canada, Australia and New Zealand pushed their combined share of world income from 25 per cent in 1820 at the outset of the Industrial Revolution to 56 per cent by 1950, with only modest increases in population, slightly above 15 per cent of the world total. This compares to a more dramatic decline in Asia, over the same period, from 58 per cent of world income to 19 per cent, with 66 per cent of the world's population, followed by an accelerating rise since 1950 to over 35 per cent of world income. Much of this recent development has occurred in East Asia.[10] While it took Britain and the United States 58 and 47 years, respectively, to double their per capita output, it has taken Japan 33 years and South Korea and China only 11 and 10.[11] According to many economists, though not all, this shift is likely to continue, with Asia and especially East Asia re-emerging in the first part of the twenty-first century with most of the world's economic activity.

As elsewhere in the world, economic growth rates as measured by Gross Domestic Product have been uneven in East Asia, although often remarkably high. In Japan, for instance, the period between 1955 and 1975 and especially the 1960s saw sustained growth at or around 10 per cent per annum, followed by a further boom in the late 1980s at around 5 per cent per annum. South Korea, Taiwan, Singapore and Hong Kong followed Japan into double digits during the second half of the 1960s and into the '70s, with Hong Kong's high rates of expansion lasting, almost without interruption, into the early 1990s. China's economic production accelerated almost immediately after its historic opening to the outside world in 1978, reaching rates of increase in excess of 12 to 15 per cent annually until the late 1990s.[12] All has not been smooth sailing, however, as Japan began to feel the detrimental effects of an 'economic bubble', in the early 1990s, inflated among other things by overspeculation on real estate, miring it in economic recession and substantial losses in personal wealth, from which it has shown few signs of extricating itself. Although acting differently, the South-East Asian currency crisis of 1997 also hit economic production rates in many parts of East Asia, and even China, buffered through a combination of stimulated internal demand, foreign investment and exports, slowed in economic production from earlier meteoric rises.[13] Nevertheless, in the decade between 1990 and 2000, the People's Republic still posted increases in economic income of 9.6 per cent, followed by Singapore with 7.8 per cent, South Korea with 6.4 per cent, Taiwan with 6.1 per cent and Hong Kong with 4.3 per cent. Only Japan fell below a comparable rate for the United States of 3.1 per cent, at 1.8 per cent.[14]

Advances in economic output per capita, a better measure of relative economic prosperity, have also been both startling and sustained throughout East Asia since World War II. In South Korea, for instance, from poverty-stricken conditions in the aftermath of the Korean War in 1953, annual Gross Domestic Product per capita – measured as purchasing power parity in 1990 US dollars – rose from minuscule levels to a respectable $17,300 in 2000, at an annual rate of over 9 per cent. This advance is followed by Taiwan at a gross rate of over 8 per cent since 1950, for a current GDP per capita, again at purchasing power parity in 1990 US dollars, of around $22,700, and by three other nations of the group, at or near the extremes of the economic spectrum, with China at around 6 per cent, although much higher recently, for a GDP per capita of $3,920 – China is, after all, still a poor country – and Hong Kong, with a similar annual advance since 1965, standing at $25,990 GDP per capita, and Japan – the second or third largest economy in the world – advancing steadily, also from relatively poor circumstances in 1950, to $27,080 GDP per capita, close to the United States at $34,100.[15] Finally, Singapore has made substantial advances since 1965, and today enjoys a relatively high GDP per capita at around $25,000. For comparison, the Organization for Economic

Cooperation and Development (OECD) nations of the developed world collectively have a per capita GDP annual growth of 2.1 per cent over a similar time period.[16] Measured in this manner, East Asian nations have progressed from almost uniformly poor conditions at the end of World War II to relative, even high, prosperity in the world scheme, with the exception of China, where effective modernization was late in coming.

Again, with the exception of China in the absolute distribution of workers, sectoral shifts away from agriculture as a primary means of production to the secondary sectors of industry and then on to the tertiary or service sector – another hallmark of standard versions of modernization – have occurred rapidly in East Asia and have been sustained. Although modernizing throughout the first half of the twentieth century, Japan still had about 12 per cent of its labour force employed in agriculture in the late 1960s and early '70s, with an additional 34 per cent of its workers in the secondary industrial sector and 54 per cent in the tertiary sector. During the last twenty years, however, these proportions have shifted further in the direction of the tertiary sector, with less than half the previous number employed in agriculture, a little less in the secondary industrial sector and with substantial increases in services. In fact, the GDP contributions among the three sectors lean still further in favour of services, standing in 2000 at 1.4 per cent, 31.8 per cent and 66.8 per cent respectively.[17]

Korea and Taiwan were both significantly agricultural countries at the end of World War II, with 38 per cent and 32 per cent of their GDP earnings in agriculture, and even higher proportions in terms of labour. Korea now has only 4.0 per cent GDP from agriculture (11 per cent for labour), 43.5 per cent (28 per cent for labour) in the secondary sector, and 52.4 per cent (61 per cent for labour) in the tertiary sector, with abrupt downturns in agriculture and upturns in secondary industry occurring from around 1960 onwards. Service sector contributions to GDP went through something of a lull during the 1960s and '70s, reaching 41.0 per cent in 1980, but are now on the rise, outstripping secondary sector production, which has shown recent declines. In Taiwan, a slightly more exaggerated transition occurred, moving from a 32 per cent, 24 per cent and 44 per cent proportional contribution to GDP, among the primary, secondary and tertiary sectors in 1950; to 3.5 per cent, 36.0 per cent and 60.5 per cent across the same sectors in 2000, although with less of a transition in terms of labour, at 8 per cent, 37 per cent and 55 per cent, respectively. Again it was by about 1980 that the tertiary sector began to outstrip the secondary in the value of production.[18]

In contrast, Singapore and Hong Kong have had little agriculture to speak of, placing emphasis instead on trade followed by manufacturing and then services. Today, Hong Kong has one of the most service-sector oriented economies in the world, accounting for around 86 per cent of GDP and 79 per cent of employment, with Singapore not far behind, at slightly above 70 per cent for both GDP and employment.[19] This compares to the United States' 77 per cent contribution to GDP and 74 per cent of employment for 2000, although with higher numbers in agriculture and a proportion of secondary output comparable with Hong Kong and slightly lower than Singapore.[20]

China, by far the slowest of the large nations in East Asia to modernize effectively, remains predominantly agricultural in deployment of its labour force, although not in terms of contributions to GDP. At present, the proportion of employment is 65 per cent in the primary sector, 22 per cent in the secondary sector and 13 per cent in the tertiary sector, whereas income value is distributed almost in the opposite direction at around 17 per cent, 49 per cent and 34 per cent, respectively.[21] These statistics underline the vast income division between rural and urban life and, in the transitions that have occurred since opening up to the world in 1978, the measured though hectic pace with which China is industrializing and modernizing.

Behind these impressive rates of economic growth, industrial expansion and transition into modern economies lie several important strategies that help define what many have labelled the 'East Asian miracle'. Some bear a strong resemblance to the 'economic miracles' of struggling economies in the West after World War II, such as those in several nations of Europe, whereas others, particularly in combination, remain distinctive. Economically, one way to catch up and advance is to practise import substitution, whereby breathing room is provided to national industries to improve and expand, in order that they might compete with and even surpass foreign competitors later. This strategy usually involves stimulation of local business combined with tariff protection from the outside world, until such time as local industries and services are competitive. Though working well in large markets, like the United States, Germany, Japan, and today in China, this practice runs the risk of producing uncompetitive industries through state protectionism. Elements of this approach were applied in Korea, especially in heavy manufacturing, in addition to China's recent tactics, at the dawn of its full entry into the World Trade Organization, emphasizing stimulation of domestic production. It was also practised selectively in Taiwan, during the infant stages of industrial development.[22]

Another approach is widespread direct state involvement, especially in physical investment and control and even operation of infrastructure and other enterprises, in order to push modernization forward and to realign productive activity. One conspicuous (but failed) example was the 'Great Leap Forward' in China, with its singular emphasis on increasing the primary means of production between 1958 and 1961. Other cases in East Asia, however, have fared far better. Singapore's early adoption of the doctrine of 'collective consumption', for instance, whereby heavy government investment in housing and infrastructure was used to underwrite labour costs, paved the way to substantial economic development, as well as improvements in material standards of living among Singaporeans.[23] The practice of off-setting the locational and operational costs of foreign firms to the area, in the Jurong Industrial Park and elsewhere, also helped move the economy forward appreciably through direct foreign investment. Both Hong Kong, through its public housing since 1971, and Korea, particularly in Seoul, had a similar, although lesser impact. Once again, however, this form of dirigisme, or state intervention, is not unknown elsewhere and at other times, as in Bismarck's Prussia towards the end of the nineteenth century.

Of all the strategies the most distinctive is the 'flying geese formation', first noted by Japanese economist Kaname Akamatsu in the 1930s, whereby nations gradually move up in technological development, one step at a time, by following the economic patterns and institutional arrangements of countries just ahead of them in economic development.[24] Certainly, this strategy is commonsensical, in that labour-abundant, capital-scarce economies will be competitive in labour-intensive industries, while also allowing the time for further skill training, education, research and development – if they choose this route – in order gradually to move up in sophistication of domestic production. It also helps to accelerate and guide the process with the assistance of multinational firms skilled in the businesses involved. Indeed, viewing the transition that occurred from clothing manufacture to household goods and other manufactured articles on to electronics, Japan, Korea and Taiwan appeared to be like Akamatsu's flying geese in a formation, led by Japan.

Then there is the important role played by an emphasis on exports and upon export processing zones, or similar export platforms.[25] Under this rubric, countries establish particular identifiable economic enclaves, which are both hospitable to foreign investors and trading partners, as well as being well integrated into the economies of the world outside. As a practical matter this usually involves the provision of special infrastructure, security,

2
A well-serviced
site in the Jurong
industrial park,
Singapore. 1997.

rule of law, open trade practices and even tax or tariff holidays in particular pieces of geography – a little like the entrepôts of old – and, little by little, allowing the practices within these special areas to proliferate and take effect more broadly. In East Asia this practice started in the 1960s, and by 1975, or thereabouts, became overwhelmingly successful as competition for foot-loose electronics firms pushed employment in the region to a substantial majority of all worldwide, offshore assembly workers. Necessary engagement with foreign enterprises can and did vary, however, ranging from direct investment to joint ventures – especially popular in South Korea. Nevertheless, it is the stable environment conducive to international business, with an export orientation, and the linkage provided to the worldwide economy, that are of paramount importance.

Finally, there was the strategy of capitalizing on local assets and what went before. In East Asia this ranged from the preponderance of small business enterprises in Taiwan and Hong Kong to the far larger corporate conglomerates of the *keiretsu* and *zaibatsu* in Japan – holdovers from the pre-World War II era – as well as governmental organization into statutory development boards, like the Economic Development Board in Singapore, inherited from the colonial period. In each case these business arrangements and institutional legacies played a role as key ingredients in how economic development proceeded. In short, it has been a combination, in most places, of well-couched dirigiste responses built on the backs of local business organizations, an export orientation, and a judicious step-wise progression following conspicuous leaders elsewhere in the region, that has been distinctive as the driving engine of East Asia's economic resurgence.

Urban Qualities of Life

Along with economic development there is invariably urbanization, and this has occurred relatively recently in East Asia, with high degrees of concentration and on a prolific scale. The proportion of the total national population who live in urban circumstances has changed appreciably. Japan became a predominantly urbanized nation in 1954, some 25 years after the United States, urbanizing most rapidly, in the case of Tokyo, during the 1960s, and resulting today in a total urban population slightly in excess of 78 per cent of the nation's total, approximately the same as the US proportion. South Korea, an even more urbanized nation today, at around 80 per cent, was only half urban in 1970 and as little as 20 per cent urban in 1945. As 'city-states', without much agricultural production, both Hong Kong and Singapore have been more or less fully urban for some time, whereas Taiwan led South Korea in its propensity towards urbanization by about five years.

Today, China, the land of a vast peasant population, is only about 32 per cent urban, although well on its way to becoming a predominantly urban nation by about 2035, before going on to stabilize, with a 60 per cent proportion of urban dwellers, probably around 2050.[26] In this overall proportion, China might be likened to Italy, with its dispersed pattern of urbanization, at 67 per cent of its total population, although given the sheer numbers involved obviously different in kind; whereas other advanced nations like the UK at about 89 per cent and Australia at 87 per cent are even slightly more urbanized than Japan, Taiwan and South Korea.[27] Furthermore, the rising proportion of urban inhabitants in China is driven by shifts in distribution towards cities rather than by overall growth. Under rigorous family planning, China's population might be expected to peak before mid-century a little above today's total of 1.3 to 1.4 billion people, before declining.[28] Population growth in the remainder of East Asia has been relatively stable, while in Japan the number of inhabitants is already in decline.

Distribution of highly populated urban settlements, however, is more concentrated in East Asia, compared to other developed places in the world, even if the proportion of urban population has converged, or is converging. The United States, for example, has some 45 urban metropolitan areas with populations in excess of 1 million inhabitants, compared to Japan with only 11 at a little less than half the US total population, Taiwan with 2 at about 8 per cent of the US population, and China with only 37 measured in a similar manner, at least so far, at 5 times the US population. Australia is even more concentrated in its urban population, with five cities in excess of 1 million inhabitants, at only 6.5 per cent of the US population. Within almost all East Asian countries one city dominates. Tokyo, for instance, has risen from 15.6 per cent of Japan's population to 25.2 per cent, Taipei from 13.3. per cent to 27.7 per cent of Taiwan's population, and Seoul from 8.4 per cent to 22.0 per cent, becoming truly South Korea's principal city.[29] The exception is largely rural China, where Shanghai and Beijing, although large cities at over 12 million and 13 million inhabitants respectively, account for only about 1 per cent of China's population each, or around 3 per cent of its total urban population. Singular concentration of urban population is not unheard of in advanced countries either, although Paris, the metropolis of France, accounts for far less of the national population, at 16.2 per cent, followed by London at 12.4 per cent of the UK's population (although much higher if the broad spread of contiguous urban areas are also accounted for), and New York with only about 7 per cent of the US total. Indeed, among the world's largest cities, one of the few higher concentrations occurs in Buenos Aires, with fully 34 per cent of Argentina's population.[30]

While Paris, London and New York might be seen among many of their countrymen and others as centres of a urban universe, for they often seem to exercise such symbolic resonance, the very character of urbanization, beyond such symbolic reference points, is almost totally embodied in a few large cities of East Asia. To all intents and purposes they more singularly represent urbanity in their national contexts by the sheer preponderance of their proportional population size, giving full meaning to the term 'mega-city' and becoming synonymous with the very idea of 'city', in a manner that is place-specific, palpable and devoid of many of the abstractions of simply being 'urban'. However, with regard to proportional population this cannot be said of Shanghai, Beijing or other major Chinese cities; they might be said to exert a more roundabout influence on China's national population, vis-à-vis being urban. Nevertheless, both Shanghai and Beijing seem to have a similar urban symbolic resonance within China, as do Paris, London and New York in their national contexts. Moreover, they are very large cities in a nation of, as yet, relatively few large cities. Consequently a similar conflation of being urban and living in a particular place might be said to occur. This kind of association is probably also sustained in Argentina, with Buenos Aires, and in Mexico with Mexico City, where 20 per cent of the nation's population now dwell. However, for an entire region to have this kind of direct association seems to set East Asia apart.

With these profound changes towards more and more urban life, material standards of living and health have improved in most cities of East Asia, although disparities in income distribution have been exacerbated and the detrimental environmental effects of industrialization and urbanization seem weakly, at times very weakly, sustainable. Ownership of consumer goods like colour televisions, video cassettes, refrigerators and mobile phones is the norm rather than the exception. Most of East Asia ranks highly, worldwide, in this regard. Not only are many of these goods produced domestically but they are also consumed internally.[31]

Standards of residential space, however, remain comparatively low, even if well above historic levels in places like Kowloon in Hong Kong, with formerly only 2.2 m^2 of livable space per person, and in China, during the 1970s, with only about 3.5 m^2 per person. By contrast, nowadays, Chinese residents enjoy about 8 m^2 per person of livable space, on average, with more advanced coastal areas and new cities like Shanghai, Dalian and Shenzhen enjoying averages of between 12 and 18 m^2 per person. In fact, most new residential development in China occurs today at or above 25 m^2 per person, regardless of venue. Availability of more ample residential space has also improved in Hong Kong, where the average is now on the order of 20 m^2 per person, and in Seoul and Taipei with similar averages.[32] Nevertheless, these space standards are still low, even in Tokyo, with 55 m^2 per person, when compared to Manhattan and Paris, to take two other relatively dense, urban living environments, at around 90 m^2 of livable space per person. Singapore, under the guidance of its Housing Development Board and where the vast majority of people live in public housing, has fared better. Today the average amount of livable space in Singapore is comparable with standards in economically well-developed nations.[33]

One consequence of relatively meagre amounts of residential space, combined with high urban densities, often involving the doubling up of households, is that physical capacities for housing many aspects of daily life commonly associated with 'house as home' are pushed elsewhere. Without putting too fine a point on it, a strong sense of 'living out here but staying there' has emerged for many urban inhabitants in East Asia. This is underlined by the relatively recent arrival of self-contained residential units, with a full complement of features and particularized spaces to support a broad spectrum of both daily and occasional activities, as distinct from dwelling space that had to be frequently reconfigured to accommodate these activities. In China, reference to the 'apartment-style' dwelling, incorporating specialized or self-contained spaces, only emerged in urban housing markets in the 1990s, becoming commonplace in Hong Kong only shortly before, and many Japanese urban families still rearrange their accommodation for sleeping. Another consequence is that distinctions between community and privacy are less sharply drawn than, say, in the US or Europe, often with a corresponding blurring of public, semi-public, semi-private and private spatial realms and a stronger social emphasis on communality, propriety and conformance. With Tokyo, at 7,099 people per km^2, ranked in the top twenty densest cities in the world, and with fifteen cities ranked still higher in Asia defined more broadly, like Hong Kong at 28,405 people per km^2, Seoul at 23,908 people per km^2 and Tianjin at 21,519 people per km^2, cities in the region have either arrived at, or are converging on, a condition of 'hyperdensity'.[34]

Disparities in income have risen in many parts of East Asia, although on the whole with less inequality than has emerged in, say, the United States during its recent period of modernization. Partly this is due to direct government policy and partly it seems due to relative stages of development and to customary ideas of social contract. Although with variation across some reports, according to the Gini Index, a measure of income inequality where 0.0 represents perfect equality and 1.0 represents perfect inequality, China, South Korea and Taiwan score 0.38, 0.36 and 0.29 respectively, compared to a recent figure for the United States of 0.43.[35] In the case of China this relatively high score is due to substantial disparities between urban and rural areas, with a city like Shanghai having a relatively low score of around 0.23 although, in the balance between social efficiency and equity, Shanghai has done a reasonable job in pursuing some modicum of equity. While stratification has increased in housing, access to support services like education, health care, open space and other social services, through location and public transportation, has been both widely and relatively evenly spread. Nevertheless, even this relatively low score represents a rise of 64.3 per cent since 1990, from 0.14, and illustrates the widening income gap among citizens in urban China.[36] Measured slightly differently according to the ratio of the highest 20 per cent income share to the lowest 20 per cent, again where a low score is a relative measure of equality, Tokyo scores 4.6, with China, South Korea and Taiwan's scores paralleling their performance on the Gini Index at between 5.2 and 6.5, but with Hong Kong and Singapore at 8.7 and 9.6, respectively, much closer to the American urban estimate at around 13.7.[37] With little in the way of a rural population, the urban–rural income divide in Taiwan, South Korea and Japan is relatively small, with Taipei, for instance, having a Gini Index score of 0.28, very close to Taiwan's overall performance.

When asked, most Japanese are self-declared members of the middle class, despite the occurrence of great wealth and rising poverty in that country. To a considerable degree this sense of parity reflects a social contract that was struck in the wake of demonstrations in 1960 over Japan's security treaty with the United States, and explicitly reflects Minister Ikeda's 'income-doubling plan', which was to double Gross National Product and personal income in a 10-year period.[38] Similar social contracts were to follow and Japan's avoidance of social instability, as it pressed forward with economic development, was not lost on either South Korea or Taiwan, which flew in a similar formation – resorting once again to the 'flying geese' metaphor – by encouraging social compliance with ambitious plans for development with the promise of a steady improvement in economic circumstances for everybody. As a central tenet of its socialist revolution, the 'iron rice bowl' compact that was struck in China, and which is only now beginning to unravel, guaranteed subsistence, or better, for everyone and employment during their working lives. Behind these cases there lurks an old and shared cultural ethos, at least partially of Confucian origin, that places the relative fortune of many at the forefront of individual aggrandizement, in addition, of course, to maintaining those responsible for community welfare in power. In this socio-cultural landscape Hong Kong and Singapore appear to be anomalies with regard to statistical income inequality, explained largely by the city-state inheritance and embrace of purer capitalist socio-economic stances. They are among the freest economic systems in the world, ranking even higher on the Economic Freedom Index than the United States, no matter how Confucian they might be in familial and other social relations.[39]

The environmental toll of rapid industrialization and modernization in much of East Asia has so far been high, with the exception, at least recently, of Japan, where concerted effort could be made affordably, and also where a certain emphasis on economic development shifted towards environmental sustainability. One measure of sustainability, which blends environmental changes relative to economic changes, is the concept of 'environmental elasticity', which expresses the relative change in an aggregation of environmental factors as a function of similar relative change in economic circumstances, like a 1 per cent change in GDP. The essence of the measure is that it equates measurable environmental detriment with economic gain. For example, a positive outcome, such as in the Netherlands, with 0.04, suggests a strongly sustainable nation and one in which the economy and the environment are improving simultaneously. By this measure, Japan at –0.01 and the United States at –0.13 are weakly sustainable; positive economic growth is slightly offset by negative environmental changes. For Singapore, the score is –0.28 and for South Korea –0.32, with Hong Kong in a similar range. China, although improved through recent efforts, scores –0.43, a very weakly and even tenuously sustainable position. Measurements on other indices yield similar results.[40]

Another index, one that combines estimates of environmental stress, human vulnerability to environmental risk and institutional capacities to improve the environment, places China and South Korea, with scores of 38.5 and 35.9, well below environmentally successful nations like Canada, at 70.6, and Finland, at the top of the list with 73.9.[41] In East Asia, it is clear, again with the exception of Japan, that improvement of social welfare is being placed above environmental cost, at least until adequate means are available to tackle both problems with the same vigour. In China, for instance, this represents a deferment of something like 4 per cent of GDP per annum, which should be invested in environmental management, in order to achieve levels of quality comparable to better performers in the West. More specifically, Beijing continues to be wracked by air pollution, now worsened by massive increases in automobile use, not to mention by emerging constraints in water supply and potential energy shortages; Shanghai still confronts substantial water pollution problems and continued land-surface subsidence, despite curtailed ground water withdrawal, probably requiring a further 150 km of flood-wall construction in order to reduce the risk of flooding to inhabited areas.[42] Shortsighted though this trajectory may appear to be from a longer-term and environmental standpoint, it is also hardly without precedent among the advanced modernized nations of the world.

In dominant versions of modernization the roles of the state, the private sector and civil society are all active and typically intertwined, operating as a system of mutual checks and balances, and yet presumably pushing forward towards human betterment. Again, these dominant versions generally favour, in no particular order: rule of law, social pluralism, representative bodies of government, local autonomy, protection of personal and property rights, meritocracy, a separation of spiritual and temporal authority, individualism and the virtue of capital markets. Certainly, some of these qualities are present in East Asia. Rule of law and an absence of corruption are evident in Hong Kong and Singapore, and Japan's performance on criminal activity is extraordinary. All East Asian nations are essentially secular states, although sometimes rhetorically on the borderline, and economic markets are usually favoured. Many, at least on paper, have representative governments. Nevertheless, at the risk of overgeneralization, it is probably fair to say that long and crucial periods of modernization have not taken place within multi-party democracies, involving successive power-sharing among opposing political groups, and that the role of the state has been very prominent, in some cases omnipresent, especially in economic development and in broadly related aspects of the lives of the citizenry. On issues of identity, as will be discussed in chapter Three, East Asian nations have been outwardly leery of Western cultural hegemony, selective in the Western traits they have sought to incorporate, or more uniformly muted in their resistance. Civil society has remained weak in its lasting impact on political landscapes, and business and political arrangements have remained diffuse and murky, with few exceptions. In addition, pluralism has not been actively and openly pursued, nor has much in the way of local autonomy.

Political regimes have ranged from outright dictatorships to one-party autocratic systems, or a democratic pretence with little practical outcome. South Korea, for instance, was a Japanese colony from 1909 to 1945 and a military dictatorship from 1961 to 1993. Indeed, during the past century it has enjoyed only about 20 years of democratic political freedom. Taiwan was a Japanese colony for even longer, from 1895 to 1945, having been ceded to Japan as a result of the Treaty of Shimonoseki at the end of the Sino-Japanese war. From 1949 until 1987 it was a Republican – *Guomindang* – stronghold under martial law, before entering its present period, largely devoid of authoritarian leadership and associated technocratic power. Hong Kong, both as British Crown Colony under a Governor, and now as a Special Administrative Region of China, has been under sustained authoritarian rule, without the enfranchisement that normally accompanies democracies, and Singapore, despite many of its other modern virtues, is still under the paternalistic single-party rule of the People's Action Party. China maintains a highly authoritarian, centralized government under the Communist Party of the People's Republic of

China, and Japan, at the other end of the spectrum with all the formal trappings of an open democracy, has remained, since World War II, almost exclusively in the hands of a single party – the Liberal Democratic Party, or various versions of it – amid constant controversy about transparency and where the real power resides. Prior to 1945 it was a fascist state, after the earlier liberal attitude of the Taishō period, combining militarism with ultra-nationalism and the effective end of civilian party rule in 1932. Outward manifestations against Western cultural hegemony have been rife in Singapore, as recently as 1988, when its National Ideological Committee promulgated a platform that included an emphasis on Asian values in spite of Western influences. Both Korea and Hong Kong pay a little more than lip service to outside cultural influences, especially where money is to be made, but remain closed and some think largely devoid of a deep modern culture. China, always balancing its cultural response to the West since the Self-Strengthening Movement of the 1860s, has adopted a pragmatic, often reluctant posture ever since, maintaining an essentially indigenous stance, while Japan seems to have moved from imitation of the West to its own recalibration of Western traits with, once again, a largely indigenous outcome.

Civil society is weak in most places in East Asia, even if places like Japan are relatively rich in associational life through neighbourhood associations – *chōnaikai* – as well as other interest groups, that have nevertheless remained largely mute in any prolonged and radical, confrontational political sense.[43] Furthermore, the diffusion and outwardly elusive nature of political, bureaucratic and business dealings in all but Hong Kong and Singapore have earned low scores on indices of both economic freedom and corruption, largely because of their intertwined nature, the emphasis placed on personal and clan-like relationships, and the comparative lack of a prevailing meritocracy. Pluralism seems to founder along similar lines, or because of rigid codes of acceptance that inhibit its progress. Japan, for instance, although including minorities like the *burakumin*, Japanese-born Koreans, Ainu and foreign workers – notably Chinese – discourages immigration and assimilation and frowns on lapses of decorum even if they are rife below the surface.[44] To a lesser extent, the same may be said of China and of Singapore, although both nations have a diverse internal population.

An underlying leaning, throughout East Asia, seems to stress a cultural bias towards collectivism and the interests of family, or company, above those of the individual, and consensus as a preferred way of reaching agreement and of achieving harmony, as distinct from debate, dissent and disputation. Also at

work is a strong sense of hierarchy, both in terms of status and vertical ranking among age cohorts, which frequently blunts a more meritocratic assign-
ment of human capital, as well as rampant clientelism, often involving the
disposal of considerable largesse if not influence-peddling. Constantly at work
among those involved in Japan are subordinate *oyabun-kobun* relations, and
among those in China, *guanxi*, or special relations. This bias has deep roots
embracing, as it does, many aspects of a well-honed neo-Confucian view
of life and personal conduct, even if, nowadays, mostly in a less principled,
habitual and degenerate form.[45] Corruption, for instance, was anathema to a
Confucian stance, even if particular relationships were to be admired among
people, and veneration of elders and exercising propriety towards others in a
non-confrontational manner were hardly surrogates for slowing progress in a
beneficial human direction. This cultural bias, however, is not a complete
explanation, for it does not readily incorporate the obvious adoption of foreign
traits, like the embrace of competitive market forces to produce efficient and
equitable distributions of goods, services and wealth, although in parts of China
this was also rife in the seventeenth century; the separation of temporal
from spiritual authority; and, increasingly, other liberal traits, such as representation in some form, protection of property rights and the belief that the
best person should get the job no matter what. Nevertheless, in spite of this
latter selectivity, conspicuous in places like Singapore, Hong Kong and
Taiwan, the question remains as to whether other East Asian core cultural
values can continue to be an alternative means to the ends of economic well-
being, material benefit and environmental sustainability. Certainly in the
recent past they have been, lifting the region from a proverbially infantile state
in most places, with regard to modernity, to one of relative prosperity and
progress.

Built Landscapes

The built landscapes of cities in East Asia are undeniably modern and are
dotted with tall buildings, extensive arrays of steel, glass and concrete, as well
as architectural trappings of contemporary life, like department stores, retail
malls, financial districts, pedestrian streets, subways and neon-lit entertainment districts – all now seemingly produced effortlessly, in spite of the varied
mechanisms of power, politics, relative economic circumstances and other
societal relations. Furthermore, at first glance they resemble anywhere else in

3
Infrastructure
snaking between
a fine grain of
urbanization in
Tokyo. 1992.

the modern and modernizing world, going back to the universalizing tendency
of modernization, although on closer inspection they do not, or at least not
entirely – an issue that will be taken up in chapter Four.

First of all, there are generally more tall buildings than elsewhere. Indeed,
Shanghai now has many more skyscrapers than Manhattan, and Hong Kong
and Singapore, from many points of view, appear to be uniformly high-rise
environments. In fact, in Seoul, after widespread government-sponsored
production, high-rise apartments became a preferred standard of accommodation, most closely associated with progress and modernity.[46] Second, the
grain of much urban building, especially in dense areas, is finer than in older
modern cities of the West, to the point that the term 'pencil building' was
coined to describe individual high-rise structures with very low aspect ratios,
defined by the ratio of ground-floor site area available for building divided by
the number of storeys. Particularly common in Tokyo and Hong Kong,
although also present in Shanghai and Taipei, this building phenomena is dictated largely by difficulties in acquiring adjacent land and financial, as well as
regulatory incentives, to build upwards. The overall effect is to produce an
urban landscape of narrow structures placed side by side, ascending upwards,
in marked contrast to the coarser grain of building in other high-rise environments including Manhattan.

Third, the discrete volumes of buildings often appear to be defined almost exclusively by external parameters on a site, such as set-back ratios, sun-angle regulations, fire-code provisions, and so on, rather than by internally driven programmatic and architecturally motivated compositional principles. Under real-estate pressure, buildings are quite literally built to the available limit, frequently without regard for much else. Fourth, highway and other transportation infrastructure often rises and snakes unabashedly between buildings, along public rights-of-way, in cities like Tokyo, Hong Kong, Shanghai and to a lesser extent Taipei and Singapore, without the attempts of disguise, occlusion and integration practised in much of the West. There appears to be a far greater acceptance of the expediency of these systems, often retrofitted into the city, as necessary and familiar parts of the urban landscape.

Fifth, cities throughout the world can be characterized by answering the question: 'What time is this place?' referring to the era or eras during which most city building took place. On this basis it is reasonable to say that New York is an early twentieth-century city, with a lot of nineteenth-century technology; that many cities in Europe were defined in the nineteenth century, if not before; and that many other American and Western cities were defined by the advent of the automobile era around the mid-twentieth century. The defining moments of most East Asian cities, however, have occurred later. Referring to the statistical analysis of urbanization presented earlier, Tokyo and Seoul were well defined in the 1960s and '70s, even if the underlay of feudal Edo has always been prominent on Tokyo's landscape.[47] Taipei, Singapore and Hong Kong are of the 1970s and '80s, whereas Shanghai in the 1990s is hardly recognizable from a decade before. This later response to 'What time is this place?' occurred around a different confluence of factors than the American automobile city of the 1950s, often involving close and visible integration with transit, and unprecedented high density.

Sixth, specific urban architectural appearances vary widely in East Asia, as they do elsewhere. However, in some cities, most notably in China, there is a jarring, outlandish, downright ugly, or 'over-the-top' aspect to parts of the urban landscape. To be sure, the pursuit of 'symbols of progress' is at work, although the garish, haphazard architecture seems to have more to do with wholesale appropriation and then amplification of styles of building from abroad. Frequently, those involved are without adequate intellectual and professional grounding and exhibit a real confusion about architectural qualities being required to stand for something else, rather than simply being architecture. Finally, historic preservation in most East Asian cities is weak or late in coming. Indeed, in the mad dash to modernize, old was often equated with being poor in quality and outmoded, as many dilapidated structures and city districts were at the time, and until recent perception of the usefulness of historic heritage for tourism. Consequently, large tracts have been destroyed, as it seemed the most expedient solution to squalor and overcrowding in many cities, and with them have gone glimpses into the past and older, sometimes nostalgic, memories.

Again at the risk of overgeneralization, the impetus for the particular physical trajectory of many East Asian cities is probably the extraordinary pressures of urbanization to build maximally to allowable and extendable limits, at a time when many other advanced nations in the world are moving in quite a different direction. Many inner areas of older cities in the US, for instance, have become and continue to be starkly depopulated, even desolated, and much lower in density. Between 1950 and 2000, for instance, the change in central city population in St Louis was –59 per cent, in Philadelphia –27 per cent and in Boston –26 per cent. The number of inner-city vacant lots under cultivation is estimated to be 31,000 in Philadelphia and as high as 65,000 in Detroit.[48] In general, in many cities in Europe and other advanced countries, where populations are stable and even declining, the emphasis in urban management has shifted towards redevelopment and away from the expansionism of the post-World War II period. Returning to an earlier point, the timing of massive urbanization in East Asia coincided with an era of widely available, sophisticated building technology and stronger means of building production, resulting in the very real possibility of constructing more building and infrastructure more rapidly – a point to be elaborated upon in chapter Five.

Under this impetus, numerous magnificent buildings have been constructed in East Asian cities: the iconic Bank of China Building in Hong Kong, by I. M. Pei; the Jin Mao Building in Shanghai, by Skidmore Owings and Merrill; and the soon to be completed opera house in Beijing by Paul Andreu and his associates. Also, interesting attempts have been undertaken to explore contemporary regional forms of architectural and urban expression, like Fumihiko Maki's incomparable Hillside Terrace development in Tokyo, and a number of contemporary reinterpretations of traditional lane living in both Beijing and Shanghai by the likes of Benjamin Wood, Wu Liangyong, Huang Hui and others. In addition, large-scale urban infrastructure projects of prodigious scope, architectural accoutrement and forward-looking programmes have been constructed in most large cities, often in association with international travel and local transportation interchange, such as Chek Lap Kok and

the Airport Core Program in Hong Kong; the Kansai terminal and Osaka connection in Japan; and the Pudong airport and futuristic airport link towards downtown in Shanghai. In the mass transit business for years, Tokyo has managed to complete an entire new subway line at the extraordinary rate, on average, of one every three years.[49]

On the less satisfactory side of the ledger, referring back to other aspects that tend to mark East Asian cities: monotonous or jumbled arrays of architecturally nondescript buildings and urban landscapes; almost casual juxtapositions of muscular infrastructure against neighbourhood communities, as well as the at times jarring, outlandish and incongruous instances of architectural production, some explanation can be offered. Perhaps with the exception of Singapore's well-manicured urban landscape and its strong belief in the physical perfectibility of the city, control of urbanization and building elsewhere in East Asia is conditioned by a top-down, managerial, functional and architecturally distanced stance, which places emphasis on relatively basic, even crude, regulatory codes. Usually these are the presumed answers to prior social problems with buildings overlaid in an uncoordinated manner in the form of specific building regulations. In Tokyo this regulatory framework is uniform across the entire city, possibly in the mistaken belief that 'one size fits all' conforms to equal treatment for all, regardless of local circumstances. It certainly has a unifying effect, although not of the kind pointed out by detractors of modernization's supposed universalizing cultural impact. Generally, little or no guidance is provided by regulators and others in authority with regard to urban design, provision of environmental amenity, or making the city add up to more than the sum of its parts. Certainly a more specifically focused communitarian outlook is lacking – more strongly emergent in many advanced Western cities – whereby urban land is treated as an irreplaceable resource and social asset, and property owners are regarded as trustees and entitled to pursue their individual interests only in ways that are deemed compatible with the public interest. This may seem odd in cultures otherwise given to collectivism and consensus as guiding lights for moving forward. However, several other societal if not cultural stumbling blocks are in the way.

First, as already noted and will be discussed further in the next chapter, almost without exception East Asian cities pursue highly centralized top-down procedures in planning and building regulation, with little in the way of local autonomy, coupled with direct provision of much of the built environment in many places. In essence, this centralized authority, paternalistic or otherwise, provides the objects of broad collective perception to be followed. Second, also

4
A symbol of progress, the Jin Mao tower in Shanghai, of 1998, by Skidmore Owings & Merrill. 2004.

as noted, civil society is often weak and has nowhere near the same density of interests and clout on urban issues, nor the local participatory processes routinely available to many in Europe and the United States that have had such a salutary effect on many public and private urban proposals. Third, widespread, broadly focused collectivism and consensus-seeking, when overplayed, has the defect of leading to least-common-denominator solutions that make everyone less unhappy but no one really happy. Perhaps more fundamental still, in a place like China, there is a comparative lack of adequate professional institutional foundations, including professional education, to resist or even fully comprehend the often haphazard, garish and untutored urban-architectural production going on in cities. Styles, as noted earlier, are often misappropriated out of context in an unknowing and indiscriminate fashion. Traditional or local ways of building, to the extent that they are even understood, are usually so thoroughly outstripped by the scale, complexity and programme of what has to be done as to render them of little apparent help.

Present and Future Dilemmas

In summary, since World War II (though Japan began long before) East Asia has modernized in most respects, often at an outstanding rate. Broad economic transition from agriculture, where it prevailed, to secondary and tertiary sectors of production took place, or (in the case of China) is taking place. This transition had distinctive, if not unique, characteristics, propelled by substantial state intervention, emulation in a step-wise progression of successful practices by other more advanced economies in the region and, at least among the four 'Asian Tigers' and China, the establishment of capitalist enclaves with a strong export orientation. Rapid urbanization followed in the wake of industrialization, resulting in very large cities dominating extensive hinterlands and characterized by extreme concentration in a national context, very high densities bordering if not crossing over into urban life of a different kind and, at least in the case of China and parts of South-East Asia, patterns of urban settlement and industrial activity, within urbanizing hinterlands, rarely found elsewhere in the world.[50] In the landscape produced by this urbanization, copious use was made of internationally available construction and infrastructural technologies, as well as styles of building. However, while superficially contemporary and universal in appearance, distinctive features also emerged through the preponderance of tall buildings, each pushing hard on the envelope available; the grain of the resulting urban fabric; the nonchalant placement of highways and other elements of city-wide urban infrastructure, as well as block configurations, in many places, that echo traditional patterns of living, again not found elsewhere in the world – an aspect to be discussed in chapter Four.

Behind these outward manifestations of modernization – distinctive in seemingly important ways from other dominant versions – resides a political, social and cultural matrix of relationships and norms that appears to allow selectivity to be practised when taking on board modern and essentially Western traits, without abandoning traditional core values bound up with collectivism, consensus, hierarchy, special relationships, and so on. Within the corresponding fabric of society, the private sector tends to operate within the framework of strong and often diffuse, though internalized, relationships with a powerful public sector (not all to the good), and civil society is weak in the execution of power and persuasion in the public arena, despite strong social capital building in some places, especially Japan.

From this snapshot in time (for modernization is still an unfinished project in much of East Asia) several further trends, dilemmas and future prospects emerge. On the economic horizon, for instance, per capita growth rates, even given plain sailing, are likely to slow down in Hong Kong, Singapore, South Korea and Taiwan during the next decade or so, as the income gap with the US and other advanced countries, like Japan, is narrowed. In contrast China, with a relatively low per capita income, could sustain relatively high growth rates over the next few decades, so long as the present overheated economy is guided into a slower, more sustainable rate of growth, without economic and social disruption. At present, the four 'Asian Tigers' are within 75 per cent of the US per capita income, whereas China is barely above 10 per cent and may be expected to rise to between 25 and 50 per cent by 2025, on its way to becoming comparable to others in the region shortly thereafter.[51]

Other factors may also come into play. Among these are the demographics that have underpinned so much of East Asia's economic success over the past 30 years, with the exception of Japan. The region's ratio of dependents – those under 15 or over 65 years of age – has fallen from around 80 per cent in 1970 to a present value of 55 per cent, on its way to a low point of around 49 per cent in 2015. The age divide with most advanced nations, again Japan notwithstanding, seems likely to continue the economic dividend for some time to come. Essentially, the falling dependency rate and greater discretionary income has fuelled an engine of consumption that has formed a virtuous circle, by channelling high savings – in the order of 40 per cent of GDP in China – into domestic consumption and, therefore, less of a dependence on exports, sometimes less reliable in recent years. However, this window of growing numbers of working-age people will not remain open forever, moving back to a much higher dependency ratio by around 2025. The implications of this shift in dealing with an ageing population, for instance, will require concerted effort and reorganization. Pension assets are very low (except for Japan, already wrestling with this issue), with a regional high in Singapore, at 47 per cent of GDP, compared to the US with 95 per cent.[52] Traditional practices of housing extended families, including the elderly, have eroded substantially in East Asia. In addition, substantial educational reform, especially at tertiary levels, needs to be made to capitalize fully on overall skill levels and professional competencies among the growing workforce.

Another much discussed factor is whether East Asia will be able to meet the challenges of governance usually associated with high-income economies as they move to narrow further the gap with advanced countries. With some exceptions, the rule of law remains weak. In the main, governments are centralized and powerful; bureaucracies are politicized; private dealings are opaquely intertwined with public dealings; the judiciary is subject to being overridden; and property rights can be disrespected. Indeed, the struggle confronting China in privatization, banking reform, legal modernization and a host of other institutional changes is likely to be long and intense. With the bold and distinctive step of establishing capitalist enclaves for export and to boost economic performance having been taken, it remains to be seen whether its virtuous aspects can be expanded. At present local government is weak in many cities, although the source of this weakness varies; when it is strong it is sometimes at cross purposes with central government directives. Within large cities in China regulatory authority is not infrequently co-opted by more powerful and larger interests. For instance, one intrinsic value of China's 'controlled detailed plans', which set out what can or cannot be done on a given property within the scope of a city's master plan, is that, in a fast-moving property market, they are surrounded by a process of negotiation to be entered into by the local government and the property rights holder for the purpose of arriving at better overall development proposals. Unfortunately, it can also usher in abuse and pave the way for corruption. So too can casual and favoured lending practices, based more on personal relationships than on well-secured investments. Indiscriminate releases of land-use rights from direct state control, sometimes to provide public development authorities with continued financial liquidity, can also skew property markets in inappropriate directions and obscure poor management practices. Local regulatory control problems have emerged in Seoul, especially on the heels of land-readjustment practices, whereby land or pieces of property can be traded backwards and forwards with private owners, or prospective owners, and inadequate resources have hampered the application of local regulatory powers in Taipei.

Another kind of weakness stems from the uniformity of control exercised from larger city-wide or metropolitan governments without inflection to meet local circumstances. This is the case in Tokyo and Singapore, where paternalism from above denies much in the way of local autonomy, a point that will be expanded upon in the next chapter. Recently, in Tokyo, tensions mounted to the point that inner-city municipal governments petitioned higher authorities for more flexibility to address local regulatory and land-use issues.[53] A third weakness, returning to the local municipal level, involves the sheer inadequacy of available financial and other resources for the purposes of addressing public open space, housing, public service and infrastructural inadequacies. Shanghai, a massive exporter of income to the central government, throughout most of its pre- and post-World War ii history, was severely hampered in its development until relatively recently. Similarly, inner-city municipalities in Tokyo make claims of unfair treatment at the hands of the metropolitan and national governments. When combined with the weak presence of civil society on the political scene, including the role of professional institutions in matters of city building, this pervasive lack of local empowerment, except during moments of extraordinary crisis, deprives most East Asian cities from an effective bottom-up capacity to resist constructively the sometimes corrupted and overwhelming weight of top-down authority. One ramification of higher incomes, higher education and both broadened career and personal horizons is rising pluralism in society and, with that rise, more diversified claims on the shape, amenity and quality of urban environments. In much of East Asia, however, the question remains whether adequate avenues for pressing those claims can be provided and in a timely enough fashion, an issue to be taken up in chapter Five.

Still another factor in the success of East Asia's past and continued economic growth and modernization is how well this performance was and continues to be leveraged. Some economists argue that the region's rapid growth was unimpressive because it was based largely on heavy investment spending rather than on productivity growth.[54] In fact, GDP growth probably has been due mainly to capital investment, although with some growth in productivity. Indeed, in 2002, Shanghai's total investment in fixed assets was over 40 per cent of GDP, with Beijing's investment even higher.[55] Capital investment and especially physical investments can be highly desirable, improving infrastructure, underwriting labour costs through provision of housing, and erecting appropriate facilities for moving industrialization forward. This holds only up to a point, however, and only so long as the rates of return from physical investment-spending are greater than the cost of capital. There have also been many wasteful capital projects in terms of long-run performance. The overly prolific duplication of serviced industrial sites, support facilities and infrastructure, as well as town centres, all in competition for outside investment, that occurred in medium-sized cities and towns throughout the Changjiang Delta in China is a case in point. The more recent penchants to establish high-technology centres, like Hong Kong's Cyberport, appear to be risky ventures, since it is not entirely clear that such physical concentration is in the best interests of what is otherwise a footloose and somewhat fickle labour market and entrepreneurial culture. Too much physical investment, at the expense of fostering human elements of productivity by improving education, developing local talent and creating conditions in which entrepreneurship and creativity can flourish, is clearly counterproductive. In some respects, Singapore's recessional exposure during the late 1980s and early '90s when it continued to pump large proportions of GDP into housing and other capital projects, while apparently ignoring higher education and the stimulus of new, forward-looking and less conventional start-up enterprises, is an instance of this failure. So too was South Korea's fostering of heavy industry, when its electronics sector proved to be a far better export performer. How many East Asian nations and cities mix and modulate their investment strategies, especially given a propensity, in some places, towards investing in physical capital rather than human resources, will also shape the future of their efforts to modernize.

In common with much of the developing and modernized world, environmental deterioration and income disparities may slow progress. On both counts Japan appears least likely to falter, although still deeply hit by economic recession, considerable loss of personal wealth, the relatively high costs of living in cities like Tokyo – at about 37 per cent above the cost in New York, although dropping – and an ageing and increasingly dependent population (17.4 per cent over 65 years of age, compared to the US with 12.3 per cent, and well up from 4.9 per cent in 1950).[56] In contrast, China's performance in environmentally sustaining its modern development has been poor and South Korea's only slightly better. As noted, at present the cost of remediation of environmental deterioration in China to acceptable and sustainable standards has been estimated at an annualized rate of around 4 per cent of GDP which, if applied, would reduce the current national growth in GDP to around 5 per cent. Cities in the east, like Shanghai and Beijing, have high costs of remediation per land area, although relatively low overall with regard to productive output. At present, the costs per GDP for Shanghai are estimated to be less than 1 per cent, whereas western provinces of the country are in much more dire straits, requiring far greater financial assistance to stem continuing environmental deterioration.[57] Put bluntly, environmental remediation can be deferred only so far without the adverse effects becoming overwhelming.

In China there is also the daunting prospect of managing urban growth, environmentally and otherwise, for an additional 350 to 500 million inhabitants by around mid-century. Especially in arable areas, like China's few large riverine deltas, this is likely to be a complex task involving the balancing of mega-city development with large-to-medium-sized city developments, simultaneously avoiding a prolific scatter of urban settlement across what remains of the agricultural landscape. China faces a rising income gap between rural and urban inhabitants, between those in the wealthier coastal region and those in the central and western provinces, and among the inhabitants of otherwise prospering cities like Shanghai, Beijing and Guangzhou. In this regard, one problem in particular worth noting is the apparent insufficiency of means for adequately 'mainstreaming' peasants and surplus agricultural workers into nearby urban circumstances, through upgrading their skills, resettling them in a dignified manner and generally integrating them into a different lifestyle. Quite apart from arresting pollution and resource degradation, pursuit of environmental quality and a harmonious social environment are becoming increasingly equated with maintaining an internationally competitive position. A city like Tokyo, for instance, has already seen its competitive edge decline in the past decade, plummeting from a ranking of number 1 in 1990 to around number 20 by 2000, due to a lack of amenity for visitors, sojourners and permanent residents alike, let alone the high costs of living.[58] Other cities in East Asia are struggling with the same problems. Seoul and Taipei remain relatively unattractive to outsiders, whereas Hong Kong has begun to embark on a substantial effort to rejuvenate its international appeal and image.

Of course, what the future holds remains to be seen. Nevertheless, in describing how the trajectories of modernization might unfold in East Asia, several scenarios appear possible. The first and most congenial to dominant versions of modernization is that a closer alignment will occur, in the fullness of time, with Western socio-economic, political and even cultural practices.

After all, with the exception of Japan, there is some way to go in modernization, compared to the most advanced nations of the world, and even for Japan, emergence from its current crisis will probably require substantial and broad reform. This is less of an issue in Singapore and Hong Kong, although still of concern in South Korea and Taiwan, with China presenting a rather different case. Almost certainly, if all goes well with the rapidly rising trajectory of wealth in China, further economic stratification will occur among urban populations, more sharply across the urban-rural divide and in disparities among rich and poorer regions. If not attended to adequately, this could engender substantial socio-political unrest, with less than certain outcomes, especially with regard to relatively transparent, Western-style versions of modernization. Moreover, for stable socio-political circumstances to remain largely as they are now, central government authority must gain greater traction in the face of decentralized abuse and subversion by poor habitual practices. The rule of law, in most cases, is already on the books. However, deeper issues of trustworthiness continue to plague daily administration, peaceful solutions to which would seem to lie more readily within the ambit of indigenous moral codes and social systems of guidance than in wholesale abandonment in favour of foreign alternatives in which the country has little experience.

The second scenario is that current and unfolding issues will prove to be largely insurmountable and modernization will gradually begin only to inch forward, making little progress relative to other advancing and high-income areas around the world. The 'complacency account' of Japan, in which the nation slowly sinks into declining yet comfortable old age, so to speak, is a version of this perspective. Finally, the third scenario is that modernization will continue, even aggressively at times, especially in China, but along its own particular path or discernible group of pathways. As noted, there are already distinctive aspects, more or less held in common, to East Asia's modernization and particularly in its urban landscape. Of the three scenarios, the region seems to be well embarked along the third and, therefore, most likely to stay its course, although jettisoning some of its socio-economic and political practices along the way and refashioning others to allow for and accommodate greater local autonomy, further meritocratic performance, some pluralism (or what might be perceived as such, relatively speaking) and, certainly, better environments. In addition, the definitional aspect of modernization itself might usefully be loosened along the way, from some of its seemingly immutable and a priori characteristics.

three

Outside Influences and Urban Patterns

Apart from commonly understood relationships, such as the linking of urbanization with industrialization, and widely shared trajectories of socio-economic and institutional transformation, modernization is also a cumulative process in which various kinds of wherewithal are added, resulting in broadened geographical reach and greater productive efficiency, as well as concomitant capacities to redress socially and environmentally regressive outcomes. Many procedural aspects of modernization appear to have been sustained in large part by the rise, rearrangement and even reaction to an orientation involving three complementary processes: a technological way of making things, a technocratic manner of managing events and a predominantly scientific way of interpreting people and their world. Far from a sudden accumulation of features, however, modernization's progress has followed a technological unfolding with recognizable episodes, spanning (in the West) roughly from the eighteenth century to the present. First came the growth of the Enlightenment through the first Industrial Revolution (*c.* 1776–1890), which saw a separation of knowledge into distinct categories (like science), and later gave rise to steam power, mechanization and the arrival of the factory system, urbanization and product economies of price. The era of the Second Industrial Revolution (1890–1970s) followed, involving mass production, mass consumption, the arrival of the corporation, labour unions, electrical power, chemical and biological agents, as well as throughput and economies of scale. Finally, the present era is characterized by computers, technical and business arrangements based on flexible production, individual consumption and economies of scope, as well as a rise in the service sector, trade, environmentalism and participatory forms of management and local governance.

The overall process has proved to be cumulative because innovations from one episode have spilled over into subsequent periods, even if their importance has been diminished. After all, railways still run, mass production still occurs and corporations continue to flourish. Furthermore, reactions from one episode have settled into the next. For instance, there is the legacy of labour's revolt against low pay and poor working conditions during the era of factories and mass production. More recently, the inevitability of modern progress in social terms and issues of basic rights and access to power were sharply questioned during widespread student and other uprisings in the late 1960s, as well as losses of confidence, in the West; from economic shocks and worries about the availability of basic resources.[1] Also in sharp debate are the environmental consequences of modern urbanization and industrialization, giving rise to a broad and lasting environmental movement. Indeed, in many Western cities, urban redevelopment, infill development, environmental mitigation and adaptive reuse of existing urban structures and property also began to emerge in importance, alongside new urban development, as urban populations in many places stabilized and even declined, and rising affluence, together with wider acknowledgement of social diversity, allowed broader expression of lifestyle preferences.

It is probably fair to say that, as modernization has progressed, its transformative power has become both stronger and more potentially pervasive in people's lives. Certainly, technological means, management wherewithal and technical problem-solving capabilities have increased massively since the early twentieth century. Longer spans of infrastructure are possible, effective communication is much faster and analytical techniques are both more powerful and widespread. Therefore, in regions like East Asia where modernization has taken place recently or is still taking place rapidly, as in China, the physical urban impact is likely to be more marked, and with less time and room for reaction or re-equilibration, than in those places in the developed West where modernization unfolded as a segmental episodic process. The suddenness, strength and comprehensiveness of recent urban modernization in East Asia is such that the palpable results probably exceed Western experiences, even though the basic concepts were borrowed from the West, and will place the region, by and large, on a different path.

Historical Underpinnings

Outside Western and modernizing influences first flowed forcefully and significantly into the East Asian region from early in the nineteenth century, initially on the heels of Western struggles for power, trade, resource extraction, and related colonial intentions and, later, from similar Japanese ambitions. In 1819, Thomas Stanford Raffles was dispatched from India to found a trading settlement on the island of Singapore, strategically located close to the Malacca and Sunda Straits between the Indian Ocean and the South China Sea – *Nanyang*. This was shortly before the signing of an Anglo-Dutch treaty in 1824, which partitioned off the Malay Peninsula from what became the Dutch East Indies and, later, Indonesia. Effectively this treaty concluded, principally in favour of the British, a protracted tussle for power and naval domination over the Indian Ocean, which began after the Seven Years War in Europe (1756–63) when the British began to project their naval power in the realization that national security required a continental balance of power supported by global naval mastery.[2] Forced engagement with the Dutch resulted in the British acquisition of Penang Island in 1786 and nearby Malacca in 1795, followed by a campaign against French privateering between 1805 and 1810, and the British capture of Mauritius in 1810. While the 1815 European peace settlement of Vienna provided some respite in the struggle, it also left the British to contend with the Dutch, at least until 1824, hence the need to base a contingent of its naval power in a location that could exert control, simultaneously and efficiently, over sea routes to the East Indian archipelago and the South China sea.[3] In this geopolitical context, however, Raffles did not push for territorial annexation to Britain. Instead, an agreement was made with the indigenous Temengong rulers authorizing the East India Company to establish a 'factory' – essentially a British-controlled trading post – in exchange for British protection and an annual monetary subvention. Those who placed themselves under the British flag (e.g., factory employees) also enjoyed British rule of law rather than local authority. After 1824, Singapore became a British possession under John Crawfurd, who replaced Raffles and took over complete control of the outpost. Shortly before, in 1822, Lieutenant Jackson, working with Raffles, completed a plan for the settlement in the form of a necklace-like string of communities stretching along 1.6 km of the coastline and dominated by the European town, reflecting the Palladianism that was rife in England at the time, and flanked by a Malay kampong, next to a Chinese settlement, on the Singapore River, and an Arab Sultanate next to the Burgis quarters on the other side of the European community away from the river.[4]

In the fourteenth century, prior to extensive contacts with the West, Singapore, then known as *Temasek*, was located in a power gap between the Srivijaya Empire, of which it was initially a dependency, and the Javanese king-

dom of Majapahit to the east. Having been laid claim to in 1365 by Majapahit, Temasek was finally taken by Malay forces in 1390, renamed *Singapora*, and made a vassal of the Malay kingdom of Malacca, remaining a remnant of the Malacca Sultanate even after the fall of Malacca to the Portuguese in 1511. Then, with the dwindling of Malay power in the area, Singapore became a meeting place for pirate fleets and the *Oranglaut*, literally 'men of the sea', who preyed on Chinese junks in the Nanyang trading zone. By 1819, when Raffles arrived, the population was around a thousand, of which several dozen were Malay rulers of one kind or another – the *Temengong* – plus some Chinese and an assortment of Burgis, inhabitants from nearby Borneo and Sarawak, in addition to the Oranglaut.[5]

Western settlement of Hong Kong and Shanghai followed within twenty years of that of Singapore, as the profitable potential of trade in China was spurred on by secure sea lanes and ports of call to Europe; the need for funds, especially by Britain, depleted by recent Napoleonic and other military campaigns, and the emergence of the United States on the international scene, out from under British hegemony. Far from being compliant, Qing dynasty China was resistive to these incursions, although shortly finding itself unequal to the task of adequately defending itself. Specifically, Hong Kong and Shanghai resulted from the spoils of the Treaty of Nanjing in 1842, which concluded the Anglo-Chinese or Opium War (1839–42), when the Chinese became the victims of gun-boat diplomacy.[6] Initially, however, the two new possessions were not equally welcomed. The largely uninhabited island of Hong Kong – after the local name, *He-ong-Kong*, recorded by the British around 1760 – was described by Lord Palmerston as 'a barren island which will never be a mart of trade'; it resulted from a withdrawal by a British naval squadron during the Opium War, under the command of Captain Elliot, below the passage leading up the Pearl River to Guangzhou (Canton).[7] A large city of over 1 million inhabitants, Guangzhou was where the East India company and other Western interests, including the Americans, had established a trading settlement – the 'Thirteen Factories' – in the late eighteenth and early nineteenth centuries. Although not congratulated for his efforts, Captain Elliot prudently settled for Hong Kong Island because it possessed a magnificent harbour, had fresh water and was sufficiently far afield from Guangzhou, as well as Portuguese Macao, to be defensible and a potential staging post for further naval operations.

Shanghai, by contrast, was one of five 'free-trade ports' – Treaty Ports – settled on by the British and other Western powers as part of the Treaty of Nanjing,

6
A view from
the peak, modern
Hong Kong on the
footprints of
early settlement.
1997.

along with Hong Kong and monetary reparations to be paid by the
Chinese.[8] Almost immediately, three settlements were formed in Shanghai,
to the north of the much older Chinese settlement at Nanshi, near the bend
of the Huangpu River and its confluence with Suzhou Creek, in Puxi, on the
west bank of the river. Administratively, these settlements took the form of
'Concessions', executed under a quasi-public corporate entity, through which
China maintained sovereignty over the land but relinquished political authority.

In 1854, land-use regulations were enacted under a single Municipal Council applicable to the British, French and American Concessions, although, in 1862, the French withdrew from this arrangement and in 1863 the British and Americans amalgamated their interests into what became known as the International Concession.[9] This situation of foreign occupation and enforced trade in China was further consolidated after the Arrow War (1856–60), and ratified by the Convention of Beijing, before expanding into additional Treaty Ports, up until the 1890s, like Qingdao, Tianjian and Dalian, that involved several other European nations such as Germany, Italy and Russia. Having become a Crown Colony in 1843, Hong Kong was expanded through the cession of the Kowloon Peninsula in 1868, placing the small, somewhat makeshift settlement on the northern side of Hong Kong Island well out of artillery range. The circular walled Chinese settlement in Shanghai, constructed for coastal defensive purposes during the late Ming dynasty, remained separate from the foreign Concessions, though they joined forces in 1862 to repel the threat of the Taiping Rebellion coming from the Chinese hinterland.[10]

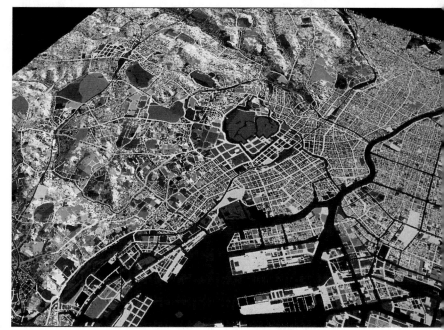

7
A collusion of topography, class and settlement patterns in Edo–Tokyo. 2001.

At much the same time, lasting Western influence arrived on Japan's shores, notably in 1853 when American Commodore Perry's 'Black Ships' sailed into what is now Tokyo Bay.[11] Quickly realizing they would be no match, militarily, for this impressive modern armada, Japan gradually opened up, with the establishment of a Western port, settlement and barracks in Yokohama, eventually linked to Shinbashi in Tokyo by a railway. Internally, the period between 1853 and 1868 was one of tension and confusion, as the Tokugawa Shogunate, established as far back as 1603, began to disintegrate under restlessness and factionalism within the aristocratic – *daimyō* – class, conflicts between modernizers and traditionalists, and the looming threat from abroad.[12] In 1868 the Shogunate came to an end, as political power moved back in the direction of the Emperor and the *daimyō* surrendered their fiefs to Imperial authority, ushering in the Meiji Restoration. Edo, the Shogunate capital, sprawling across the Yamanote plain and along the Sumida River, was renamed Tokyo – 'Eastern Capital' – and, with the modernizers in ascendancy, modern institutions were installed quickly. Compulsory education was instituted in 1872, around the same time as coinage, banking, taxation and railroads. In 1885, the Imperial Diet was constituted as the parliamentary arm of a constitutional system of imperial rule, following Western precedents. Industrialization followed during the last decade of the nineteenth century, primarily supported by the government and, technically, again along Western lines.[13]

Prior to the Meiji Restoration, Edo spread from the Shogun Ieyasu Tokugawa's castle to become one of the largest cities in the world at the time, expanding in population from a few thousand in 1600 to half a million in 1650 and to 1.3 million inhabitants by 1720. Much of this was due to the Shogun's doctrine of *sankin kōtai*, whereby the *daimyō* families, including many of their vassals, were required to be housed in Edo, together with a significant number of the *hatamoto* – the Shogun's standard bearers – and their soldiers. With this influx also came merchants, craftsmen, tradespeople, and so on, supporting and being supported by the burgeoning population.[14] 'Edo-Tokyo' was not old, by international standards, and yet not really young, but always very large. Geographically it was also superficially proto-modern, with the Yamanote, 'High City' or 'Garden City', sprawling across the hinterlands of the Kantō Plateau, composed principally of a loose arrangement of *daimyō* estates, temples and monastic quarters, and the adjacent Shitamachi, 'Low City' or 'City on the Water', compacted across lowlands running along the coast and up the Sumida River, composed of dense development, criss-crossed by canals and waterways, housing a majority of common people. However, far from being modern, Edo was a mirror of feudal power, with the Shogun's castle at its centre and around 600,000 people inhabiting the Yamanote, with 69 per cent of the land area, and the other 600,000 crammed into the Shitamachi, sharing only 16 per cent of the land area, the remainder consisting mainly of water and unreclaimed wetlands.[15]

Such was Japan's emulation of Western technology and related practices, together with its own ambitions to take its place on the world stage, that it became the principal initial conduit for modern ideas and practical applications in both Taiwan and Korea. Japan began making territorial encroachments on the northern East Asian mainland late in the nineteenth century, starting to open up the Korean peninsula by force in 1876, and precipitating an armed struggle with China, settled in 1895 by the Treaty of Shimonoseki, with the ceding to Japan of Taiwan (Formosa), Korea and the Liaodong Peninsula. Then followed the bloody conflict between Japan and Russia, also pushing territorial claims into northern China in pursuit of natural resources, that ended in the 1905 Treaty of Portsmouth and the re-ceding to Japan of Korea, along with Port Arthur and the remainder of the Liaodong Peninsula, which Japan had reluctantly been persuaded by Western powers to turn over to Russia in 1902. In addition, Japan gained control over substantial parts of Manchuria, from which it became a threatening force to inner China, as well as a general understanding with the British, in 1902, whereby Japan would have a 'free hand' in the region in exchange for favoured nation status for the British in the lucrative ongoing modernization of Japan.[16] On the heels of these colonial acquisitions Taipei was quickly established as the colonial capital of Taiwan and, with the arrival of Gotō Shimpei, first as a public health officer and then as the chief civilian administrator of Taiwan in 1898, substantial renovations were made to existing Chinese settlements. Government quarters were constructed, often with neo-Classical edifices; the walls of the administrative centre were torn down; public sanitation and lighting were improved considerably; and roadway alignments were constructed along neo-Classical European lines favoured, at the time, in Meiji Restoration and later Taishō Japan. Indeed, it has often been noted that the strong Western influence prevailing in Japan was more readily and more extensively imprinted on its colonies than at home in a city like Tokyo. For his part, Gotō Shimpei was strongly influenced by his medical studies in Germany during the late 1880s, and remained an avid advocate of Western-style public-works projects throughout his career, including a stint with the Southern Manchurian Railroad in 1905, before his return to Japan in 1915.[17]

Prior to the Japanese colonial arrival, the Taipei Basin was composed of village settlements dating back to indigenous populations and remnants, in the case of Keelung and San Domingo, of the struggle between the Dutch and the Spanish for the island that concluded in favour of the Dutch in 1662, along with the pronounced Chinese presence in what became known as the Tri-city area. After the fall of the Ming dynasty in 1644, many Chinese fled to Taiwan, settled there and later began agitating against the Dutch, eventually displacing them. In 1709, Mengchia was established as a trading post near the confluence of the Tamshui and Keelung rivers as a loose pattern of relatively rudimentary settlements, with streets terminating on temple and market places. Later, in 1853, a second settlement – Ta-tao-chen – was established further downstream on the Tamshui for improved navigation, in the form of a regular layout, with streets and canals parallel to the river, alongside which stood trading houses and shops. As the importance of the Taipei Basin increased it gained prefecture status in 1875, with Chen Hsin-chu as governor. Shortly thereafter a third settlement – Chen Nei or the 'Inner City' – was constructed, this time in the classical form of a square, walled enclosure, with a regular layout of streets and gates and in a relationship to surrounding mountains and water bodies deemed propitious under geomantic *Feng Shui* principles.[18]

After increasing pressure and occupation, Korea was officially annexed to Japan in 1909 and the old capital of Hanyang, now Seoul, renamed Kyongsong. Again the Japanese colonists began dismantling surrounding walls around the city, making roadway improvements, improving sanitation, lighting and transportation, as well as generally bringing a geometric, Western-influenced order to the otherwise organic qualities of the existing urban area.[19] They also built imposing government structures, including their colonial headquarters, again in the manner of the Meiji Restoration and later Taishō period, with strong Western neo-Classical influences, and importation of modern institutions, already well underway in Japan.

Hangyang had been founded by General Yi Songye, who unified the Shilla and Koryo Kingdoms into the Chosun dynasty in 1392–4. According to old accounts, the site of Hanyang was selected as a propitious place for a capital and organized spatially according to Hyongsedo Korean cartographic principles – based on geomancy brought to Korea from China in the nineteenth century – whereby the city was conceptualized as an organic body subject to natural forces and flows of the earth's energies. Under this rubric, mountains and streams were regarded as conduits for these forces and flows, primarily in the form of wind, water and solar orientation. What emerged was a city site

Central Beijing's
persistent form.
1996.

surrounded by mountains, with walls following the ridge lines for added protection and demarcation, several water courses, generally flowing in an east–west direction, and generous and well-ventilated south-facing slopes as future locations for palaces and shrines. Subsequent settlement incorporated four major and four minor gates in the surrounding wall; the main Kyongbok palace complex and garden on a north–south alignment near the centre, on a northern slope with the preferred solar orientation; nearby a rather loose arrangement of other aristocratic enclaves; and a much denser 'lower class' community, including merchants, craftsmen and some literati, primarily on the centre-to-southern side of the city. In this spatial arrangement the Chosun dynasty remained in almost glorious isolation, often referred to as the 'Hermit Kingdom' because of its closed-door policy, until severely shaken and then dislodged by the Japanese in the 1900s.[20]

Unlike Hong Kong, Shanghai, the other Treaty Ports, extensive parts of Manchuria, Vietnam and Taiwan, all under Western or Japanese hegemony by the early twentieth century, Beijing and what was left of China remained solely in the arthritic and increasingly helpless grasp of the Qing dynasty and, therefore, further away from Western influence, until 1911. Not that the China of the Qing was unaware of the West. Internally, the Self-Strengthening

Movement, which began in 1860 as a way of taking up foreign modern technology, although in a non-essential or ideological manner, was followed by the
Hundred Days Reform of 1898 and then the Constitutional Movement of 1901,
successively enlarging the scope of foreign influence to encompass social and
political institutions. Nevertheless, these efforts proved to be too little too late
for the reluctant Qing, who were brought down by civil disorder and revolt,
ushering in a tumultuous early Republican period of warlord and other
factions that eventually gained some modicum of tense stability in large parts
of China by 1928, under Chiang Kai-shek's Nationalists.[21]

Between 1911 and 1918, amid mainland strife, modernization began under
the influence of figures like Zhu Qiqian, a reformer and modernizer who
became Republican Minister of Internal Affairs in 1913, having served prior to
that as the Minister of Transportation. Once again roads were constructed,
paved and widened, transportation and sanitation improved and some building
projects embarked upon, largely in emulation of modern Western practices.
One significant contribution was the creation of parks for residents of Beijing,
through the transfiguration of imperial gardens, ceremonial sites and the
Forbidden City, the outer walls of which were pulled down. Consistent with
prevailing Republican rule, social and political institutions also received attention and were gradually modernized. However, given the uncertain times and
the scarcity of resources, exacerbated further by the removal of the capital
from Beijing to Nanjing by the Nationalists in 1928, which also siphoned off
funds that had formerly flowed into Beijing, the condition of the former capital
– now called Beiping (Northern Peace) – was poor, with little modern infrastructure or industry.[22]

In its imperial glory, Beijing (Northern Capital) was defined by a large city
wall encircling a square enclosure, dating from the Yuan dynasty (1271–1368),
penetrated by imposing city gates and, over time, laid out in a relatively regular pattern of streets, running east–west and north–south, between which ran
lanes – the *hutong* – flanked on either side mainly with single-storeyed, four-
sided courtyard houses – *siheyuan* – some commercial establishments and
special buildings like temples, pagodas, palatial enclaves and humbler buildings of the less well-to-do. Adjacent to this square enclosure and to the south,
another rectangular wall component of the city was formed and reinforced
during the Ming dynasty (1368–1644) and the Qing dynasty (1644–1911),
although with a more irregular internal pattern of streets and lanes. The
imperial compound of the Forbidden City was aligned along the central
north–south axis of the city, and to the west was constructed an extensive

necklace of lakes and gardens, stretching from the northern city wall to the city centre near the Forbidden City, and to the south, again close to the north–south central axis, the magnificent Temple of Heaven and several other large temple complexes. According to some, Beijing's most famous ruler–planners were Khubilai Khan (1215–1294), whose Mongols conquered the Jin, firmly establishing Beijing in the Yuan Dadu period, when the city was called *Khanbaliq*, and the Emperor Yongle (1360–1424), the accomplished Ming ruler. In any case, the early layout of Beijing closely approximated the cosmological ideal of a square-shaped universe with the Son of Heaven at its centre, also physically incorporating, in the self-similarity of house-to-lane, block-to-street, palace-to-city, and so on, Confucian principles of propriety – *li* – and the one and the many from the *Book of Rites*, or *Liji*, also allegedly derived from the earlier *Zhouli*. Both in its layout and architectural embellishment, Beijing was quintessentially a classical imperial Chinese city and capital, housing, by the time of the Qing, well over 1 million inhabitants.[23]

Modern Prefaces

From these initial and uneven beginnings, when modern influence was forced on East Asia by the West and carried forward by Japan's own colonial ambitions, processes of modernization and urbanization unfolded in a roughly parallel manner, encountering different levels of resistance or impediment and with varying degrees of purchase and impetus from place to place, before coming to a virtual halt amid the sea changes of power and calamitous destruction that took place during and shortly after World War II. Planning ordinances began to be enacted and public improvements made to major cities during the latter nineteenth century, much like counterpart regulation and public projects in the West. First came consideration of public health and safety, through so-called light, air and building code regulation and provision of water, sanitation, electricity, gas, transportation and other municipal services, together with institutional buildings, such as educational facilities and hospitals, as well as public parks. While these provisions were not as uniform or as comprehensive as those undertaken in many if not most Western cities, improvements to urban living conditions were made. In Singapore, for instance, which had experienced suburban expansion and ribbon-like trolley-car urban development since the 1860s, a municipal ordinance was enacted in 1887, followed by a housing trust, in 1917, to deal with slum clearance and more adequate provision of dwellings.[24] Hong Kong also enacted district ordinances in the late nineteenth century, although some were for the purposes of segregation, such as the Peak Residence Ordinance of 1887. By 1912 a rail connection from Kowloon through the New Territories to Guangzhou was complete and hospitals, schools, a botanical garden and even a university were founded, all consistent with the Victorian colonial image of the time.[25]

Similarly, the European-dominated Municipal Council of Shanghai provided a broad array of municipal services by 1880, in part to stem the risk of disease from the neighbouring Chinese settlement and including assistance to the Chinese in this regard.[26] Beijing began to embark on road construction, sanitation and public park provision during the early Republican period, including the creation of Central Park (Zhongshan Park) by Zhu Qiqian, in 1914, from the imperial Altar of Earth and Grain, immediately to the west of Tiananmen in the centre of the city.[27] Despite substantial institutional modernization by Japan, at least on the surface, physical modernization in Tokyo was largely piecemeal. Several Western-style projects were completed, including the Ginza Brick Quarter after a fire in 1872, by the British architect Thomas Waters, and Mitsubishi Londontown in 1890, by another British architect Josiah Conder, on the site of a former *daimyō* estate near the imperial palace. Ryōunbaku, a twelve-storey tower, was constructed in Akasaka in 1890, as a symbol of Japan's growing technical prowess, and further *daimyō* estates were appropriated for construction of government buildings, ministries and the Diet.[28] Prompted by rapid population growth, overcrowding, peripheral expansion and public safety, a Town Planning Act and an Urban Building Act were promulgated in 1919. With abolition of the *sankin kō tai* doctrine of the Shogunate, Tokyo's population had dwindled to about 500,000 inhabitants in the 1870s, to rise to 1 million in 1890 and 2.7 million by 1907.[29] On the Japanese colonial front, Taipei and Kyongsang (Seoul), followed suit, with piecemeal adjustments, although an urban planning committee was put in place in Taipei in 1898, which among other things later provided policies calling for arcaded structures – *tingzijiao* – along streets for reasons of climate control.[30] There was a prevalent belief, at least in those areas influenced by the West – stemming largely from Western contention with ills produced by the first Industrial Revolution – in the redemption of squalor and blight in cities by virtue of safer building conditions, adequate provision of light and ventilation, as well as more convenient transportation and provision of public open spaces. These efforts were also an attempt to make cities more efficient and to redress at least some social issues behind mounting unrest from the lower classes, largely in the name of continuing stability and economic progress.

9
The Bund in
Shanghai during
the 1930s.

Meanwhile, industrial development took hold, particularly in places like Tokyo and Shanghai and under increasingly independent Japanese involvement. Manufacturing started in earnest in Tokyo, around 1890, along Western lines, with the bulk of equipment supplied by foreigners, mainly the British, and with strong state involvement both because of the capital resources required and the belief that a rich and strong enterprise should not be left entirely in private hands. Around World War I, which proved to be a boon to Japanese industry, foreign influence diminished considerably and was replaced by government subsidy to favoured and also indebted private enterprises or, rather, cliques – the *zaibatsu* – organized on the base of a resurrected samurai class, such as the Mitsubishi, Mitsui, Sumitomo and Yasuda.[31] Geographically, industrial districts in Tokyo stretched south along the shoreline of Tokyo Bay to Yokohama and on the eastern side of the Sumida River in Senja and Fukugawa, all well served by port and railway access.

After 1895, Japan entered into Shanghai's commercial fray alongside its Western competitors and, although commerce was strong, the city soon became dominated by manufacturing. Quickly, Japanese firms surpassed the British in the number and scale of their cotton mills – a primary source of industrial production – and flour mills, chemical plants, mechanical workshops and shipbuilding also flourished.[32] Again the centres of industrial production were located adjacent to the city proper – the foreign Concessions and the Chinese town – with textiles concentrated immediately to the north, chemicals and mechanical production along the Huangpu River, also to the north, and ship-building to the south in a modern harbour constructed in 1901 on the Huangpu.[33] At this time Shanghai enjoyed several competitive advantages as a site for manufacturing. It had close proximity to raw materials, principally cotton from its hinterland in the Changjiang Delta. It possessed a cheap supply of electricity and other fuel stocks, as well as an extensive readily skilled, yet low-cost, labour force. It also enjoyed the benefits of financial institutions – concentrated on the Bund, along the Huangpu waterfront, in front of the business centre of the Concessions – capable of handling sophisticated transactions, including the largest bank in China.[34] Finally, technical know-how was readily transferred and it was a place conducive to technical and cultural experimentation.

In comparison, Japan's colonies provided more in the way of raw materials and product than industrial production, and both Singapore and Hong Kong remained entrepôts, the economies of which were battered by the cessation of free trade by Britain, followed by the United States and Japan, in the 1930s. Of the two, Singapore probably fared better, because of its more strategic location and by having been buoyed up by the need for rubber and tin from the Malay Peninsula as early as 1900 for such things as vehicle tyres and tins for food preservation. By 1903 it was the seventh largest port in the world and its population doubled between 1900 and 1930, rising from 225,000 to around 550,000.[35] Hong Kong, on the other hand, declined from around 28 per cent of the China trade in 1911 to only 16 per cent in 1925, about the time it also suffered a boycott by Guangzhou, a primary source of products, as well as severe labour unrest. An ascendant Japan had garnered 40 per cent of the China trade by 1918.[36]

In a second round of urban planning and development, following this time on the heels of the Second Industrial Revolution in the West and related urban improvement practices from about 1920 onwards, more comprehensive approaches to urban regulation and management were gradually introduced into East Asia, largely along already established conduits of influence. In Tokyo, Gotō Shimpei became mayor and between 1920 and 1923 began to modernize the city more thoroughly with the development of what became known as his 'big handkerchief plan', because of its extensive scope. This plan for substantial infrastructure improvement and land readjustment, following the German model, was intended to provide improved circulation and wider and better distribution of public services. He was assisted by the American

Charles Beard, whom he brought to Tokyo as an advisor and to head up the Tokyo Institute of Municipal Research, dedicated to problems of improved urban management.[37] In the end, however, this effort largely failed; it proved too costly and became too entangled with well-entrenched private and corporate interests.

Shortly after the disastrous Kantō earthquake of 1923, during which 44 per cent of Tokyo's land area was flattened or burned and 63 per cent of all houses destroyed, further headway was made in the direction of adopting Western procedures of zoning against landowners' indiscriminate land use, stricter building codes, and more effective use of land readjustment for improved infrastructure investments. The more important and lasting consequence of the earthquake, however, was the suburban boom that took off to the west and the relative safety of the westerly Saitama Prefecture. There, real-estate development took the unusual form of railroad companies building railroads as far out as 30 km from the city centre and constructing department stores, other commercial ventures and even nascent communities at primary transit stops. Indeed, in these arrangements, the railroad was the pretext for profitable land development, giving rise to the beginnings of prominent contemporary urban centres, like Shibuya, Shinjuku and Western-style garden suburbs.[38]

Elsewhere in East Asia, Singapore formed its first comprehensive town planning body under the Singapore Improvement Ordinance Bill of 1927.[39] Beijing extended its planning and modernization efforts under the energetic leadership of Yuan Liang – a graduate of Waseda University in Tokyo – who served as mayor between 1933 and 1935.[40] In 1932, Japanese authorities unfurled their land-use zoning and transportation plan for Taipei, and land readjustment schemes and related improvement mechanisms for Kyongsang (Seoul) in 1934. Hong Kong, always shy of strong intervention by the public sector in 'free market' circumstances, made minimal alterations to its urban codes, while Shanghai, now under pressure from Chiang Kai-shek's Nationalist forces, literally sealed both the French and International Concessions from external Chinese interference in 1927.[41] Nevertheless, Shanghai remained the 'model of modernity' in China, with an expanding population reaching 2.6 million by 1927 on its way to around 5 million by 1949, and with volumes of trade and manufacturing that accounted for a substantial portion of China's total, prompting the Nationalists to extract funds from the city to help support public projects elsewhere in China, like their new capital in Nanjing.[42] Under a shift in influence, away from the British, the United States and France, towards the modernizing Chinese Nationalists, a northern annexe was planned for

Shanghai by the architect, Dong Dayou – a University of Minnesota and Columbia University graduate – following Beaux-Arts principles and in the traditional style of building promoted by the regime.[43] Nevertheless, construction techniques and practices were modern, involving steel frames, reinforced concrete, macadam road building, elevators, and so on.

Resistance and impediment to urban modernization came essentially in four forms. First, there was distrust and social unrest aimed particularly in the direction of colonizing authority and exploitative capitalism. In 1925, for instance, there were widespread strikes at Japanese mills, which were dominant engines in Shanghai's industrial production. These strikes led to, or became bound up with, broader civil unrest, pitting students and workers against the police.[44] Demands for broader Chinese representation in the governance and affairs of the Concessions also escalated, resulting in their becoming sealed off with the arrival of the Chinese Nationalists in 1927. At much the same time labour unrest erupted in Hong Kong, during which eleven people were killed. Underlying this unrest was a considerable amount of agitation from (then communist) Guangzhou, resulting in the 1925 boycott of Hong Kong, and significant interruptions in its entrepôt trade.[45] Enforced Japanese colonial authority and presence in Korea hardly led to full compliance with their plans for modernization by the Koreans, although Japan fared better in these regards in more out-of-the-way Taiwan.

Second, there was local contextual resistance to urban modernization, even in places like Tokyo, in spite of broad state-level commitment. As we saw, Gotō Shimpei's ambitious planning efforts in the early 1920s were not very effective, especially when they encountered a multitude of entrenched private interests deeply ingrained in the prior urban patterns of Edo. One source of this failure, which serves to illustrate the entanglement, was land adjustment or expropriation of property for widening streets, creating public open space and modernizing other elements of infrastructure, especially in the dense urban fabric of the Shitamachi. This was proposed under the theory that such improvement would benefit adjacent landowners and, therefore, compensation would only be made when the amount of property taken exceeded 10 per cent of its lot area. However, this formula was resisted by many, either because they were dubious of the positive returns of the proposed improvements, lacking clear examples, or because they would not be adequately compensated.[46] Moreover, the cost of fuller compensation quickly proved to be prohibitive. Similar resistance was met in Kyongsang (Seoul) after introduction of land adjustment there in 1934. In fact, as in most parts of the world, public taking of private property was generally resisted, particularly throughout well-established urban areas in East Asia, since the public purposes and benefits were probably far less clear than they are today, or than they were then in more developed parts of the world.

Third, remoteness and underdevelopment proved an impediment to modernization, especially in broad reaches of China with little or no contact with the outside world or, at that time, with the powers in China itself, in any organized, progressive way. Although modern up to a point under Western control, both Singapore and Hong Kong failed to progress beyond being well-oiled entrepôts into indigenously based industrialization, due to their colonial perception only as remote sources of raw materials and outlets to markets for finished goods produced elsewhere, mostly at home.

Finally, political–cultural reaction to Western influence, and conceptual compartmentalization of this influence for applications and practical purposes only, was rife from the start in China, as well as appearing in Japan. The Chinese phrase that emerged from the Self-Strengthening Movement, *zhongxue weiti xixue weiyong* – 'Chinese learning for essential principles, Western learning for practical functions' – erected a collective mental compromise that allowed simultaneous pursuit, or so it was thought, of indigenous and fundamental essences alongside exogenous organizational, managerial and technical forms of development.[47] Simply setting one set of cultural values against the practicality of doing things, however, did not last long. As one distinguished observer put it, 'gunboats and steel mills bring their own philosophy with them'.[48] Nevertheless, this largely bifurcated emphasis persisted in the philosophical mindset of the Chinese. Even Sun Yat-sen, the modern founder of China during the early Republic, initially saw China as resistant to modern nation building precisely because of indigenous neo-Confucian traits of individualism – stemming from the habits of mind of autonomous scholars, rather than as it might be understood in the contemporary West, notably in the United States – and loyalty to clan and family, but changed his mind when he became critical of Western materialism and adjusted to the ingrained nature of Chinese tradition.[49] Sun Yat-sen was taught in Western schools, spending years in the West, and was not classically trained in the Chinese manner or had much working knowledge of Chinese thought. This state of compromise was interrupted by the May 4th Movement, which sprang up in Beijing in 1919, embracing all manner of positivist Western thinking and modern practical reasoning. However, with the rise to power of the Nationalists in 1927, and their political arm the *Guomindang*, orientation to the West moved again in the opposite direction. The New Life Movement, launched by Chiang Kai-shek in the early 1930s, called for greater adherence to traditional Confucian values of politeness, righteousness, integrity and self-respect, together with a capacity to endure hardship, as well as love of country and loyalty to national ideals.[50] In urban-architectural terms it also came to mean glorifying China's past accomplishments while looking forward through the use of modern materials and techniques. Certainly, Yuan Liang's modern city of tradition, incorporated in

Beijing's Tourist District Plan of 1933, took this stance by being, at once, critical of early Republican destruction of imperial historical patrimony and yet distancing Chineseness from the self-same imperial past, through modern technical intervention. Similarly, early periods of modernization in Japan took place against a backdrop of *wahon yōsei* – 'Japanese spirit and Western technique' – although later this type of East–West bifurcation disappeared almost completely.

Towards the mid-1930s, Japan pressed further forward with its territorial and colonial ambitions, while entering at home into what is now referred to as the 'Dark Valley Decade' – a time of militarism, nationalism and, ultimately, of fascism.[51] With increasing force, the Japanese moved south across the East Asian mainland. In 1933 they defeated a Chinese army, stopping just north of Beiping under the Tangqu Agreement, before more fully exerting their power and influence, under the Hu-Umeza Agreement, over the newly designated 'North-China Autonomous Zone', including Beiping. By 1937, the full-scale 'War of Resistance' against Japan was underway in China, enjoined by both the Communists and the Nationalists. Shanghai fell to the Japanese in 1941, followed by further expansion of what they called the 'Greater East Asia Co-prosperity Sphere', with the fall of Hong Kong, also in 1941, and Singapore in 1942 – renamed *Shōnan*, or 'Light of the South'.[52] Incursions by the Japanese inland from the eastern coastal region of China proved to be difficult against stiff and numerous opposition, although by then Japan had control over most of the Chinese productive assets. Generally, Japanese hegemony was executed forcefully and often brutally. In Singapore, however, they attempted to create indigenous self-sustaining industry for the first time.

Then the tide of war turned, resulting in Japan's unconditional surrender to the Allies in 1945. Japan was severely damaged. Incessant Allied bombing had destroyed in the order of 760,000 houses in Tokyo, not to mention the ghastly and grotesque atomic destruction of Hiroshima and Nagasaki.[53] Thus early modernization, with Japan in the vanguard, came to a sudden end in East Asia, followed by widespread anti-colonialism and autonomous nation building. The process of decolonization in the Malay Peninsula, for instance, began immediately after World War II with armed insurgence against the British, primarily by the Communists. The United Malay National Organization (UMNO) was founded in 1946, led by Tunku Abdul Rahman, and Lee Kuan Yew formed the Malayan Forum in 1947, arguing for an independent socialist Malaya, including Singapore. In 1954, he founded the People's Action Party (PAP) in alliance with the Malayan Communist Party and won a general election in 1959, although with the Socialists as his allies, not the Communists. Against this

political progress, however, urban living circumstances were deteriorating badly. Immigration down the Malay Peninsula boosted the Singapore population by over 50 per cent in a very short period of time and, combined with neglect of municipal services during the past twenty years, resulted in some 300,000 squatters and a further 250,000 living in slums.[54]

Immediately after World War II, together with anti-colonialism in many quarters, the other major influence on East Asia was the outcome of the long festering civil war in China. Beiping, now again Beijing, fell to the victorious Communists in January 1949, followed by Shanghai in May. Suddenly Hong Kong became a refuge for Chinese from the mainland even after the border was closed in 1949. The Crown Colony's population jumped to above 1.5 million, compared to about 1 million in the late 1930s, and resulted in large numbers of shanty towns and squatter settlements, often perched precariously on marginal hillside slopes that were dangerously susceptible to mudslides.[55] Similarly, Taipei became a Guomindang refuge and eventual stronghold, with mainlanders often acting as callous carpetbaggers. Soaring prices, deterioration of public health and squatter settlements, mainly displaced Taiwanese, resulted in demonstrations in 1947 and declaration of martial law. Shortly thereafter, the Nationalist governor – General Chen Yi – was replaced, under pressure from the United States, and executed for his heavy-handed mishandling of the situation. With circumstances going badly for Chiang Kai-shek and his Nationalist supporters, more and more mainlanders poured into Taiwan.[56]

Meanwhile, Kyongsang, finally named Seoul in 1949, was also under intense pressure of immigration from rural areas, from the north, and from expatriate Koreans returning from Manchuria, China and Japan after World War II. By 1949 the population in Seoul had doubled from its total in 1935, and squatter settlements – 'moon villages' as they were called – sprang up on vacant sites, marginal lands, public rights-of-way and up precarious hillsides of the city. Then civil war broke out between North and South Korea, with China and the Communist bloc aligned with the North and the US-led United Nations coalition on the side of the South. For Seoul the result, when the dust finally settled in the stalemate of 1953, was around 47 per cent destruction of its buildings, as well as massive dislocation of vital elements of infrastructure.[57]

It was from the ashes of wartime destruction, heady movements of post-war decolonization and, above all, from massive migration that the first real autonomous and full-blown period of modernization began in East Asia, resulting in the high rates of industrialization and urbanization mentioned in chapter One. To put precise dates on this period is difficult. But, outside China, it took somewhere between 1950 and 1965 for sustained modern capitalist production to start becoming effective, and sometime after 1970 for social and equity issues of this modernization to be more fully appreciated and considered. In Japan, for instance, adverse consequences of Ikeda's Income Doubling Plan included poor air and water quality; acute housing shortages, with 34 per cent of Tokyo's population poorly housed and 24 per cent living in what some Western visitors to the 1964 Olympic Games called 'rabbit hutches', at less than 5 m² of livable space per capita; as well as massive transportation congestion, running at something like 250 per cent of capacity.[58] Civil unrest mounted, resulting in riots during 1968 and 1969, before matters began to be redressed in the 1970s. Similarly, in Hong Kong, negative social and environmental effects of the laissez-faire economic boom of the 1960s, deeply coloured by sweatshop labour and rudimentary housing resettlements, were administratively recognized and at least partially addressed only after 1971, with Governor Maclehose's reforms. Within China, now the People's Republic of China, modernization also began in the 1950s, although under a different Communist guise and with substantial Soviet expertise. Amid gross mismanagement and a strong drift to the political far left, early progress was halted, however, before the onset of the disastrous 'Cultural Revolution' and its aftermath, during the last half of the 1960s and on into the early 1970s, only to be recommenced after Deng Xiaoping's historic opening to the outside world in 1978.

Revolution from the Top

As discussed briefly in chapter Two, a distinguishing feature and central reason for the success of rapid post-war and contemporary modernization in many parts of East Asia is the very direct and positive correlation of collective consumption, such as government provision of housing and often social services, with processes of capital accumulation and economic production. In contrast with the West, at least in the degree of application, modernization has taken place largely outside of the liberal pluralist paradigm of the standard model described earlier, and usually has been a case of 'revolution from above', resembling, perhaps, industrialization during the nineteenth century in parts of continental Europe. Today, in much of East Asia, the state continues to be the midwife of capitalism, and the state role, alongside the system of private market forces, has been crucial to much of the region's economic success. This said, however, there are significant differences between one place and another. In fact, several quite different responses have emerged from the interaction between collective consumption and market forces, due mainly to differences in historical circumstances. In Singapore, Lee Kuan Yew and the ruling People's Action Party found themselves in an unenviable predicament during the early post-colonial period. In 1963 they were strenuously campaigning to join the Malay Federation, strongly believing, in spite of some wide differences with other member states, comprising what is now Malaysia, that Singapore would have great difficulty going it alone as an independent nation. This, however, is what happened in 1965, when Tunku Abdul Rahman and others passed the 'Singapore Amendment', summarily ejecting the island province from the federation. Suddenly confronted with nation-building, Lee Kuan Yew and his followers hastily assembled a plan to transform the fragmented island society, with massive socio-economic problems, into an independent and self-reliant modern state.[59] It is difficult to imagine worse circumstances from which to begin.

Basing their path forward on economic prosperity, Lee Kuan Yew and the young nation's leadership decided to capitalize on the country's assets, primarily a low-paid, yet reasonably well-educated, labour force, and to move the nation forward from a commercial trading post to a fully industrial state.[60] They quickly recognized the need for substantial direct foreign investment, since all sectors of Singapore were relatively poor at the time, and the need to encourage this investment by remaining very open to international trade. More specifically, decisions were taken to keep labour costs low, while

continually improving productivity, through massive programmes of collective consumption in housing and transportation, thereby underwriting rising costs of living. The decision was also made to make foreign investment as attractive and as easy as possible, through state construction of roads, port facilities and other infrastructural improvements, in addition to construction of export processing and other factory facilities. The huge Jurong Industrial Estates, on the south-west corner of the island, mentioned earlier in chapter One, were a conspicuous example of this approach. There a highly functional gridiron layout of well-serviced sites was provided to foreign enterprises and investors, adjacent to up-to-date port facilities with large and expandable cargo-handling capacities.

Key to this collective consumption in support of economic production and capital accumulation was the creation of two very powerful statutory boards: the Economic Development Board and the Housing Development Board. Far from being entirely new, however, this type of practice drew upon prior statutory board traditions from the earlier colonial period. Nevertheless, the planned interaction between these two entities was new and largely unprecedented. Essentially the Economic Development Board provided a climate conducive for capital investment and productive employment, while the Housing Board provided the living environment for those engaged in these economic activities. Moreover, the extent of the Housing Board's influence over time cannot be underestimated when one realizes that 85 per cent of all Singaporeans in 1986 lived in public housing, provided for them in Housing Board estates, the largest programme of its kind among all urban systems within the capitalist world on a per capita basis. In comparison to Hong Kong, where there was also and continues to be a very large public housing programme – second within the capitalist world on a normalized basis – home ownership, at 66 per cent of the total, is high in Singapore, further emphasizing the strong social contract between the state and its citizenry.[61] Over time, the Housing Board's functions expanded from basic housing relief into close coordination between new town developments and transportation improvements, together with extensive programmes of urban renewal. The Urban Redevelopment Authority, one of the most influential entities of its kind anywhere in the world, was formed in 1974 to preside and guide many of these latter efforts into what was termed 'A Tropical City of Excellence'.

For at least 25 years, Singapore's strategy of collective consumption enjoyed uninterrupted economic success. Standards of living were raised appreciably across the island. Housing conditions were vastly improved over the 'dark days' of the middle 1960s and employment opportunities continued to increase and diversify. By 1985, Singapore had emerged on the world scene as a leading modern industrial and commercial nation. By 1987, however, financial overcommitments to collective consumption had become evident. The real-estate market started to go into decline and a mismatch was experienced between the housing preferences of a burgeoning middle class and standard housing estate units. In comparison to other parts of East Asia income redistribution also remained a problem, in spite of sustained efforts to improve the situation, although it was on a par, as noted earlier, with most Western nations. More recently, adjustments have been made in the nation's overall development strategy to account for some of these shortcomings and to move more fully into the contemporary era of high technology and new technology. An earlier posture of relatively low spending on local tertiary education, for instance, has been reversed in order to equip the labour force more fully, together with a programme of government backing for promising start-up, high-tech companies. Realizing that a more highly educated and potentially footloose labour force may resist a strict regime of political and social

pressures, the government has also been at some pains to modify its hard-line ideological position.

In China the institutional trajectory of development and modernization has been different, although as one might imagine under the Communist Party, remaining strongly committed to collective consumption and a strong central role for the state. Since the beginning of Deng Xiaoping's economic reforms of 1978, there has been a shift away from a consolidation of state-owned enterprises towards a more instrumental stance, whereby work and political units throughout the nation have begun to enjoy greater levels of autonomy and freedom of economic action. This has provided China with broader opportunities for economic experimentation under Deng's rubric of 'let's go and see', or 'one country, several systems', and has certainly hastened the nation's economic growth and modernization. It has also caused something of a loosening of authority between the central government in Beijing and provincial and municipal governments, especially in rapidly modernizing areas like Guangdong Province, Hubei Province, the Changjiang Delta and the Bohai Bay Region, and in cities like Shanghai, Dalian, Shenzhen, Suzhou, Wenzhou and Qingdao. Indeed, there is often some resistance on the part of these wealthier eastern provinces and cities to share their new-found income with other parts of the country, and simmering debate in central government regarding the efficiency of 'slipstreaming' the nation's economy behind the burgeoning coastal region, or of pursuing programmes to subsidize poorer regions.

One of the first attempts in China to be more open to the outside world was the creation of a number of special economic zones and other export platforms during the late 1980s, along the lines of those described in chapter One. These occurred in places like Da Bei, adjacent to Dalian in the north, Pudong, near Shanghai in the central coastal region, and in Shenzhen and Hainan in the south. Within these zones, new infrastructure was provided, together with manufacturing and warehousing facilities, somewhat along the same lines as Singapore and earlier successful experiments in South Korea and in Taiwan. The clear advantage over extensive urban renewal to existing urban and industrial centres was the significant lowering of both the cost and time necessary to provide improvements in the hopes of attracting external, foreign investment. Places like Pudong were then further subdivided into specific zones, such as the Jinqiao Export Processing Zone, due east of Shanghai; the Waigaoqiao Free Trade Zone, to the north, which operates explicitly as an entrepôt with extensive facilities for exporting, importing and processing; and the Lujiazui financial District, now the central business district of Pudong, as well as for much of

Shanghai.[62] With planned office space improvements almost completed, on the order of 42m² of space, Lujiazui is a very large development, as is Waigaoqiao, with around 10 km² of land area and some 2,000 enterprises already in place.[63] Most special economic zones have experienced rapid early economic success, although with varying later success. The GDP of Hainan, for instance, grew at a rate of around 20 per cent annually, increasing almost three times between 1987 and 1993. Recently, however, this boom has subsided substantially, calling into question, among other things, the appropriateness of Hainan's location, especially in comparison to other better placed and longer established places like Shanghai.

The general reform of state-owned enterprises and a redefinition of property rights in several sectors have also hastened the processes of modernization in China.[64] The family responsibility legislation, for instance, providing legal contracts for farming families and giving them responsibility over the land, in return for compensation linked to production, was an economic boon to the countryside and to the nation's peasantry. Soon small rural towns and neighbouring small cities became diversified centres of production, service provision, education and information for farmers. A good example of this type of development is Zhangjiagang, located next to the Changjiang River in the delta region east of the old capital of Nanjing. Until recently a relatively underdeveloped rural area, this county is now made up of towns and villages with a population in excess of 800,000 and thriving township-village enterprises, largely small rural industries. Urbanization there has been very rapid, changing from around 16 per cent in 1980 to about 20 per cent in 1986, and close to 50 per cent today. Nationally some estimates place the contribution of township-village enterprises to GDP as high as 30 per cent, although as China moves into a more conventional pattern of modern urban production this contribution has begun to decline.[65]

These developments in China, however, have not been without their problems. High levels of competition between towns and cities, many with almost exactly the same profiles of economic activities in spite of locational and geographic differences, as well as the existence of market forces, like the transference of property rights and flexible pricing of goods and services in relation to supply and demand, have created considerable duplication of effort, potential waste and significant social cost. One unfortunate outcome of the family responsibility system was the 'development zone fever' and 'real-estate fever' which occurred, in the absence of normal market constraints, as farmers attempted to find more productive uses for their land, as well as surplus labour, and competed furiously with one another for outside investment and markets for their goods. Many were successful, in spite of an inherent lack of demand for investments, with the upshot that many areas are grossly over-built, especially with regard to high-end commercial and residential develop-ments, owned mainly by hapless foreign investors. More serious has been the sudden erosion of agricultural productivity in a nation that already has only one-fifth of an acre per capita of cultivated land, or about 30 per cent of the world average. Indeed, only about one third of China's land mass can be read-ily cultivated. Between, roughly, 1978 and 1994 something like 19 per cent of cultivated land was lost to urban and industrial development, some of it prob-ably indiscriminately.[66] Overall, national emphasis remains on economic pro-duction, now including substantial stimulation of internal demand, as the first priority, with a tendency to defer environmental protection and remediation, as described in chapter One. Also, the social security net is beginning to fray under the mounting market orientation and it remains to be seen whether income production can be rapid enough and sufficiently well spread to bal-ance rising income disparities and environmental costs.

Under the aegis of different systems, both Hong Kong and Taiwan also engaged in considerable state-directed economic efforts and collective con-sumption. In Taiwan, as noted in chapter One, there were very active policies of import substitution and import restrictions on cheaper goods from else-where, in order to achieve self-sufficiency, after the Guomindang takeover in 1949 and subsequent periods of unrest and power consolidation. The Taiwanese also took a relatively distinctive approach towards industrializa-tion, maximizing the value added to output, particularly in products like textiles and 'white ware', as well as building up state enterprises, already well established during the Japanese colonial era, through substantial subsidies and the consignment of expensive imported goods to promising private enter-prises. Throughout there was also a conscious emphasis on production for export.

Similarly, Hong Kong was highly successful in the export orientation of its manufacturing and was also a prolific state partner, like Singapore, in collective consumption of housing, transportation and other social services, especially after Governor Maclehose's reforms of 1971.[67] As discussed, Hong Kong ranks second only to Singapore in the relative amount of public housing production in the capitalist world at around 70 per cent of its total. At a time when govern-ment departments were not spending available funds, Maclehose's reforms included massive expenditure on housing, aggressive new town development, significant public infrastructure improvement and considerable investment in social services. Development of new towns, for instance, began around 1973 with settlements in the New Territories like Tsuen Wan, Tao Po, Tuen Mun and Sha tin, with target populations of 500,000 or more. The aim was to stem overcrowding of central areas and to construct much needed mass housing in an efficient, cost-effective manner.[68] Even more significant was the relationship that developed between Hong Kong and neighbouring Guangdong Province, through which Hong Kong became active as a financial and service centre to the outside world, while manufacturing, using cheaper labour, took place across the border in China proper. Rapidly, in the order of 80 per cent of industrial investment in Guangdong came from Hong Kong, encompassing around 23,000 joint ventures, and 50 per cent of the workforce in the province was employed by Hong Kong-based firms. Rural–urban migration among a population of some 60 million was also rapid; consequently cities like Guangzhou began to expand and prosper dramatically, becoming flagships for New China's market-economy experiment. Perhaps even more remarkable, the city of Shenzhen rose up out of paddy fields close to Hong Kong's border, reaching a population of 1 million in a very short space of time. Today, since the handover of Hong Kong to China in 1997, the so-called Hong Kong-Guangdong Joint Venture continues to flourish in an increasingly well-integrated region.[69]

From the wartime ashes, a markedly top-down reconfiguration of substantial aspects of Japanese society began to unfold during the Allied occupation. In 1947, shortly after the 'Tokyo Spring' – a buoyant moment of liberal democratic promise and fervour, during which attempts were made to dismantle thoroughly the lingering presence of entrenched pre-war corporate interests – the so-called reverse course was chartered, in which the United States shifted its focus towards encouraging accelerated economic recovery and, therefore, social stability. As the 'Cold War' with the Communist bloc intensified, the US needed a bulwark against what they saw as impending Communist aggression in the East Asian sphere and quickly sought to shore up Japan in this regard, in spite of some earlier desires to move more slowly and deliberately in the direction of a robust framework for an entirely newly constituted democracy.[70] In 1948 the 'Yoshida Deal' or doctrine was struck, under which Japan's security would become largely the responsibility of the US and Japan would concentrate on rebuilding its capitalist development.[71] Consequently, dismantlement of the *zaibatsu* and *keiretsu* was abandoned, or rather the reformation of huge business federations, consisting of large enterprises with subcontractors and suppliers, was encouraged, bringing members of the pre-war political and industrial elite, as well as elements of the pre-war bureaucracy, back into power. These federations, with their networks, quickly became the engines for priority production of ships, steel manufacture, automobiles and electrical appliances, etc., through a concentration of available resources. By the official end of Japan's occupation in 1952, with the signing of the Japan–us Security Treaty, almost every aspect of Japan's post-war economic machine was in place. Over time, close ties and mediation of the business federations' corporate and financial interests with those of government ministries became commonplace and dominant in Japanese society, within which the Ministry of International Trade and Industry (MITI) became a conspicuous handmaiden. The so-called 1955 System of almost singular rule by the Liberal Democratic Party also became well established and, for many in Japan, 'identity association' shifted sharply away from the state to close association with corporate entities.[72] As Japan profited from the Korean War and continual upward economic trajectory from 1960 to the oil shocks in 1973, including the Ikeda 'Income Doubling Plan', an array of white-collar workers was formed – the *sararimen* – and nurtured throughout their working lives by the corporations and agencies to which they belonged. The younger working generation of the 1970s and '80s effectively entered into an enterprise society with little knowledge of much else and to such an extent that the nation was sometimes labelled as 'Japan, Inc'.

In keeping with high levels of government and corporate complicity, urban planning was also highly centralized, beginning with Tokyo's 1946 War Rehabilitation and Post-war Recovery Plan, in which the city and its metropolitan area quickly became a national concern.[73] Subsequently, little power involving autonomous determination has been devolved downward from a supra-regional level to local municipalities and to community-wide groups. In contrast, management of Tokyo's urban development has been strongly administered through the Tokyo Metropolitan Government and the office of its governor, more or less since the promulgation of the National Regional Development Law in 1956 and the first physical plan for the region in 1958.[74] Similarly, negative public reactions against the urban effects of rapid re-industrialization and economic development were dealt with in a top-down 'one size fits all' manner, including: overcrowding and poor residential space standards; incidence of photochemical smog which became a grave concern by 1970; opposition to distinctive neighbourhood and environmental impacts of radial road building beginning in the same year; and petitions for the right to sunlight in 1973, resulting in enactment of a special ordinance – *Hiatari-Jōrei* – in

1976.[75] Indeed, when viewed from a perspective of equal justice or rights for all, such an overbearing orientation has a certain efficacy. However, when seen within the widely differing urban circumstance prevailing in Tokyo, this total dependence on a uniformity that could not help but result in rather crude treatment vis-à-vis local circumstances and needs has proved far less appropriate. For instance, a relatively poor, haphazardly built district like Kyōjima in Tokyo's Sumida-ku, with many shabby and illegal structures, is vastly different from the general opulence and planned construction of nearby Minato-ku. In the aftermath of the collapse of the 'bubble economy' in the 1990s and a loosening of the hold of the corporate state, considerable agitation has occurred, particularly within inner-city wards of municipalities like Minato-ku, Sumida-ku and Chiyoda-ku, for higher degrees of local autonomy and corresponding financial wherewithal, well in excess of the relatively mild concessions made by the national and metropolitan authorities to citizen participation through the Town Planning Act of 1968 and the Local Autonomy Act of 1975.[76] Moreover, rising national concern about Tokyo's declining international competitiveness would seem to argue for higher degrees of local amenity, positive distinction among local areas, and for a capacity to tailor urbanization locally, especially in the inner city, to meet external needs as well as those of local populations. According to several sources, the city's competitiveness ranking has slipped behind both Singapore and Hong Kong in the East Asian sphere. New listings on the stock exchange, on a par with New York in 1992, are now about one third as many, and the number of international conferences held in Tokyo has slipped 30 per cent since 1993 and is now only about half as many as in Singapore. As described in chapter One, average residential floor space in Tokyo is well below that in other major international cities, as is the quality and scale of available office space. Parks and other public-space amenities are also comparatively less extensive and accessible.[77]

Top-down rule over South Korea and Seoul's urban circumstances has also been both strong and persistent, even outside the framework of the military dictatorships. In a manner similar to Japan's *zaibatsu*, South Korea's *chaebol* have enjoyed strong ties, not always obvious, with ministerial and other governmental officials. As in Japan, the *chaebol* became the principle source of manufacture for export, so important to South Korea's economic growth, and construction of major urban infrastructure and building in cities like Seoul. Strong mayors, like Seoul's Kim Hyon-ok, during the late 1960s, nicknamed the 'urban bulldozer', ensured a seamless tie between central government interests and those of big business.[78] South Korea and Seoul's wholesale commitment to modernization and to architectural modernism, including Western-style apartment buildings and dwellings, resulted from the governing elite's determination to progress the nation and the city forward. One upshot was the eventual popularity of modernism in housing and other forms of building, especially in Seoul, in the hands of the massive Korean Housing Corporation.[79]

Spatial Orthodoxies

The spatial model that was married to this top-down urban managerial response was borrowed largely from the West and, with some local modification, filled the gap caused by the lack of any useful traditional guidance and little to no prevalent legacy in modern metropolitan planning. The scheme that was generally adopted conformed to master planning practices, internationally rife at the time, embodying functional separation of land uses at a relatively broad grain across the surface of a metropolitan area; efficient provision of ring and radial transportation infrastructure to ensure even distribution of high horizontal mobility; hierarchical establishment of concentrated centres of special activity, including satellite settlements near the periphery to relieve population and other pressures on existing inner urban areas; and provision of green belts to bring needed open-space amenity to metropolitan areas and to establish useful and legible boundaries between pockets of urban development. Specific land-use zoning plans were prepared in accordance with this general scheme, with accompanying regulations and plans for roadway and other infrastructural improvements. Later modifications included broad-scale accommodations between real-estate market forces, transportation accessibility and ecological considerations. In short, the master plan formed a common blueprint from which urban development could be envisaged and managed. Moreover, in the West, during building booms of the 1950s, '60s and early '70s, considerable attention was placed on the management of prevailing urban dynamics under this overall rubric. In fact, by the 1920s, German cities were developing extensive satellite communities; comprehensive zoning plans were being introduced into United States cities, followed by green-belt towns in the mid-1930s, as well as similar applications in the United Kingdom; and intra-urban circumferential and radial expressway systems were being envisaged, certainly by the early 1940s. From similar roots, although with a different ideological response to the rational

allocation of resources, physical planning in the Stalinist Soviet Union –
planikova – also often ended up with similar spatial results.[80]

Between 1958 and about 1962, shortly before the birth of Singapore as a
nation state, the Norwegian planner E. E. Lorange provided United Nations
assistance to prepare a concept plan for future urbanization and industrial
development. In 1963 further work was done on this plan by Otto
Koeningsberger, Charles Abrams and Susume Kobe, stressing the need for an
integrated approach and, in 1965, a contract was signed between the United
Nations and Singapore to develop the scheme further, with an ad-hoc committee of government department heads representing Singapore's interests.[81]
What emerged from this process became known as the Ring Concept Plan, a
spatial strategy for accommodating different levels of population, ranging
from 2 to 4 million people. One of the principal components of the plan was
the establishment of a concentrated belt of development on Singapore's southern coast, including the existing city and stretching from Changi in the east
to Jurong in the west. Another key component was the delineation of two
north–south corridors for urban development around a central freshwater
catchment and natural preserve. These corridors were imagined as high spines
of urban development consisting of a sequence of new towns – like Ang Mo
Kio, Yishun, Woodlands, Tao Payou and Bishan – each with a population of
some 100,000 to 200,000 and defined by major roads with a town centre in
the middle, surrounded by high-density residential communities and service
functions, and with a green 'buffer' zone around the outside. Internally, the
dwelling community was built according to theories about neighbourhood
design and the required mix of residential and non-residential functions
prevalent in Britain and other parts of Europe at the time. The third major
component of the overall plan was an island-wide expressway and mass-tran-
sit system, including heavy rail, linking the new towns together and providing
easy access to the centre of Singapore. Finally, a redistribution of employment
was organized in accordance with this physical plan, with heavy industry concentrated in Jurong, light industry distributed among the new towns, and
commerce concentrated in the traditional centre of Singapore, as well as more
locally in the new town centres.[82]

This Ring Concept Plan served Singapore well, at least until recently, and
became something of a model for others in the region. Through strong regulation, extensive public construction and maintenance of housing, as well as
major infrastructure improvements, the urban growth of Singapore was guided and largely conformed to the plan. As the housing and related needs of a

growing population were felt, new towns were developed in a manner that attempted to minimize the time of travel to employment centres. As automobile use increased, 'cordon-taxes' and other economic disincentives were put in place to push transit alternatives and, over time, as the new towns became more heterogeneous in the activities that they supported, their earlier role as bedroom communities diminished substantially. However, as Singapore contemplates a future population in excess of 5 million, and as the more affluent society begins to demand more varied and improved housing, as well as becoming more concerned about environmental amenity and sustainability, the Ring Concept Plan has begun to undergo revision. Recently a Blue–Green Plan was prepared, in outline form, better to address emerging issues of more developable areas for urbanization, environmental sustainability, continued conservation and fresh water supply. Plan x has also been devised, including substantial urban expansion to the north-east as well as the possibility for extensions into nearby Ubin and Tekong islands. Further shoreline reclamation has also been undertaken under the plan, along with consolidation of housing and commercial development along expanding rail transit corridors. In addition, industrial parks in Jurong are now beginning to include multi-storey prototypes for manufacturing, assembly and storage, further to increase capacity without additional land demands, and higher-rise commercial development continues, especially in desirable central areas.[83]

With an eye towards Singapore, although well in the train of international urban-planning practice, Hong Kong also began constructing a dispersed pattern of concentrated satellite new-town developments to meet the growing needs of an expanding and more affluent population and to relieve pressure on existing older commercial and industrial centres. What has emerged, since 1973, is a nodal pattern of dense, high-rise residential developments and local commercial centres on buildable or reclaimed land amid the sharply hilly terrain that stretches northward from the island of Hong Kong and the Kowloon peninsula to the border of the Special Administrative Region. By the 1990s, this interconnected network of new towns had shifted the centre of Hong Kong's population substantially, with 1.14 million residing on Hong Kong Island, 2.23 million in Kowloon and 1.69 million in the New Territories.[84] Second- and third-generation new towns have also been either constructed, or planned, at Yuen Long, Tai Po, Junk Bay and Tin Shui Wai and, in a manner similar to Singapore, these and other earlier new towns are now linked across and through the intervening terrain by rail and other forms of mass transit. Hong Kong has a transit system with one of the highest riderships per capita of total population in the world. Also, over time, a transition has been underway within the new towns from bedroom to full-service communities. Sha Tin, for example, with a population of 591,000 in 1991, now well on its way to a target population of 700,000 to 1 million, is the site of the Chinese University, and amid the linear configuration of high-density development that extends along the valley floor beside an extensive waterway are numerous non-residential institutional, recreational and commercial functions.[85]

When confronting urban growth rates of around 10 per cent per annum by the 1960s, Seoul also adopted an urban growth management strategy based on a physical plan involving ring-radial roadway circulation, multiple centres and green belts. The 1966 Comprehensive Development Plan proposed four ring roads at varying distances from the city centre with some thirteen radial arterials, the junctions of which were to become subcentres for surrounding community developments.[86] In this plan, Western new-town planning and garden city ideas – both coming from more or less the same root – seemed uppermost in the planners' minds. Again according to prevailing orthodoxy, industrial development was to be concentrated in the south-west of the city, with direct access to coastal port facilities, and both tax incentives and favourable infrastructure improvements were provided to spur this development along. Slum clearance and urban renewal also formed part of the Comprehensive Plan, especially in Seoul's dilapidated central commercial and mixed-use area. One project that caused some controversy but also made an emphatic architectural statement on behalf of advanced forms of modernism was Sewoon Sangga, designed in 1967 by the architect Kim Soo Geun, along the lines of architectural principles of members of Team 10, like Peter and Allison Smithson.[87] Essentially, Sewoon Sangga was a 1-km long, internally integrated megastructure, ranging from eight to ten storeys in height, constructed along a former fire break created by the Japanese through their Air Strike Defence Law of 1937. Originally, Sewoon Sangga, opened with much fanfare by Mayor Kim of bulldozer fame, comprised space for around 2,000 stores and businesses, a 177-room hotel and 851 apartments. Over time the surrounding area changed and the progressive, though large-scale and peculiar, structure became something of an eyesore and today stands as a reminder of the failure of Seoul's early heavy-handed urban renewal projects. Even the 1988 Olympics had little positive impact, apart from being a showcase for the *chaebol*'s symbols of progress.

From the 1970s through the middle 1980s, urban growth in Seoul pushed quickly south across the Han River. By 1986 the proportion of urbanization had shifted from 80 per cent to the north and 20 per cent on the south to around equal numbers on either side of the river.[88] Again a spatial orthodoxy of urban satellites was pursued with separating green belts and access provided by a ring-radial system of major roads. The satellite communities of Magdok, Yongdongpo, Kangnam and Jamsil were quickly constructed along the southern banks of the Han River, and Yoido Island, near the centre of Seoul, was developed as a municipal and commercial centre. Throughout, a high-rise Western mode of apartment living was adopted, although the monotony of repetitive tall structures became an issue to be addressed through more varied yet high-rise structures in later more economically prosperous times. In comparison to some other East Asian cities, mass transit connections were poor and one of the weaknesses of the follow-on 1972 National Development Plan was a green belt scheme easily leapfrogged by unplanned development. Where it did function it had the effect of driving up the cost of land in central areas of Seoul.[89] A further round of decentralization occurred in 1989 with the construction of five new towns – Islan, Joongdong, Sanbon, Pyunchon and Bundang – roughly ringing the metropolitan area from the west through the south, within 20 to 25 km of Seoul proper. Built as relatively dense, self-contained communities, ranging in density from 176 to 406 people per hectare, these towns have a planned variation in population from 390,000 in Bundang, to 170,000 in Sanbon. However, there has been a certain feeling of isolation, at least among earlier residents.[90]

Throughout these successive rounds of efforts to decentralize effectively the metropolitan urban development of Seoul, the city has remained attractive to residents and immigrants from elsewhere in South Korea alike. If anything, the new towns and other additions to the metropolitan region have added to Seoul's attractiveness through comparatively better schools, community services, employment opportunities and housing. Many problems, however, exist. Over the years, economic 'growthism' as a driving doctrine, set against incremental, piecemeal and uncoordinated growth management, not to mention the fallacy of green belts and their unintended centralizing effects on decentralization, have produced unequal and unbalanced urban growth at the regional and national scale, as well as many inefficiencies in daily life. To some extent, Seoul's geographic location, very near to the border with North Korea, has also hemmed in the spread of urban growth, skewing development further to the south.

In 1958 the first regional metropolitan plan for Tokyo was promulgated, along similar lines as Tokyo's Post-war Recovery Plan of 1946 – the Ishikawa Plan – which envisaged satellite cities along ring roads with green areas in between, in order to limit the older ward population of Tokyo to 3.5 million. Based on Sir Patrick Abercrombie's 1944 Greater London Plan, the initial National Capital Region Improvement Plan recognized and made provision for upgrading and rationalizing existing urban areas, developing a suburban 'green' zone around the older 23 wards, and creating satellite developments in neighbouring peripheral regions, all to be connected through an integrated network of expressways and arterial roadways, together with extensions of mass transit. Although green space aspects of both plans drew upon an earlier 1939 Green Space System Plan for Tokyo, the 1958 plan was much broader in scope and more authoritative in its definition then any prior plans for the city.[91] Unlike the Greater London Plan, however, new towns like Tama and Kohuku were conceived of largely as commuter settlements, or single function new towns with populations of 200,000 to 300,000, focusing on employment in the central city. The one exception was Tsukuba Campus City, initiated in 1963, with Tsukuba University research institute at its core.[92] The upshot was that while housing pressures may have been resolved, commuting pressures were not. Moreover, with exacerbation of outward overall urban expansion through leapfrogging and urban development of designated green belt zones, as well as excessive use of specialized land-use zones, the plan proved less than successful, forcing a new round of planning in 1968. Meanwhile, the Shinjuku Sub-Centre Corporation was formed in 1960, with considerable private sector

15
Central Tokyo
with Marunouchi
in the foreground
and Shinjuku in
the background.
1985.

funds, and in 1961 legislation was passed allowing construction of higher-rise buildings; the first real skyscraper – the Kasumigaseki Building – was erected in 1968.[93] One result of these activities, as well as pent-up real estate pressures, was development of concentrated commercial and mixed-use sub-centres in Tokyo at Shibuya, Shinjuku, Ikebukuro and Osaki. In an attempt to resolve the pressures of urban development on inner-city Tokyo, Kenzo Tange released his Tokyo Bay Plan in 1960, showing an intricate network of infrastructure, road-ways and reclaimed islands of developed land stretching out from the Shitamachi into the adjacent bay.

The Second Capital Region Improvement Plan of 1968 expanded to four the number of designated zones within the metropolitan area, in efforts to pro-mote and control orderly urban growth.[94] This four-zone policy included: the built-up area of the city, a suburban development area, satellite towns on the periphery, and a suburban green-zone conservation area. Clearly, the attempt was to persist with a modified version of green belts as controlling devices on land use, to deconcentrate the city still further, and to make allowances for inevitable suburban development. However, this plan also failed in many respects, for many of the same reasons as the 1958 plan, leading to the Third Capital Region Improvement Plan of 1976, with an emphasis on an urban–regional complex of multiple centres. This was followed in 1986 by a fourth iteration of the Capital Regional Improvement Plan, further reinforcing

84

this multicentrism away from central Tokyo with policies and programmes to relocate government institutions, educational facilities and the like.[95] In addition, much-needed suburban upgrading was placed higher on the metropolitan agenda, addressing both dilapidated inner-city areas, as well as older post-war peripheral expansion.

In the aftermath of the recent economic collapse, the Tokyo Metropolitan Government is undertaking the development and implementation of what has variably been called its 'Vision 2000 Plan' or 'Ring Plan'.[96] Projected towards a 25-year time horizon, this plan finally accepts centralization of Tokyo into a single centre made up of the several earlier subcentres – Shibuya, Shinjuku, Ikebukuro, etc. – as well as subcentres located on the metropolitan area's periphery, in and around remaining green zones. Completion of both an inner and outer ring of transportation is envisaged to improve accessibility. Further elaboration of the large central core area, consisting largely of the 23 wards inside the circumferential Yamanote subway line, includes a central business zone flanked by a historical–cultural zone to the north, around Ueno and Asakusa; an information technology and media zone centred on Minato-ku to the south; and a waterfront zone of mixed use and entertainment on further reclaimed land in Tokyo Bay, in and around Rainbow Town. Nevertheless, the spatial logic remains much the same – multiple centres, green conservation zones, ring-radial transportation systems, and broad, area-wide designations of preferred, largely single-use functions. Again what the future might hold remains to be seen. However, a much higher degree of bottom-up local municipal autonomy and project-plan making seems to be in order. The centralized top-down approach has had to reckon with the emergence of numerous subcentres and other local aberrations that were not exactly within their plans, now finally recognized in the more variegated urban panorama of the contemporary 'Vision 2000 Plan'. However, this impetus should be capitalized upon and pushed forward well below the broad metropolitan master-planning level.

More or less from the onset of the Communist regime in China, physical master planning, with standards promulgated from on high, has been de rigueur throughout the country, closely following the orthodoxy of ring-radial roads, green belts and core-periphery, as well as satellite modes of physical planning, initially adopted from the Soviet Union. Basically, a prescriptive set of criteria have been developed at the national level as the yardsticks against which specific city plans will be judged and approved.[97] These criteria cover a broad range of spatial specifications for master planning, including ratios of

16
The central
business district
in Hankou, Wuhan.
2003.

required residential and other district densities, templates for the layout of major and minor roadways, designations of use under given urbanizing circumstances, and specifications for open space allocation. For a typical case, in a city like Wuhan, the provincial capital of Hubei province in central China, master planning exercises have been conducted at roughly five to ten year intervals according to this standard formula. Currently Wuhan has a metropolitan population of 8.31 million with a core city population of 3.92 million and a floating population of non-registered people in the order of 1.5 to 2.0 million.[98] The present master plan, developed in 1996 and finally approved in 1999, consists of a ring and radial thoroughfare system, with four ring roads, organized concentrically around the city centre, and contiguous districts of existing and new urban development zoned broadly according to dominant uses. Within this overall plan, multiple nodes of concentrated activity are located, logically enough, at the intersections of major radial and ring roads, and several satellite communities are designated beyond the city periphery and separated from the city by a green belt, also provides a spatial armature for introduction of greened 'buffer zones' back into the city. The overall effect of the master plan is a cohesive carpet-like conformation of urbanization that appears to smooth over local inconsistencies, while providing pre-designated zones for needed new development. Below this master plan level, 'controlled detailed plans', mentioned in chapter One, were prepared to

86

provide regulation and guidance at a local and site-specific level, again in conformance with standard criteria of designated use, floor area ratio, site coverage, open-space allowance, building height and setbacks from adjacent streets.

On its face, this approach may not seem extraordinary or inappropriate. Indeed, in many respects, such as the pressing need to provide an orderly blueprint for rapid expansion of the metropolitan area to attract and accommodate new industry and to move current residents out of overcrowded, dilapidated and downright squalid living conditions, the master planning exercise may serve its purpose. It is certainly little different in its spatial configuration from other similar master plans operating elsewhere in China. Wuhan, however, is a rather particular place, like many other cities in China. It spreads across the confluence of the Changjiang and Han rivers, about 1,000 km from both Beijing and Shanghai, and incorporates many lakes, including the magnificent East Lake, as well as hilly natural outcroppings of land. It consists of three settlements – Hankou, Hanyang and Wuchang – each with its own historical character, and was a Treaty Port, with six foreign concession powers. Furthermore, Hankou was a bustling capitalist enclave during the Qing dynasty in the seventeenth century, probably well in advance of similar economic enterprises in much of the West, and Wuchang, across the river, was the site of the beginnings of the revolt against the Qing dynasty in 1911 and the early seat of the subsequent Republican government.[99] In short, there is much that is unique about Wuhan, both topographically and historically, a clearer recognition of which would argue for a much higher degree of local and district-level inflection in the current homogenizing master plan, and for finding ways to recognize and, spatially as well as urbanistically, exploit the inherent mosaic-like qualities of the city and its underlying history and geography.

A style of recent master planning, which still incorporates many aspects of the overall Chinese master-planning orthodoxy but in an exceptional way, is the 'side-by-side' pattern of development adopted by cities with strong export platforms, like Suzhou, located in the Changjiang Delta, about one-and-a-half hours drive west on the expressway between Nanjing and Shanghai. Suzhou is an ancient city, dating back as far as 514 BC, which gained sustained prominence as Pinjiang in 1229. The overall layout of Pinjiang was a well-ordered tartan grid of alternating streets and canals, enclosed by a regular rectangular encirclement of walls, located not far from the Grand Canal – a major public works project during the early dynastic times that provided commercial and other water-borne access from Hangzhou to Beijing. A prosperous city, Suzhou became renowned for silk manufacture and, within its grid of streets and

canals, numerous magnificent garden villas were erected, primarily by wealthy merchants, 55 of which remain on the city's historical register.[100] In the 1970s, primarily in response to population pressures, the city expanded well beyond its walls, mainly to the west, largely in the form of parallel rows of housing blocks for workers – *danyuanlou* – prevalent at the time throughout China. Following Deng Xiaoping's well-publicized tour through Southern China in 1992, Suzhou was given permission to adopt a new planning strategy and to experiment with a 'socialist-market' and then 'market' economic forms of development. In fact, two cities in the south were designated as part of this experiment – Suzhou in terms of direct foreign investment, and Wenzhou in terms of responding to rising domestic demand.

The primary dilemma facing Suzhou at the time was fourfold.[101] first, there was pent-up demand for urban growth, although with shrinking local capacities to service that demand adequately. Second, local industry was in dire need of upgrading and replacement. The prominence of sunset industries, like silk and textile manufacturing, needed to be repositioned and Suzhou's industrial base diversified considerably. Third, the continual overcrowding and dilapidation of the central Pinjiang sector of the city needed to be eradicated, with its historical significance preserved and exploited for tourism. Fourth, surrounding and encroaching rural settlement growth needed to be contained and the city's competition with nearby township-village enterprises for production eliminated. Suzhou's 1996–2010 master plan, which emerged alongside aggressive and successful negotiations with foreign investors and enterprises, followed the concept of what became known as 'one body with two wings'.[102] Spatially, and urbanistically, the historic core was to be preserved, conserved and upgraded. Simultaneously, two extensive new districts were to be developed, directly to the east and west of the existing city, in a manner that allowed environmental conservation areas and agricultural preserves to surround the city and to interpenetrate significantly between existing urbanization and the two new districts. The planned district to the east, in the direction of Shanghai, encompassed 70 km² of land and water area. It became a joint venture with Singapore and, particularly in its early planning stages, had support from Singapore's Urban Redevelopment Authority. It was to be a full-service adjunct to Suzhou, but with an emphasis on industrial development built to international standards – the Jurong approach – with a twenty-year build out and accommodation for 600,000 residents and 360,000 jobs.[103] On the west, the Suzhou New District, as it was called, was more of a local concoction, incorporating 25 km² during its first phase, with an eventual build out of 52km².[104] More mixed in the spatial distribution of uses than the Sino-Singaporean joint venture, this district also included development opportunities for commercial, residential, industrial and recreational functions.

The fate of Suzhou's 1996–2010 plan remains undecided, although the city and its mayor at the time – Zhang Xinsheng – deserve high marks for a bold strategy, as well as attitudes towards environmental quality and historic conservation. Economically, both new districts got off to a brisk start. By around 2000, some 300 enterprises had been established in the Suzhou New District and, at one point, the Sino-Singaporean joint venture – Suzhou Industrial Park – was receiving investment commitments of around $2 million per day.[105] Substantial renovation and environmental improvement also occurred in the historical urban core and the average residential livable space standard for inhabitants was raised considerably, well above national norms. However, a bumpy road to success has been experienced. Front-end infrastructural investment in the Suzhou Industrial Park was very high and the plan proved difficult to phase smoothly and incrementally, prompting criticism from the Singaporeans. Many early promissories of development commitments were never transacted in both districts, and the inherent competition between the two satellites was problematic, especially when viewed against early overestimation of demand, with the Suzhou New District perhaps faring slightly better. Nevertheless, in the longer term, the overall planning still holds promise.

Underlying much urban planning in China are institutional problems or mismatches with practical and desirable realities. Mayors, for instance, have considerable power in their locales and, despite considerable planning from above, are usually under heavy pressure, again from above, to achieve immediate and high-profile, demonstrable results. Often this responsibility translates into short-term planning practices and special projects that fail adequately to address longer-term issues and planning needs, as well as taking paths of least resistance that prove to be economically, socially and environmentally unwise. In addition, the range of institutional, regulatory and financial mechanisms available to meet the rising needs of market forces, public-private participation and productive subsidy of particular disadvantaged groups are very limited in comparison to municipalities in the West, hamstringing more sophisticated assaults on pressing problems. Furthermore, property markets and their self-regulatory properties, though much improved, are still in the early stages of development, allowing very little to be reasonably projected into the future.

Uncharted Territory

In summary, modern urbanization in East Asia has occurred largely under the aegis of borrowed Western planning models and practices, with some modification and adaption to meet local circumstances. During the contemporary era, this has meant adoption of a thoroughly technological temperament and outlook, especially in order to meet the challenges of rapid modernization and explosive regional urban growth. Moreover, underlying this rapid modernization, almost without exception, is a sudden onslaught of all the transactions, occupations and interrelationships associated with modernization, processes that were more gradually evolved in the West. At the risk of oversimplification, within this technological orientation there is a belief in empirical understanding of issues at hand, the plausibility of being able adequately to project future outcomes, and ready adoption of problem-specific and administratively tractable measures, and then to move on to another round of decisions. But often the sheer size and scope of these operations have exceeded similar applications in the West. Moreover, when contemplating the urban growth management and associated issues nowadays confronted in East Asia, one wonders whether the technical apparatus in play is simply being outstripped by the dynamic urban circumstances they are meant to address. This certainly seems to be the case in Tokyo's overcentralization and, with similar dynamics, in Korea's chief city of Seoul, but it is also applicable to parts of China for somewhat different reasons.

As outlined, China is still very rural and underdeveloped, with a settlement pattern, at least in its fertile river valley regions, that largely conforms to what is sometimes characterized as a '*desokota* region', or 'urban–rural continuum', incorporating numerous hamlets, villages and small towns into a fine-grained network of economic and social activities, separated at relatively short distances by agricultural production and conservation areas.[106] In fact, unlike most other parts of the world, many of these settlements, in a place like the Changjiang Delta, west of Shanghai, each house and otherwise service tens of thousands of people, many working both on the land and, when in surplus supply, within often thriving township-village enterprises. There, the overall population is in excess of 73 million people and it is in regions like this that some serious issues of urban formation must be confronted. At present, there are about 669 cities in China with populations of around and in excess of 100,000. Within this number, the distribution of cities by class size drops away dramatically, with only some 37 cities, measured as one might in the West, with populations in excess of 1 million, including large metropolitan areas like Shanghai and Beijing. In short, urbanization in China is composed of literally hundreds of settlements with populations below, say, 500,000, in addition to a myriad of much smaller settlements, with many located in productive regions like the Changjiang Delta.[107]

Now, as the proportion of China's urban populations moves upwards rapidly, the sheer number of cities will undoubtedly increase, as existing smaller-sized settlements become larger and others are formed. Indeed, one estimate of this increase was from around 400 to 900 cities, with populations in the range of 100,000 over the next 30 years or so, depending upon assumptions regarding the trajectory of proliferation, with the number of cities with future populations of 1 million or more ranging from 114 to 203, again roughly comparable to the current distribution, per capita, in the United States.[108] Certainly, this proliferation will be subject to interlocking bundles of constraints concerning resource availability, economic wherewithal, availability of materials and provision of infrastructure, and may not result in the overall 60 per cent proportion of urban population cited earlier, at least in the timeframe that has been suggested. Nevertheless, the sheer prospect of this proliferation, and expansion in existing city scale, especially in a relatively confined arable context like the Changjiang Delta, may very well exceed the present growth control limits placed on large metropolitan areas like Shanghai, and the convergence of a footloose urbanizing population on small to medium-sized cities like Suzhou.

Recourse to further developed Western experiences in order to resolve these kinds of urban growth and reorganizational problems may also be hampered by the differences in the conditions of urbanization now present in much of Europe and the United States and those currently dominant in East Asia – an issue noted in chapter One that will be expanded upon in chapter Four. First, the urbanizing rates of change requiring redress, along with concomitant urban management problems, are generally much less strongly felt nowadays in the developed West than in East Asia. Second, the prevailing orientation towards city building is different and has been for some time. As some would have it, the Western focus is now on the 'post-modern city', or on the other side of modernization's push to growth and expansion that began to rise to prominence in the 1970s, as outlined in chapter One.[109] Instead, differences, rather than similarities and cohering urban conditions, have become strong vantage points for urban management and building. Nowadays, issues like social diversity, local identity, specific continuities with the past, as well as preservation and local environmental awareness, have come to dominate Western urban agendas and planning preoccupations. There has been a significant loss of faith in big plans, and top-down procedures have been replaced by bottom-up, incremental participatory processes. Indeed, there are even intellectual suspicions abroad about generalizing accounts of urban phenomena like this text. To be sure, in well-developed cities like Singapore, Hong Kong and Tokyo there are signs, as discussed, of something of an emerging focus on local issues, plurality and local identity. In general, however, broader aspects of East Asian modern urbanization appear to be out of phase with Western local concerns about modernization – an observation again to be taken up further in chapter Four. Furthermore, the sheer suddenness, resulting scale and attendant management problems associated with East Asia's contemporary urbanization – the concatenation of modernization's transformatory power again – coupled with as yet untended issues potentially arising from more effective local participation has moved, or is moving, many East Asian cities into uncharted territory, with less than readily predictable outcomes.

four
Urban Forms and Local Expressions

In principle and often in practice, broad, technically inclined and managerial orientations to orthodox modern urban planning allow local interpretations to be made, particular needs to be met, and the aspirations of local citizenry to be addressed with regard to a sense of place in the world. The extent to which this occurs, however, is often a matter of the interested and forceful presence of local constituencies, together with the ready availability of institutional processes and practices for ameliorating and redefining the overarching features of big plans and urban management strategies. As described so far, the prevalence, indeed dominance, of top-down urban planning in most parts of East Asia has tended to stunt the growth of highly articulated and well-organized bottom-up influences on local urban outcomes. Well-organized elements of civil society, elsewhere a strong potential bottom-up mediator of homogenizing influence, are either generally weak or disinclined towards matters of urban-architectural expression, save at relatively rudimentary levels of safety, public health, nuisance and necessary provision of shelter and basic services. Local governments, within a broader metropolitan area, also often lack autonomy, being regarded as instruments of higher authority, usually at national level. Furthermore, the blueprints supporting master planning, as well as many aspects of urban regulation, usually originated in the West and were borrowed, in both a wholesale and piecemeal manner, to meet the challenges of burgeoning modern urbanization. During this process an underlying technocratic, non-specific and architecturally disinterested orientation not infrequently passed over, rather than collided with, indigenous practices of place-making and valuation, often effectively downgrading the latter in favour of an overall drive to modernize.

Nevertheless, despite these shortcomings in institutionally formalized, widespread and concerted local reaction to modern top-down planning, many instances of ad-hoc local responses and adaptation have occurred in East Asia, imbuing cities there with unique urban spatial characteristics, especially at the scale of particular districts, sub-districts and building complexes. As outlined in chapter Three, East Asian cities have histories and local manners of city-making that persist in the otherwise relatively ill-defined and unstructured aperture between urban master planning and individual building. Moreover, as sketched out in chapter Two, they are different-looking places. Patterns and propensities of use and property ownership, dating back to pre-modern and early modern eras, still exert an influence on physical environments. Ideas of social community, rooted either in broad politico-cultural ideologies, or simply as habitual ways of being in the world, well below concerns of upper-level planning, also operate in East Asian cities, creating the grounds for localized instances of urban shape and appearance that are potentially unique. Individual aspirations towards situatedness, placedness and representative-ness, even when coping with massive pressures of urbanization, invariably come to bear on the myriad of local construction activities and architectural forays that shape cities, including issues of urban-architectural expression and incremental vernacular modification of public and semi-public urban spaces. So far, anyway, the sum total of ad-hoc local reactions to larger-order forces of urban modernization has produced a local physical urbanity that is both local-ly distinctive and different in notable ways from that found in other regions of the world, especially the developed West.

Upward Extensions

Returning to an observation made in chapter Two, regarding the grain and spatial character of urban form, particularly in well-established inner city areas, what transpired with remarkable uniformity was straightforward upward extension of earlier patterns of property ownership. *Mutatis mutandis*, it often seemed as if a small sprig was watered and nurtured into a tall stalk and, space allowing, a flourishing tree, with land rent and capital flows as the nurturing ingredients. Where rent was high and capital plentiful, following in the wake of rising property values, taller buildings sprang up. The mimicry and competitive aspects of the biological plant analogy also seemed to come into play. Individual property owners vied with each other to construct tall buildings, in order to capitalize fully on land rent, while also copying and incrementally extending others' earlier successes. Fierce competition around the profits to be made pushed some property owners out and allowed others to aggregate parcels together and to compete on a larger scale or broader property footprint. These gains, however, were usually relatively minor, since few owners wanted to leave, with the result that footprints remained relatively small, even as specific real-estate developments became very tall, like the 'pencil buildings' mentioned earlier. Overall, a fine grain of otherwise tall building volumes materialized. The underlying logic of this form of upwardly extended urban development corresponded to where the ground was most fertile, returning to the biological plant analogy again, and that was typically defined by relative location in a city and more specifically by high transportation accessibility vis-à-vis other locations within the city. Consequently, geographically central locations were favoured, as were less central locations well served by transit, returning to mechanisms of polynucleation of urban form discussed in chapter Two.

In some places, like Hong Kong and Tokyo, the result was hyperextension of property ownership patterns and hyperdensity as a living and working condition. Particularly in Hong Kong's case, these conditions appeared to cross over into another plane of living existence, where well-established ideas about privacy, self-containment and association were altered considerably. In a less than positive light, the recent outbreak of SARS – Severe Acute Respiratory Syndrome – that befell Amoy Gardens, a high-density high-rise dwelling in Hong Kong, illustrates the often unwitting and dysfunctional closeness of this association. On the positive side, however, a sense of community caring, solidarity, security and just plain belonging clearly also come into play.

During the 1980s the so-called pencil buildings, renowned for their slim vertical profile, emerged out of the circumscribed pattern of property right ownership and tiny urban sites in older urban areas of Hong Kong, like Central, Wanchai and Kowloon. As outlined in chapter Two, these buildings have an 'aspect ratio' – gross floor area divided by the number of storeys – that is very low when compared to other high-rise buildings.[1] Ranging in height usually between 20 and 25 storeys, each floor typically consists of two dwelling units, with the bottom three or so floors usually dedicated to non-residential functions that merge into the commercial domain near street level. Specific types of buildings are sometimes called 'airplane' or 'butterfly' plans, referring to the elongated or spread configuration of the symmetrically disposed apartment units around centrally located elevator shafts and stairways. Units are often small, on the order of 40 to 50 m^2 of livable space, and building construction usually embodies concrete and steel frames with infill planes, or curtain

18
Pencil buildings' in
Hong Kong. 2001.

walls, for the outer skin. Nearby commercial and residential buildings, of a broader site footprint and larger scale, also have relatively low aspect ratios, responding again to remnants of the earlier pattern of property ownership and because of the enduring profitability of retaining use rights, especially given Hong Kong's relatively laissez-faire attitude towards building height limitations and the economic dictates of high degrees of concentration.

Recently, however, with the construction of very tall buildings on reclaimed land along the waterfront of Hong Kong's Central district, like the

International Financial Centre by Cesar Pelli, questions have been raised regarding the need to protect the background profile of the rugged peaks that have defined the natural setting of Hong Kong for so long.[2] This debate may well result in new height limitations. Across the harbour, in Kowloon, building heights were constrained by the airspace of Kai Tak airport, although with the removal of the airport function to Chek Lap Kok many high-rise buildings have begun to appear. An ensemble of building characteristics, consisting of tall buildings on relatively small site footprints, built close together and merging near ground level with a high volume of bustling commercial activities, criss-crossed by narrow roads, invariably of historical origin, as well as by elevated walkways and through-block malls and arcades, give central areas of Hong Kong a distinctive urban appearance. Mass transit use and service is very high, with only about one in twenty people having cars, and the circulatory pavement area per capita in Hong Kong is around one tenth of that in American urban areas.[3] As will be shown later, this ensemble of characteristics also extends, by and large, to newer housing estates and new town developments in other parts of the Special Administrative Region.

In East Asia, however, upward extension of historically rooted patterns of property ownership, across several different kinds of site circumstances, is perhaps most manifest in Tokyo. There, both the feudal and natural topography of Edo became congealed into a persistent underlay for much of the city's modern urban expression, particularly within extensive areas of the older inner-city wards, as well as in newer urban areas spontaneously developed after the 1923 Kantō earthquake. One kind of site circumstance coincides with the highly developed lowlands of the Shitamachi, described in chapter Two, and the valleys between the headlands that extend from the upland Kantō Plain towards Tokyo Bay. In the Shitamachi settlement was very dense, almost from the onset of the Tokugawa Shogunate, often built on patches of reclaimed land along the edge of the bay and in low-lying areas adjacent to the Sumida River, resulting in numerous canals spanned by bridges, many of which were filled in later to become roads. Regularly shaped, relatively wide rectangular urban blocks of buildings were constructed, usually encircled on the outside by slightly taller commercial structures, facing the streets and canals, with living quarters tucked in behind, often entered through gates and served by a less regular network of narrow lanes. Often particular blocks were the domain of specific craft guilds, or associations of merchants plying their trade in particular items, as well as certain areas for entertainment – the so-called ludic zones

of Edo.[4] The modern district of Kajichō, for instance, was the realm of black-smiths, and parts of present-day Asakusa, up river, were set aside for entertain-ment and night life. In the successive hands of numerous property owners, tenants and small entrepreneurs, properties in these urban blocks became extended upwards, especially on the edges of the original blocks, adjacent to major surrounding streets and roadways. Many traditional urban blocks took on an *anko-gawa* configuration, analogous to the local confection, with a 'soft', or low in this case, core surrounded by a 'hard', or high, outer shell of building.

This *anko-gawa* urban configuration also arose in many parts of the valley lowlands, adjacent to hills and headlands emanating from the higher Kantō plain on the west of Tokyo. Again, as described in chapter Two, these were historically densely packed, though not tall, settlements for merchants, peasants and other commoners, close to the aristocratic *daimyō* estates on the nearby hilltops, as well as the quarters for some lower-ranking soldiers. Typically, the commoner districts were composed of regular though discontin-uous networks of lanes to either side of a roadway running the length of the valley or lowland area, lined by two- and sometimes three-storey shophouses, with commercial space on the ground floor and living quarters above. The depth of each lot was on the order of 35 m, although the street frontage could be quite narrow, maximizing the exposure of shops to those passing by. Typical lot sizes for the *daimyō*-class retainers and soldiers were about 20 by 40 m, set out in regular blocks of around 80 by 120 m or more.[5] One result of the modern upward extension of this historical pattern is often a very sharp gradation from tall, thin, 'pencil' buildings, placed side-by-side along the major streets, to low-rise dwellings in the interior of urban blocks and, with this reconfiguration, the equally sharp disjunction of moving from bustling, high-rise urbanity to quiet, small-scale traditional circumstances. This is the case in the *Banchō* area of modern Tokyo, immediately to the west of the castle compound. Although not a lowland area – it was the residential district for the bannermen of the Shogunate – many of the interior lots and blocks away from major roads, usually facing down a broad slope towards Mount Fujiama, seem little removed from earlier traditional patterns of settlement.

Another result of this selective upward extension of the underlying historical pattern of Edo is the endurance of the *chō*, or neighbourhoods, of Tokyo and of the *chōkai*, or neighbourhood associations and smaller subdivisions of the *chōme*.[6] Becoming official administrative units in 1909, as part of Meiji Restoration reforms, the *chōkai* gained firmer status in 1934, during the dark days of national mobilization, before being almost banned, after World War II, for their complicity in fascist community affairs. Today, stripped of their earlier ideological orientations, they usually provide social services, fire and crime protection, as well as organizing annual religious and other festivities. Generally, a *chō* consists of a grouping of households, anywhere from 2,000 to 5,000 people, and conforms to several of the large urban blocks of the underlying land parcel configuration of Edo.[7]

Before leaving the lowland site of Edo–Tokyo, one district that deserves further elaboration is the Ginza, in the heart of Tokyo, because it clearly illustrates several phases of development and redevelopment found elsewhere in the city. Originally, the Ginza was the *chō* of the silversmiths, with some masonry though largely timber residences, workshops and shophouses, organized tightly along and between a regular layout of streets. After a tragic fire in 1872, the area was razed and quickly renovated into the Ginza Brick Quarter under the supervision of the British architect Thomas Waters mentioned earlier, retained by Tokyo's governor to make the area 'fire proof' and imposing to foreigners (i.e., modern).[8] Consisting of about 1,000 European-style buildings and replete with gas lights and paved streets, the Ginza certainly lived up to its original commission, at least in outward appearance. But, many houses were damp, poorly ventilated and poorly built, resulting in high vacancy rates. Dismayed, the government provided subsidies to convert the quarter to retail commercial uses during the 1880s, a state of affairs that continues today. In the 1920s, the Ginza became the hangout of *moga-* and *mobo*-style modern youth who, through their antics on the street, raised the ire of older generations and earned Ginza its first taste of trend-setting fashion, still persistent today.[9] Finally, in the aftermath of World War II, the district changed rapidly in scale. Pressured by rising real-estate prices, because of its central location, proximity to transit and allowable use, high-rise contemporary glass and steel structures were constructed, often on the small original footprints of earlier buildings. Today, it is filled with high-rise department stores and other retail outlets, including work by Renzo Piano and other notable contemporary architects, and, at least until recently, enjoyed one of the highest commercial land rents and volumes of retail sales in the world.[10]

Another set of site circumstances that made a physically distinctive transition from Edo to modern Tokyo were the hilltop sites of the former *daimyō* estates. These sprawling, often walled, compounds, together with monastic quarters of similar splendour, were loosely organized along the ridge roads that meandered around the tops of the hills and headlands of the Yamanote, or upper city of Edo, as well as in a few locations near the Shogun's castle in the lowlands.[11] They were large tracts of land and, with the demise of the Shogunate, were suitable for building government industries and other complexes, as well as museums, such as those in Ueno Park, sprawling across the headland of the same name. They also became sites for foreign embassies and large business enterprises, sometimes stemming from the same *samurai* families of original ownership. Today, given recent upward pressures on property values and the low interest rates during the recent economic downcycle, many of the properties have been developed or are undergoing development as high-rise building complexes, with large footprints, adjacent car parking, as well as retail and entertainment space (i.e., largely as contemporary, American-style, high-rise mixed-use complexes). Unfortunately, in other areas, especially during the 1980s boom, entrepreneurial desires to assemble land parcels for larger-scale structures were so great that practices of intimidation were visited on defenceless property owners.[12] Nevertheless, today in Tokyo, projects like Minoru Mori's Roppongi Hills complex are beginning to make their mark, albeit awkwardly, often developed in an effort to appeal to overseas companies and to satisfy contemporary needs for well-serviced, large-scale and up-to-date office space with other supporting accompaniments. Even the venerable Mitsubishi company's Marunouchi district, built on a lowland *daimyō* estate, first as Londontown and more recently as an array of concrete and glass moderately high-rise buildings, is slated to undergo upward revision to suit better contemporary international business practices.[13]

Another large-scale building conversion of a relatively open site occurred in Shinjuku, now one of the dense sub-centres of Tokyo. As mentioned in chapter Three, the primary underlying impetus for high-density and high-rise development came on the heels of railroad and subway development, within which Shinjuku continues to be a major stop and multi-modal transportation interchange. In fact, it is one of Tokyo's major hubs. Earlier, however, from the time of Edo up through the Meiji Restoration, Shinjuku was predominantly a pastoral and forested setting, with grassy slopes, offering splendid views of the city and bay in the distance to Tokyoites from various walks of life. Dotted with shrines and *daimyō* estates and later the site of a large water reservoir, Shinjuku was part-playground, part-preserve and part-entry into Edo–Tokyo, from a westerly direction, along the Koshu Kaidō roadway, having been made a post town as early as 1698.[14] With the railroad came the real-estate developer's initial outward and westward push from Tokyo, and during the post-war restoration this began to change the area, at first slowly and then rapidly and radically. The Shinjuku Subcentre Corporation was created in 1960, although the land to the west of the station, *Nishi-Shinjuku*, remained largely vacant until the late 1960s, followed by a substantial building boom, under less constrained height limitations, which produced the largest concentration of high-rise buildings in Japan. During the late 1980s the Tokyo Metropolitan Government's office complex was constructed, and opened in 1991. Designed by Kenzo Tange, the main tower of the complex rises 243 m, splitting into two symmetrical smaller towers at the 33rd floor, and now superseding Tokyo Tower as the premier vantage point for viewing the city. The railroad station itself is immense, interconnecting some five main lines through a sprawling network of underground passages and above-grade pedestrian crossings. The busiest terminal in the world, the Japan Rail facility serves in excess of 760,000 passengers per day.[15] To the east of the station lies the older traditional shopping and entertainment district of Kabukichō, now also the home of some of Tokyo's few foreign workers, like the Chinese. Remnants of the earlier open landscape setting can be found in the serene setting of the Shinjuku Gyoen garden and Shinjuku Central Park, adjacent to the Tokyo Metropolitan Government's complex.

Finally, in Tokyo, there are neighbourhoods like Kyōjima in Sumida-ku, on the eastern side of the Sumida River, that formed as spontaneous settlements by those from lowland areas who escaped the Kantō earthquake and fire of

20
Tokyo metropolitan government building, 1991, by Kenzo Tange, in the contemporary high-rise context of Shinjuku, Tokyo. 1998.

1923. Originally wetlands and sparsely occupied agricultural lowlands, often below sea level and protected by dykes, the organic layout of these neighbourhoods reflects the underlying pattern of rice fields and stream meanders, now covered by streets, across which major roadways, like Meiji Dori, have been inscribed, pulling the district into a more uniform, rectilinear spatial order.[16] Once again an *anko-gawa* configuration of urban form has materialized, with construction of taller and larger structures along the major roads that bound the dense, though low-rise, neighbourhoods. In fact, across its land surface Tokyo can best be seen as a sprawling mosaic of locally defined neighbourhoods and sub-districts, of more or less intense urban development, bound together by roadways, rail lines and waterways. Indeed, it has often been referred to as congeries of villages.[17] In this layout, it also appears to present a dualistic perceptual frame, without much mediation or resolution, as well as a sort of spatial parenthesis between locally identifiable topographic features, together with traditional patterns of settlement, and the unifying topology of relative position created by the underlying subway system. Within the dualistic perceptual frame one can often encounter a bucolic, traditional, small-scale and village-like setting alongside an outwardly modern, up-to-the-minute, showy, bustling and high-rise environment, with nothing much in between. Negotiating the city requires two mental maps – one topographic and the other topological – in contrast to the singular cadastral view that predominates in much of the West.

In Taipei, upward extension of historical patterns of settlement and property ownership has taken on a dispersed and less dense, extended form, coincident with the earlier distributed patterns of villages, hamlets and towns in the Taipei Basin. As described in chapter Three, what became Taipei was earlier three relatively distinct settlements of foreign immigrants, mainly Chinese – Mengchia, Ta-tao-chen and Chen Nei – as well as numerous indigenous agricultural settlements. As Taipei expanded during the last quarter of the twentieth century, this polynucleated pattern was perpetuated, along a loose gridwork of major roads, mainly to the west of the original Chinese settlements.[18] Once again the result has a loose mosaic-like quality of different places agglomerated. The shophouses of Mengchia, for example, were extended upwards, more or less in place, whereas the regular footprints of urban blocks in Chen Nei and parts of Ta-tao-ken became host to high-rise structures, with all three original settlements expanding according to their own internal spatial logics, becoming distinct though adjoining districts. Similarly, the modern western expansion of Taipei, operating under relatively laissez-faire, market-driven controls, has solidified into a patchwork of specific residential and commercial developments and precincts, with density and scale varying largely according to intra-city location and transportation accessibility, as happens elsewhere in modern urban expansions.

A characteristic of a traditional Chinese city, like Beijing, or the Concessions of Shanghai, is the presence of relatively large urban blocks, criss-crossed by lanes – Beijing's *hutong* and Shanghai's *lilong* – bordered by major streets and roads, providing two distinct spatial orders of traffic circulation and adjacent building. Typical blocks in inner-city Beijing, for instance, are on the order of four to five hectares, with similar sizes in Shanghai. Dimensionally, these blocks also tend to be square or broad, rather than narrow and long; in Beijing they were traditionally composed primarily by the *siheyuan* – single-storey, four-sided courtyard houses – made up of pavilions and arcades around one or more square open courts, depending on the rank and wealth of the household. Access to the *siheyuan* was from gateways on narrow lanes, typically running

21
Upward extension
in contemporary
Taipei. 1996.

east–west between the broader streets and roads, with so-called reverse rooms, having ancillary functions, facing out to the lanes with few if any openings.[19] The overall visual effect of this urban landscape was a horizontal village-like appearance, which scrupulously maintained the privacy of inhabitants, and was often heavily vegetated by trees inside the open courtyards and along the lanes. In Shanghai, conditions were more urban and more modern. The *lilong* houses, of which over 200,000 were constructed since the end of the nine-

teenth century, were a hybrid between the traditional Chinese courtyard houses and Western-style row houses.[20] Usually rising two or more storeys in height, these dwellings also faced on to narrow lanes, entered from an adjoining street through a gateway in the façade of shophouses lining the streets, and then through a smaller courtyard at the front of each dwelling. Broad expanses of the foreign Concessions were occupied by single houses on individual lots, again varying in size and grandeur, as did the *lilong* houses, according to the wealth and status of the occupants.

Over time, in both cities, through hardship, neglect and overcrowding, this earlier building stock and urban landscape became severely dilapidated and in many cases beyond repair. Given the high intrinsic property-right values in today's burgeoning real-estate market in central locations, substantial redevelopment has occurred, resulting in wholesale erasure of these traditional and early-modern dwellings. Indeed, for many inhabitants, the squalid, run-down conditions are reminders of a way of life they would rather forget, preferring contemporary high-rise living, with superior amenity and space standards. The broad dimensional characteristics of the urban blocks, regulation notwithstanding, allows and even promotes new commercial, mixed-use and residential construction, often on a tall and massive scale. In Beijing, for instance, two substantial commercial districts have emerged recently, on the urban blocks once host to numerous *siheyuan* – the Central Business District to the east of the Forbidden City and the Financial District to the west. Such whole-sale conversion of land use is also fuelled by the high dependency of inner-city municipal districts, like Xicheng and Dongcheng, on the sale and lease of property rights as a source of general income. Belated efforts in both cities to preserve and conserve the *hutong* and *lilong* environments has resulted in conservation zones, such as the Shichahai area in Beijing's Xicheng district, within which gentrification has begun to occur, and the conservation and preservation plan for 25 historic areas now underway in the city.[21] In Shanghai, otherwise large-scale contemporary redevelopment has been matched with concerted restoration efforts, such as Vincent Lo's Xintiandi project designed by the American Benjamin Wood. Nevertheless, again in both cities, the under-lying, broad urban block configuration has given scope for both upward extension and conversion of earlier land use.

As in other parts of the world, earlier suburban ribbon development along streetcar lines and major roadways, leading in a radial pattern outside central cities in East Asia, has also been subject to upward extension and expansion to make way for contemporary urban developments. In Singapore this phenom-enon is particularly pronounced in locations like Orchard Road, one of the first suburban routes leading inland, away from Jackson's original plan. Lined by rows of single houses, often on relatively capacious lots, with the arrival of the streetcar, narrow shophouse districts were constructed closer in towards

23
The Xintiandi
Lilong restoration
of 2001 by
Benjamin Wood.
2003.

previous page

24
Terraces and the
'five-foot way',
Singapore. 1997.

the city centre on both sides of the road. Basically, as elsewhere in South-East Asia, the Singaporean shophouse was two to three storeys in height, with a gabled roof, often behind an ornate front façade, and with separate establishments joined together in rows, sometimes sharing the same unifying façade treatment. The lower floor was usually dedicated to commercial activity, often serviced by a lane at the back, and crossed in front by a continuous arcade allowing customers shelter from inclement monsoon weather. The upper floors were typically the living quarters of the shop owners, or used for back-office functions and storage. Within this dense mix of commercial and residential functions, multi-storey row houses were also constructed, again often with arcades along the front – the so-called five-foot ways leading from relatively narrow side streets, adjacent to a major roadway.[22] Today, Emerald Hill, adjacent to Orchard Road, is a well-restored example of this latter form of residential development, many units of which have double-hung 'Dutch doors' behind the arcades and balcony overhangs, adding a further layer of spatial mediation, or layering, behind the interior of the houses and the outside street. There is an old-world, serene quality to this living environment, just a stone's throw away from the bustling commercial activity along Orchard Road. During the recent building boom, however, this general urban pattern was radically changed in height and building volume, if not footprint, with the result that the former relatively narrow strips of shophouses and suburban lots along Orchard Road are now lined with high-rise hotels, department stores and commercial buildings, with an underground subway replacing the streetcar, making it a major hub of activity in Singapore. Nevertheless, on closer inspection, the underlying template can also be discerned.

Finally, upward extension of inherent patterns of development sometimes have very particular expressions in East Asia, perhaps nowhere more exaggerated than in the conversion of old marketplaces in Seoul. One such is the Namdaemun Market, which was located beside one of the old gates of the city. Historically, it was important for food and clothing, as well as the location of two seventeenth-century storehouses for rice storage, used as a form of taxation. Today the market covers about 4 hectares of land and houses 10,172 registered shop owners.[23] Mainly the stores are hybrids of the *chango*, or traditional store located inside the old wall, and the *jangshi*, or temporary market located outside the wall. In contrast, in the Dongdaemun area, also a site of traditional markets, high property rent and real-estate opportunity have pushed the commonplace market function into the Keopyong Freya – a 22-storey 'megamart' with an additional six floors of parking. Dwarfing neighbouring stores, this multi-use structure houses some 3,000 wholesale and retail outlets, vertically arranged in market-like stalls across thirteen floors of open interior space, centrally served by elevators and escalators. Above are nine further floors of office and apartment space.[24] This and others, like the Doosan Tower completed in 1997, offer customers in contemporary, automobile-oriented Seoul the convenience of market-style shopping, choice and mass supply.

District Making

Apart from local adaptation of foreign models, the making of modern urban districts within East Asian cities has also been strongly influenced by the internal logic of dominant social organization and what constitutes a community within a broader, national scheme, as well as by progressively widening and refining early local attempts to cope adequately with the sudden urban population increases. Nowhere was this interest in community more thoroughgoing than in China, although in places like Hong Kong, Singapore and South Korea, residential districts and communities also took on distinctive local appearances, mainly dictated by the evolution of strong public-housing programmes. After the civil war, China's economy was in a shambles, urban infrastructural services were at a very low ebb and there was an acute and mounting housing shortage. Consistent with their socialist ideology, as well as to control inflation, reduce the financial deficit, promote industrial production and supply the basic necessities of life, the People's Republic established a centralized planned economic system. Priority was given to quick and extensive development of heavy industry, drawing from the Soviet experience.[25] The construction, distribution and management of urban housing was centralized, paving the way for establishment of a welfare housing system, although it was not until after 1956 that the real conversion to wholesale public ownership occurred.[26] In theory, the central economic idea was to expand the reproduction of the means of primary production (i.e., primary industry) and to avoid rivalry from non-productive urbanization (i.e., housing) for scarce resources. Under the dictum of 'production first, livelihood second', a policy of high industrial accumulation and low consumption was put into effect with welfare supplements, including housing and urban services, provided in order to meet the basic needs of urban dwellers. Along the way, cities, including Beijing, were to be converted from centres of consumption to centres of production, resulting in an almost exclusive concentration of municipal works in newly built industrial cities, mainly in the north, as well as in new industrial suburbs of existing cities and towns; together with piecemeal industrialization of available sites within those cities and towns. No less a figure then Mao Zedong was reputed to have said that he wanted to see smoke stacks as far as the eye could see, referring to his government's new capital of Beijing.[27] However, the state alone did not have sufficient resources to build the public infrastructure to support the urban expansion and conversion, so specific departments, public enterprises and work units were called upon to contribute. Soon, work-unit communities (*danwei*) began to spring up around the edges of established urban areas, as well as within cities, where the cost of building was cheap and where sufficient self-containment could be achieved, again reducing the need for external infrastructure and related service costs. Functionally, work-unit communities, initially modelled after the Soviet *rayony*, were usually relatively large and highly mixed-use environments, incorporating centres of production (i.e., factories), living quarters, social services, leisure-time activities, and easy access to daily and occasional shopping necessities. Larger work units also included hospitals, a full range of primary and secondary schools, as well as public utilities and extensive roadways. The relative priority given to a work unit in the overall scheme of things usually dictated what could be afforded by way of available welfare subsidies, like housing, community services, household necessities, etc., and gave rise to a certain amount of social stratification, in spite of the prevailing socialist rhetoric.[28]

Initially, the physical layout of the work-unit communities was one of two kinds. The first was composed of a grid-iron pattern of roads and streets forming large urban blocks occupied by multistorey perimeter blocks, each on the scale of a neighbourhood, with communal open and recreational space at the centre. Factories and other facilities for production, like workshops, were located in the blocks with the most advantageous external access and community facilities and services above the neighbourhood level were concentrated at or near the centre of the entire community. The second type had more or less the same overall configuration and roadway network, but the housing was lined up in repetitive rows of north–south facing multistorey buildings with communal open space in between. By the mid-1950s a strong debate broke out over the efficacy of each physical layout, finally decided in favour of the parallel-block scheme of worker housing – the *danyuanlou* again – on the grounds of consistent north–south orientation and, therefore, better environmental performance at a time of little possible investment in climate control; less noise

and other disturbance from nearby streets; and an absence of bourgeois architecture, allegedly to be found in perimeter block approaches. With a Floor Area Ratio of about 1.0 and upwards, the *danyuanlou* were relatively dense, with in the order of 600 people per hectare, and often reaching up to seven storeys in height, all in walk-up conditions.[29]

The accompanying social organization of these work-unit communities was hierarchically defined in an overlapping manner according to a relatively consistent management formula. In an early example, Caoyangxincun, built between 1951 and 1988 on the then outskirts of Shanghai, the community as a whole eventually consisted of some 107,000 people, with nine village communities ranging in size around 12,000, and further subdivisions into work groups of about 2,000 and small groups of 300 to 500.[30] Spatially, this social organization and management structure was organized into four housing clusters, or several rows of *danyuanlou* around one work area – the so-called four dishes and one soup formula – with community facilities, kindergartens and a school in central locations. The housing clusters, in turn, were spatially organized, again roughly in four segments, around larger-order production facilities to form a village, again with higher-order community facilities at or near the centre, and so on, up to the full-scale district level of the entire community, replete with administrative, medical, banking, entertainment and cultural functions. Comparatively, Caoyangxincun was large. The more normal formula, using slightly different nomenclature, was for a residential district on the order of

30,000 to 50,000 inhabitants, residential quarters of 7,000 to 13,000, and housing clusters of from 1,000 to 3,000.[31] It is interesting to note that this spatial and social formulation closely coincides with the idea of 'neighbourhood units', first promulgated by Ebenezer Howard and the Garden City Movement, where 30,000 or so people was seen to be an ideal community size, supporting a broad complement of work-related facilities, schools, shops and other community facilities.[32]

At first, the Chinese also emulated the Soviet Union's mode of production and standard method of design for housing. This involved semi-industrialized methods of building construction, both to lower assembly costs and to release labour for more productive purposes. Standardized housing designs also took full advantage of construction efficiencies, with a fundamental design module conceptualized around the residential unit or block itself. Typically, these units were of simple concrete slab-and-wall construction, six bays in length, served by stairs and straightforward vertical risers for utilities. Each unit accommodated on the order of 100 to 120 people, with some doubling up. By the late 1950s, however, the Chinese found they could not continue to afford the Soviet prescription, abandoning the internal corridor configuration and interior unit space dividers as 'rational design yet irrational use' for their purposes, and thenceforth providing only the most basic 'sleep type unit' (i.e., not self-contained and with the nominal provision of multipurpose space and sleeping niches) at around 4 m^2 per person of livable space.[33] By then, any architectural pretence in either wall or roof articulation was considered non-productive and, as economic circumstances worsened under conditions of absurdly imbalanced production, urban housing was reduced to a very basic form of shelter.

From the early to middle 1970s, when Deng Xiaoping began to take charge of the Communist Party Central Committee, more attention was paid to urban development and residential districts began to make a comeback, although this time also with the appearance of high-rise dwellings, especially in Beijing with the Qianmen Dajie project, where well-serviced land resources were scarce and population pressures for new or better housing were high.[34] The many residential districts constructed in China during the late 1970s and into the 1980s, still took the form of relatively large, integrated and even self-contained communities, although the housing stock improved, with more variety, better livable space standards, and with the monotonous slab-block configurations interspersed with 'point-block' towers, served centrally by elevators and stairs. Episodically, through the shift in 1978 from class struggle to socialist modernization, followed in 1984 by a planned market economy and in the 1990s by a fully fledged socialist market economy, commercialization of housing, as a commodity and not as a welfare good, substantially loosened the hold on housing by work-unit communities.

Nevertheless, urban residential districts continue to be built to provide low-to-middle-income housing for incoming urban workers and to provide better housing opportunities for existing urban dwellers, although now often out towards the urban periphery. Indeed, the *Anju*, or comfortable housing programme, which began around 1995, has been responsible, in industrial towns like Wenzhou, for providing well-built, amenable and spacious residential districts, with kindergartens, communal gardens, schools and adjacent commercial areas.[35] Typically, these districts occupy broad blocks, surrounded by roads and large streets on which commercial activity is usually located on the lower floors of six- or seven-storey buildings situated around the perimeter with apartments above served by elevators. Parallel blocks of self-contained apartments, with balconies and private outdoor space, usually occupy the interior of blocks, served by minor streets, and also spatially help define outdoor communal recreation spaces and community facilities. Although by no means literal copies, many up-scale, residential gated communities in places like Shanghai's rapidly developing Pudong New Area, form large enclaves of tall, mid- and low-rise buildings, interspersed with flourishing gardens, recreational and communal facilities. Far from being anti-urban, the sense of enclosure appears to have deep roots in China, dating back to the *siheyuan* and traditional patterns of settlement described earlier. In any event, adjacent streets formed by the complexes are usually the domain of commerce and often bustle with street life.

A less comprehensive, though only slightly less ideological attitude towards housing and community development is apparent in Singapore's new towns and Housing Development Board heartland, where tall towers of apartment blocks are the rule rather than the exception, carefully grouped around outdoor recreational spaces and hierarchically organized into ensembles that support various levels of other community functions and public facilities.[36] Space standards are well in excess of China, although a puritanical ethos seems to pervade these complexes, pushing unplanned and spontaneous activity, oxymoronically, to specially designated spaces. Singapore's Housing Development Board, although not without strict controls on personal use of public and commercial space, has managed to provide bigger, better equipped and more varied dwelling units, in keeping, until recently anyway, with user preferences.[37] Hong Kong, also with a strong commitment to public housing, has followed a similar

26
Resettlement
housing in the
Sanlinyuan resi-
dential quarter of
Pudong, Shanghai.
1997.

evolutionary trajectory of refinement and space provision, although with more
proverbial bumps in the road and often with less fixation on hierarchical,
pre-planned and controlled arrangement of community services, as well as
the social models of 'neighbourhood' that lay behind them.

The year 1954, or thereabouts, marked the point in Hong Kong's housing
development when the public sector entered the business of public housing.
Prior to that, most housing conditions in Hong Kong were dense and often
poor. The majority of the housing stock was row houses, shophouses and the
five-storeyed so-called cantilevered boxes with gallery access around the
perimeter, built in large quantities after 1940. Living standards were very low,

with sleeping cubicles on the order of 2 by 2.5 m sometimes rented to three to six people. The overall average ranged from an appallingly low 2 m² per person of livable space and the spot density of many three-storey tenements, dating from the 1880s, was over 2,000 people per hectare.[38] In retrospect, the period from 1954 to 1970 witnessed the evolution of a high-density, yet relatively low-rise city, to one of ten- to twenty-storey public housing projects. Following the very basic shelter provision of the earlier resettlement estates, mainly for cross-border immigrants, the Mark I public housing projects went into effect. Around eight storeys in height, each housing block had floors typically containing 62 single-room flats, with gallery access, and a provision of about 12 m² of living space per flat, with communal bathrooms and kitchens located in the link between one housing block and another.[39] In 1956, following a change of regulations allowing building heights to reach from ten to twenty storeys, the so-called Massive Blocks came into existence. Each was rectangular in overall plan configuration, usually housed 24 units or more per floor, with stairways, elevators and double-loaded corridors located along the centre of each floor plate, forming an eight-unit basic module. Space standards were increased slightly to around 3.25 m² per person on average, but again with what can only be described as sleeping cubicles, separated from a single multi-use space towards the front of each unit. Local densities were up to 4,000 people per hectare and the rather elongated form of each dwelling unit tended to impede adequate light and ventilation.[40]

From 1970 to the present, and especially under the Maclehose reforms discussed earlier, the evolution of out-and-out tower blocks predominated, as existing buildable parcels of land became scarce and, thus, more costly. Building regulations changed in 1966, in response to the excesses of density of the prior Massive Blocks, to decrease and fix maximum site densities at 2,500 people per hectare. In addition, provision for adequate light and air to each unit, as well as to the street level and lower non-residential floors below, ushered in an era of thinner towers. Indeed, a typical private sector product at the time was the omni-directional point-block tower, or from 30 to 40 storeys of residential functions, with central core service, to eight units on each residential floor. The second generation of public housing, by contrast, were the 'H and Twin Blocks', with from 30 to 32 units per floor, each providing about 40 m² of living space per unit, with staggered gallery access, and a rise in height of from 20 to 24 storeys.[41] Each wing or tower of the 'H' or 'Twin' plan configuration was narrow – one apartment thick for light and through ventilation – with a stair and elevator core forming the cross-arm between the stacked

27
Mark I public
housing in Hong
Kong in 1957.

living units. Each unit was also self-contained (i.e., bathroom and kitchen facilities), although no ground-level podium was provided for non-residential functions. Instead, those services were typically located in separate buildings within the residential complex.

With the third and subsequent generations of public housing, the overall configuration of tower blocks converged more substantially with those provided by the private sector, although space standards and other amenities remained well below those of higher-priced condominiums and rental apartments. The 'Trident Series' of the 1980s, for example, rose as high as 40 storeys, with from 16 to 24 units per floor, but again with freestanding unattached non-residential functions as a part of an overall complex.[42] With increased space standards, the dwelling units began to approach the standards of middle-class housing and all units were self-contained and usually set up for tenant 'fitout'.[43] The typical floor plan was an omni-directional pin-wheel arrangement of three wings leading from a central service and elevator core. The internal corridor was double-loaded and the floor plans of each unit were articulated to provide better views, balconies and adequate light and ventilation. The 'Harmony

Series' of the 1980s reduced the number of units per floor to sixteen while maintaining the height at around 40 storeys.[44] Slightly larger units were also provided, at around 55 m^2 in area, and the overall configuration of four wings leading from a service core was much closer, in concept, to market-rate housing. finally, the 'Concord Series' of the 1990s typically incorporated from six to eight units per floor, again in a four-wing omni-directional configuration and at a height of some 40 storeys.[45] Except for issues of unit size and other amenities, this series closely approximated private sector housing and was, in fact, designed specifically for the Housing Authority's Home Ownership Scheme. Each unit came fully prepared and no tenant 'fit-out' was allowed.

Viewed over time, this progression of public housing maintained high densities, after the excesses of earlier periods, with large numbers of dwelling units per building, at least up until the late 1980s and '90s, when the building size declined to equalize more with private sector models. With high-density housing now the norm in so much of Hong Kong, several social aspects warrant comment. First, overcrowding was a serious issue during several phases of Hong Kong's development. Often appalling and sub-normal living conditions, at least by international standards, were the plight of many in Hong Kong and even the more capacious contemporary standards are minimal at best, in spite of government efforts to turn the situation around. A certain 'normalcy', as it were, of individual household living conditions did not really occur until the 1980s, when the prevailing 'sleep-type' unit was abandoned in favour of larger 'apartment-like' units, with a full complement of relatively specialized rooms and services within each unit. Certainly the available living space of 3.25 m^2 per person during the 1950s and '60s was very low, comparable to a similar level in mainland China during the depths of the 'Cultural Revolution'. Earlier lower levels, prevalent before that time, can only be regarded as deplorably sub-human. As in China, the provision of a basic shell within which tenants fitted out their own units was economically expedient, allowing more units to be brought on line each year and allowing modifications to be made, over time, as household needs changed. Recently, the convergence of public housing and market-rate housing in both layout and appearance is encouraging, and the prevalence of high-rise living, in almost all walks of life, has allowed Hong Kong's less well-to-do to avoid quite the same stigmatization as their counterparts in high-rise living environments elsewhere in the world. In fact, progressive public-housing development, since about the 1970s, appears, in many respects, to have imitated middle- to upper-income housing, albeit with far greater economy and lower amenity.

28
Mixed-income,
high-rise housing
in Aberdeen, Hong
Kong. 1999.

Second, notions of community and privacy often provide the prospect of finely graduated distinctions between private, semi-private, semi-public, communal and fully public realms of living environments. It is well known that different cultures, *ceteris paribus*, have different preferences in these regards. For instance, the difference between the public and private realm of housing is often sharply drawn in many European residential circumstances when compared to American suburban counterparts, or even to dense residential organizations in other places like the Middle East.[46] How these distinctions come about is an ongoing function of the 'push' and 'pull' between what the physical circumstances of housing will allow and how that housing is configured by cultural preferences and living habits. In Hong Kong, like other places in East Asia, such as Seoul, the economic imperative to build tall and dense housing has gained the upper hand, and strongly and perhaps narrowly defined the possibilities for community and privacy, with a strong distinction between the privacy of the dwelling unit and the public realm outside the building itself. This is not to say, however, that the realm of smaller community interaction has been ignored entirely. There is some room for it to take place on each floor, with populations of, say, 50 to 100 people, and at the scale of each building, although there the potential population involved is much higher at around 3,000 to 4,000.[47] Indeed, the existence of tenant associations and similar organizations gives credence to these possibilities. As elsewhere, however, the sense of being a neighbourhood is registered most strongly in people's lives among the non-residential uses, in and around the building complex, where the potential scale of such an operation is on the order of a not-so-small town. The point is that it is the increments of scale, and ultimately the scale itself, that sets Hong Kong apart from most, if not all, other living environments and offers the prospect of a different way of life.

Third, another aspect of the realm of everyday life, returning to a point made in chapter Two, is how the dwelling unit might be perceived. In many cultures the 'house' is seen as a 'home', with a full complement of features to support a broad spectrum of both daily and occasional activities. In other words, there is a high degree of concentration of the spatial needs of relatively specialized functions in a singular enclosure. Distinctions between home, workplace and places of shopping and recreation are often sharply drawn and spatially self-contained. In Hong Kong for many, at least up until the time of fully fledged provision of regular apartments, this ensemble of relatively discrete spatial environments was largely absent. The very meagre space standards of dwelling units, not to mention instances of doubling up, pushed the responsibility of housing many aspects of daily life, commonly associated with 'house as home', elsewhere. Consequently, many of the distinctions between otherwise different environments used during the daily life cycle were blurred. Conversely, the impact on 'street life' and multiple destinations during a day was equally profound, lending an intense vitality to the city. While this phenomenon is certainly not unique to Hong Kong, for it has occurred in other parts of China and elsewhere in East Asia for similar reasons, it does again begin to define a difference in the kind of living environment, rather than simply a difference in degree.

In Tokyo, another model of community living emerged in the aftermath of the 1923 Kantō earthquake, which, as described earlier, precipitated flight from the inner city to the apparent safety of the western agricultural hinterlands. Contrary to the dense, crowded *yashiki* neighbourhoods, built on the underlying settlement pattern of Edo, this was a suburban recipe with strongly Western ingredients, although also with a distinctly Japanese flavour of the countryside and preference for village-like living. Directly connected by rail to central Tokyo, this suburban development afforded an escape from inner-city work environments and the dominant traditional style of life–work arrangements. Impetus for the model, however began much earlier from Ebenezer Howard's Garden City idea, first introduced to Japan in a newspaper article titled 'Floral Garden City' – *Hanazono Tōshi* – and later became advanced through a Ministry of Internal Affairs publication titled 'Garden City' – *Denentōshi*.[48] Governmental interest was perhaps not surprising,

29
Denenchōfu
garden city, 1923,
in the western
suburbs of Tokyo.
1995.

in the aftermath of the Kantō earthquake's devastation and fire, for reasons of promoting public safety, as well as presumably returning to a more bucolic and garden-like image of earlier Edo. Nevertheless, Eiichi Shibusawa, a developer of note, and Ysuneta Yano, a publishing magnate, embraced the garden city's apparent balance between city and countryside, forming the Garden City Corporation Founding Association in 1916 and Garden City Incorporated in 1918, with Shibusawa as president. Through this non-profit development corporation and with its financial backers, they purchased about 154 hectares of farmland on Tokyo's western outskirts and planned Denenchōfu, targeted at a middle-class residential market, as a demonstration of garden city principles. Although planning was completed in 1923, inauguration of the project was delayed by events surrounding the earthquake and completion of the Meguro–Kamata railway, linking Denenchōfu to Tokyo.[49] In layout, Denenchōfu resembled Howard's earlier diagram for a garden city, with concentric rings of streets intersected by radial streets emanating from a central park adjacent to the railroad station and a commercial centre, eventually established around the station. Residential lots were modest at the time, on the order of between 360 and 1,000 m², to match the middle-income market, and later became further subdivided, accommodating in the order of 30,000 people.[50] Today Denenchōfu remains a model neighbourhood, one of many predominantly residential developments pursued by the Tokyu Corporation, among others, in suburban Tokyo. In contrast to inner-city neighborhoods, this model continues to offer a more open concept of urban landscape, with gardens in the front of dwellings and relatively broad tree-lined streets and, although overtly Western in many of its characteristics, it harkens back to the *hatamoto* and lower samurai-class estates of Edo described earlier.

Spaces In-Between

On closer inspection, among the defining characteristics of the East Asian urban scene are the spaces in between many of the buildings and urban blocks that make up the constructed fabric of cities. Often a study in contrasts, they frequently convey either an ambience of repose, communal serenity and gentle interaction that one might associate with village life, or the hustle and bustle of a teeming anonymous crowd amid glaring signs and symbols of seemingly endless commerce. Emblematic of the former condition is the traditional 'lane life' that seems to lurk behind major thoroughfares and among the contemporary labyrinths that connect adjacent parts of the city together, while the other cacophonous condition can be readily appreciated in the nearby broad swaths of 'neon life', also so much a part of East Asian cities. Although not unparalleled elsewhere, this bifurcation of urban experience between homely respite and crowded encounters with the world outside, between the ethos of the farmer and that of the merchant, is particularly marked by the sheer density of many East Asian circumstances and by the truncation of much of any mediating experience in between.

Although the spatial configurations of lane life in East Asia vary from city to city, in scale and modulation, all bring aspects of the traditional village to the city and appear intended to foster good relations among people living together in close proximity, returning to the overriding considerations of social propriety. The *roji* of Tokyo, for instance, are narrow lanes that provide access from adjacent and surrounding streets – *tori* or *dori* – to dwellings inside the semi-enclosed neighbourhoods. A substantial feature of lowland areas, like Sumida-ku and Tsukishima in contemporary Tokyo, *roji* are also very present around upland areas such as Akasaka, Roppongi and the older 23 wards. Many *roji* have posed problems for fire protection, as they often 'dead end' and have widths of less than 2 m across, requiring widening to around 2.7 m, to allow two firemen

to pass in parallel with fire hoses.[51] The blocks lining each *roji*, usually on both sides, are also narrow, sometimes on the order of 4 m wide, or less, and are occupied by two, and sometimes three-storey dwellings, in poorer areas often constructed primarily of timber, with narrow gaps in between. Façades facing the *roji* invariably screen the interiors of dwellings with layers of screens, sliding doors and narrow entranceways. Often the *roji* are heavily planted and scrupulously maintained in a kind of informal order. Safe for children to play, usually under watchful eyes from the inside, the *roji* also form useful communal spaces for adjoining residents and have a semi-private quality that makes one hesitate before entering. Indeed, within the system of the *tori* and *roji*, the importance of orientation and its implied meanings is expressed by being *ura* with respect to the *roji*, conveying the idea of participating in a community space, and being *omote*, or more formally disposed in alignment beside the *tori*, or street, beyond.

Along major routes across neighbourhoods, the *tori* also often assume a commercial character along the ground floors, and sometimes host markets. The term *ma*, which has many uses in Japanese, including the idea of 'face', or of not being embarrassingly conspicuous among the social group, can also convey the idea of 'space in between' and be deployed conceptually and perceptually to define objects, like buildings and parts of buildings and rooms, as much as they are defined intrinsically.[52] *Ma* can also be transgressed, as through the prorogation of nuisance or the heedless occlusion of sunlight but, in the case of well-functioning *roji*, is represented by a subtly differentiated sense of private from semi-private and semi-public space, without many of the sharper physical distinctions experienced in the West. In short, an appropriately orchestrated network of *roji* and *tori*, in at least the senses of orientation and *ma*, provide neighbourhood residents with both capacities to express themselves sufficiently and to participate in a well-ordered sense of community.

The *lilong* or lanes of Shanghai also imbue one with a moment of hesitation before entering and also often terminate within a relatively short distance, and are usually lined on either side with two-storey, three-storey and sometimes higher dwellings. They are, however, typically wider, from 4 to 5 m across and can, although they seldom do, allow for vehicular access. Literally meaning 'block lane', *lilong* or, in earlier incarnations, *shikumen* – named for the decorated gateways in the lines of shophouses that marked their entry from outside streets and roadways – similar configurations of lanes and lane houses can be found among other cities, like Wuhan and Guangzhou, referred to there as *xiangzi*.[53] Broadly synchronous with urban development of foreign concessions, from before the turn of the twentieth century onwards, many of the lanes resulted from speculative real-estate ventures, where the large urban blocks typical of inner-city Shanghai and other cities in China were subdivided into three or four portions and each developed as a separate lane-served residential complex, with adjacent commercial activity along a boundary street or road. Generally, each venture was in the order of 100 dwelling units, some, like Si-wen Lane, which began construction in 1916, were as large as 3.2

hectares in area, accommodating around 600 dwelling units.[54] Most often the *lilong* ran perpendicular to the outside street, as short spines providing convenient access, a modicum of privacy and respite from the bustle of activity outside, as well as a communal space for adjoining neighbours. In other, larger, configurations lanes separated by blocks ran perpendicular to the entry spines and parallel to the outside street in a spine-rib layout, sometimes referred to as a fishbone pattern. Entry to adjoining houses in each block row invariably required passage diagonally across a shallow courtyard, enclosed by walls above head height, thus preserving the privacy of a dwelling interior. This arrangement also provided an often well-shaped parenthesis with the lane outside, in which visitors could be properly received. *Lilong* houses varied in size and in material opulence. Basic units, however, were typically on the order of 60 to 105 m², spread across two to three floors, with typically two rooms per floor. Over time, the types of *lilong* housing expanded to include the so-called New *Lilong*, much closer to European townhouses, although still with the entry court, and Garden *Lilong*, incorporating side yards and larger plots of land.[55] Like the *roji*, the *lilong* played host to a variety of community uses, ranging from neighbours gathering in the evening to children's play and the staging of occasional festive events like marriages. In their bare essentials, though, they also provided gradation from the public life of the street to the privacy of the house, again in a manner that facilitated proper use and conduct, by allowing residents largely to control and orchestrate their contact with visitors and strangers.

Historically, the *hutong*, described briefly in the context of Beijing's urban block structure, had a low-rise single-storey configuration and was often more continuous and well-travelled, although no less well-mannered in intended use. The term *hutong* probably originates from the word *hottog*, meaning 'well' in Mongolian. In essence, villagers, or early urban settlers, dug out a well and lived there, pointing to the early evolution of Beijing as having a strong agricultural base inside its great walls. Certainly by the Yuan dynasty (1271–1368), nomenclature for Beijing's streets and roads had become fairly standardized – a 36 m wide roadway was called a 'standard street', an 18 m wide roadway was called a 'small street', and a 9 m wide lane a *hutong*.[56] Through the vicissitudes of early settlement and changes over time in property ownership, both resulting in rearrangement, enlargement, diminution and so on, of adjacent courtyard houses and other urban structures, Beijing's *hutong* proliferated and diverged from the original regular arrangement, sometimes taking on a maze-like configuration within the relatively large city blocks described earlier, with the result that the ideal east–west alignment disappeared. Widths of *hutong*

varied from 40 cm to 10 m. So-called 'slant', 'half' and 'blind' *hutong* were also created, and at least one continuous *hutong* incorporated more than twenty twists and turns. Typically, the entrance to a private family courtyard complex – the *siheyuan* again – was on the right-hand side of the complex from a *hutong*, through a gateway – ornamented according to rank – then through a smaller courtyard into a forecourt, leading thence to the major courtyard, or courtyards, in the heart of the family compound. The circuitous zigzag movement through this entry sequence was very deliberate, as in Shanghai and elsewhere in China, allowing the propriety of the household to be preserved and visitors to be welcomed with appropriate grace. The usually blank wall along the *hutong* on the outer side meant that street pedlars and traders made specific noises – ringing a bell, banging a drum or crying out in a particular manner – to let those inside the *siheyuan* know what was on offer outside, a practice that continues today.

Similarly, the lanes among the *hanok* of Seoul had a walled-in character, with gates and doorways indicating the presence of family compounds beyond the walls.[57] They were, however, often even more dendritic and discontinuous than *hutong*, forming an intricate network of passages away from nearby streets. Insadong is one of the few remaining areas of Seoul where this pattern

125

has been consciously preserved. Formerly following an old ditch in the city, Insadong is a street, on both sides of which are lanes and alleys leading to what were once residences for literati and minor bureaucrats during the Chosun dynasty, located not far from Kyongbok palace, in the heart of Seoul. Once renowned for bookstores, Insadong and its offshoots now cater for antique stores and galleries. Similar dendritic patterns of lanes and alleys are to be found in older, often dilapidated commercial areas of Seoul, criss-crossing the larger and newer urban block structure. The *hanok* is the traditional Korean house or household compound, like the Chinese *siheyuan*, with rooms, or pavilions, arranged around an enclosed courtyard, although usually without the same high degree of architectural development. Often the *on-dol* raised floor provided heating to the rooms. An urban neighbourhood was usually made up of ten to twenty *hanok* sharing the same lane. Usually heavily vegetated, the *hutong* and the lanes of the *hanok* bring, even today, a rural feeling to city life. To the idle passer-by from elsewhere, it might seem incomprehensible that the *hutong* and the lanes among the *hanok* appear so serene and almost vacant in what are otherwise very populous and dense cities. At other times they are more active, as people from the neighbourhood stroll and loiter in the public right-of-way, children play – sometimes in Beijing on furniture set up for that purpose – and pedlars ply their trade.

Dense commercial and high-rise concentrations, like central areas and some new-town centres of Hong Kong, as well as places like Shinjuku, Ikebukuro and Shibuya in Tokyo, are laced with pedestrian through-block connections and passageways that are analogous in circulation pattern to traditional lanes and also seem to encourage modes and manners of every-day life more closely associated with a communal realm than with outright public space. In Hong Kong, the proliferation of multi-level and intensively developed pedestrian-circulation systems within dense urbanized areas is probably second to none. In addition to the literal ground level of streets and sidewalks, which are comparatively narrow, due to little historic realignment and surrounding development densities, there are numerous pedestrian street overpasses, skywalks, vertically organized shopping complexes with open access and underpasses. Partly because of the steep terrain, exterior stairways, people movers and even exterior escalators carry pedestrians through parts of the city, often several storeys above ground, in a largely unprecedented manner. Unlike other cities with similar ad-hoc pedestrian connections, such as Houston and Minneapolis, this is not a matter of climatic convenience, although it has that aspect also, but one of both necessity and opportunity.

Lane and
hanok in Seoul.
1997.

Direct pedestrian entry into the upper reaches of the 'Mid-Levels' would be arduous without mechanical assistance, and commercial and residential densties, above and below, are such that horizontal access at plus three to five storeys above ground, and even higher, are commonplace. Furthermore, both horizontal and vertical connection of various layers of the city is necessary to support the pedestrian traffic of surrounding development and to compensate for the narrow street rights-of-way below. Through-block connections, again on multiple levels, increase the amount of accessible pedestrian area open to small as well as larger commercial outlets, without interrupting the wider and differently shaped floor plates of commercial and residential developments above.

The result is a convenient, highly compact, perforated podium of commerce, without much in the way of architectural rhetoric. Unlike the Futurist modernist dream, the interconnection between buildings is ad hoc, although economically highly rational, and almost entirely unselfconscious in its effect. Moreover, 'verticality' and its experience have become widespread, particularly when one remembers the tall buildings above, and accompanying this accentuated vertical experience are several sensibilities that set Hong Kong apart as

another kind of place. First, the cone of vision, in addition to moving from side-to-side, is given free reign to move up and down, with the result that horizontal floor and ground planes can have much the same status as vertical planes, or walls, in other perhaps more conventional circumstances. Second, verticality is a ubiquitous yet appreciable dimension of urban life, offering an anonymous cross-sectional and often voyeuristic encounter with one's surroundings, much like that dramatized so well in the film *Chungking Express*. Conversely, vertical movement forms a sort of parenthesis where life literally stands still, between the often well-ordered circumstances above and the hustle and bustle below. Third, the persistent vertical dimension often conveys the sense of inhabiting a strong Cartesian space rather than a largely Euclidean realm. Not only is this a matter of changing position, up and down, but also a question of address and a mode of belonging. Finally, there is a certain giddiness that goes with the vertical rise – a feeling of vertigo – another way of measuring displacement in urban space. Many of these aspects are not unique to Hong Kong by any means, but when they become overwhelmingly prevalent conditions of urban living, as they do there, then differences in kind emerge to replace differences of degree.[58]

In the contemporary labyrinths of Tokyo's Shinjuku district another ad-hoc arrangement prevails, although perhaps not with such an extensive and persistent experience of verticality. There, commercial alleyways snake up between and around tall buildings connected in a continuous flow of potential pedestrian movement, with passageways serving the widespread transportation facilities below. Cross-street connections also extend the flow to neighbouring commercial blocks, further creating a fine-grained web of possibilities for pedestrian movement, and opportunities for retail commerce, that hovers above, lies below, or passes through the more staid and regular urban structure of large department stores and major ground-level traffic arteries. Particularly in Ikebukuro's Sunshine City, the potential dizzying effects of vertical experience also return. The Toyota Auto Salon, for instance, offers a system of ramps for buyers and sightseers alike, moving through a very tall, multistorey space, enclosed from the street below by a sheer glazed curtain wall, and a Cartesian web of pedestrian movement proliferates throughout the larger complex.

By contrast, the realm of what might be called 'Neon Environments' and places where no expressive holds seem to be barred typically occupy many of the outright public spaces along well-travelled roadways and outside major transit destinations in East Asian cities, often immediately adjacent to the well-mannered lanes and other residential enclaves. These places of merchand-izing and frequent hard bargaining, though deemed necessary in older times, were never given much status in a social scheme of things that prized scholars, landowners and farmers more than lowly merchants and traders. Even today, frenetic mass retail and entertainment activity seems to take place without much social approbation. Along Nathan Road in Hong Kong, for instance, the central spine of Kowloon, as well as on smaller commercial streets on either side, there is a veritable hive of merchandizing activity, on both a large and a small scale, with advertisements of wares plastered four, five and even more storeys high across the façades of buildings, placed cheek to jowl, usually encroaching over the thronging sidewalk below. At night these signs come alive in a neon and incandescent glow of profuse colours, images and move-ment, as the double-decker buses continue to rumble, close behind one another, up and down the road. Behind, in the neighbouring narrow streets, the assault of neon and the shouts of hawkers on the senses is sometimes even more intense, with many signs jutting so far out into the street above the ground-floor level that they form a close succession of images, combining together to form a sort of canopy over the jostling crowd below. Once a low-rise ribbon of shops stretching north towards Kowloon Tong, interspersed with schools, churches and other institutions, many of which still remain, Nathan Road has undergone the kind of vertical transformation described earlier in this chapter. A broad emporium, where all manner of goods and services are on sale, especially in lower-cost markets, stores of the same kind are often grouped together as if to give further emphasis to a particular line of products and the illusion of comparative shopping.

However, as far as visual effects are concerned, probably nowhere on earth rivals the exterior of intensely developed areas of Shinjuku, in Tokyo, followed closely by Roppongi, the Ginza and the commercial zone in front of the entrance to Ueno Park. Several orders of magnitude more extensive and resplendent than Times Square in New York, Shinjuku leads the way in high-tech sign animation, dot screens and other devices, as well as the sheer size of specific advertising installations. Versions of these hyper-intense vernacular neon landscapes can also be found in Seoul and Taipei, as well as in Shanghai, especially among shopping areas and older established districts of commerce. Lower-key versions abound in more local areas where merchants ply their trade. Singapore has Orchard Road, a marvellous, though more sedate, multi-layered concoction of sidewalks and seating places at different levels set back from the street, shaded by huge trees, and further enclosed by lines of stores,

34
Neon and other
street signs,
Kowloon, Hong
Kong. 1998.

130

35
The multiple
layers of Orchard
Road, Singapore.
1997.

hotels and arcade entrances. Although less ad hoc in its profusion of signs, the one regular exception is the holiday season, running through Christmas, Buddhist and other religious observances, when the road is further festooned with lights and huge temporary, three-dimensional salutes to festive spirits, literally draped across the entire fronts of buildings.

Nevertheless, Singapore aside, in all this frenzied assault on the visual senses some order does seem to prevail. First, signage and other advertising conforms to property boundaries, often conveying a strong vertical dimension, especially against the background context of 'pencil buildings' and other upward extensions of relatively small property holdings. Second, it covers where possible and without excessive intrusion on inside inhabitants, the entire façade of a building or, put another way, it tends to incorporate, one way or another, all available elements of the building façade behind. Third, many signs can be read side by side, as a kind of running text, by people either walking down the street on the same side, or from across the street, regardless of background context. In other words, there is a coherence of parts, if not the whole, at work and a high degree of specific legibility is exhibited, regardless of differences in colour, shape and luminosity among the signs.

This profusion of signs and building-size advertising installations can run to several explanations. First, photographs from bygone eras suggest that it has almost always been that way within intense merchandizing enclaves and districts. Banners and flags stretched far up the outside of façades in many East Asian cities, as well as over narrow streets, and carved and coloured wood designs were emblazoned across the fronts of buildings.[59] Second, otherwise unregulated competition between neighbouring establishments to entice customers inside – the no-holds-barred aspect – would probably result in the use of all available space for signage and advertising. Again this would probably be reinforced by the appearance of establishments selling the same wares side by side, a practice that began in older times in many East Asian cities, among the Chinese during the Ming dynasty, if not before, and in Korea, often for purposes of taxation and control.[60] Third, there is an element of self-perpetuation and expectation in this practice. Once begun, it was followed, elaborated upon and came to be expected and to symbolize retail districts. This kind of explanation might cover the similarity of almost all Chinatowns, or Asiatowns, in various parts of the world.

Another use of 'space in-between' that has begun to occur in East Asia is the provision of more extensive 'green' public open space, often in the margins created by public infrastructure projects, like major thoroughfares, or along the edges of existing and recovered water bodies, in addition to the recent outright provision of large public parks, like Renmin Park in central Shanghai, Century Park in the same city, the proposed Olympic Green by Sasaki and Associates in northern Beijing, and Kowloon Park in Hong Kong. Shanghai has made ambitious plans to renovate the existing linear pedestrian platform along the Bund, through Vittorio Gregotti, as well as redeveloping the North Bund area, with well-orchestrated public open-space proposals by the SWA Group, including docking facilities for cruise ships, as well as constructing Riverfront Park along the Pudong side of the Huangpu River and planning for extensive landscape modifications to Suzhou Creek, by the American-based firm of EDAW. Long in the making, but almost complete, is central Shanghai's Yan'an Central Green Space – an ambitious project, extending intermittently through a series of smaller parks and then more continuously, from Hongqiao Airport to the Huangpu River, a length of some 20 km. Running in parallel and sometimes beneath the Yan'an expressway, which essentially transects the central city from west to east, this undertaking was first mooted by Huang Fu Xiang, the Director of the Shanghai Urban Planning and Research Institute, and includes a delightful 28-hectare segment, adjacent to the city administrative centre and Renmin Park, by the Montreal firm of WWA. In concept this transect of the city also continues on the Pudong side, through Century Avenue to Century Park on the east.

Hong Kong is also now looking to recapture public open space and park amenity along the shores of Kowloon, more or less from the old Kai Tak airport in the east, around and past the Hong Kong Cultural Centre, including the edges of Norman Foster's proposed West Kowloon Cultural District. More modest in scope are the recently completed Nanheyan Dajie linear park in central Beijing, along the site of an old wall, plans to 'green' several of Tokyo's old and moribund canals, including areas around Nihonbashi, and Seoul's recent plans to recover linear parks along several major thoroughfares, south of the Han River, as well as to uncover and refurbish the ancient waterway running through the centre of the city. The pressure to undertake these public improvements is understandable, given the density of surrounding areas and the relative scarcity, mentioned earlier, of accessible green open space. From a design perspective, the responses vary from singular spatial and landscaped conceptions of specific links – almost all the improvements are linear – to simply allowing the park space to accommodate local exigencies and recreational needs along their length. The sheer scale, certainly of the Yan'an Central Green Space, is impressive, comparable to large parkway projects recently contemplated or constructed in, for instance, the United States. In most instances the motivation for the projects appears to be similar to that found in the contemporary West, namely recovery of abandoned and under-used sites with the potential of splendid recreational and environmental amenity.

Finally, a relative newcomer to the streetscape of East Asia and particularly to China, is the street dedicated to pedestrians, usually along what was once a heavily travelled vehicular and pedestrian thoroughfare. In Shanghai, a lengthy segment of Nanjing Road, just beyond the Bund, was pedestrianized in the 1990s, to an urban design scheme by Jean-Marie Charpentier and his associates, in conjunction with Zheng Shiling, that also included substantial renovation and upgrading of the old department stores and other retail establishments that lined both sides of the road, beginning during Shanghai's previous commercial heyday of the 1920s and '30s, when the road was the main westerly route out of town leading eventually, as the name suggests, to Nanjing.[61] The scheme involved dismantling extensive ungainly pedestrian overpasses, installed to resolve traffic congestion, paving the road with granite, installing a fountain to the delight of children, providing a variety of seating areas for weary passers-by, and generally following many of the same

36
Fountain and
pedestrianization
along Nanjing
Road, Shanghai.
2000.

pedestrian improvements to be found in similar locations in Western cities. Although not intended to start a trend, the success of Nanjing Road's pedestrianization quickly spawned other similar projects, like long segments of Wangfujing Street in central Beijing and Jianghan Road in the heart of the Hankou district of Wuhan, both also suffering from problems of congestion and mixed modes of pedestrian and vehicular traffic. However, the pedestrianized street seems to have proliferated beyond these large cities as a status symbol of municipal modernization, without the same underlying circulatory and commercial rationale. In Asakusa, Japan, in contrast, the double-width pedestrian street with stalls in between – *Nakamise* (literally, in between shops) – leading to the Sensōji Temple, has maintained its historical market function. Although not denying movement other than by pedestrians, this ensemble of essentially a pedestrianized market zone and temple complex was common in days gone by, especially towards what was then the outskirts of Edo–Tokyo.[62] The broad and short market street, usually leading to buildings of governmental importance, was common in Chinese cities, like the old Tiananmen in old Beijing, apparently obviating the need for the plazas and squares of the West, almost never to be found in East Asia before the modern era. The occasional broadening of T-intersections of prominent streets also typically accommodated a pedestrian market function in traditional China.

Urban-Architectural Expressions

Moving further down in scale to the level of specific buildings, matters of urban-architectural expression no longer appear such natural outcomes of indigenous cultural developments in East Asia as they did in the past, with or without the transformatory effects of earlier outside influences. Nevertheless, the tension between universalism and localism is not infrequently drawn, returning to a line of argument pursued in chapter One, sometimes appearing to come from an overly self-conscious search for a suitable contemporary urban-architectural identity. This is particularly apparent in China, where there is a strong tendency for some to hold on to the architectural character of the past and for others to pursue contemporary architectural explorations, sometimes wildly.[63] Patrons and the powers that be in Singapore also seem actively to pursue a sense of local architectural identity, as well as placing the city squarely on the international architectural stage; not surprising, perhaps, given the controlling influence from the top exerted on most aspects of life there. Japan, with long-standing encounters between tradition and modernism, including stints at the forefront of modern architecture in the hands of architects like Tadao Ando, Fumihiko Maki, Yoshio Taniguchi, Kenzo Tange and Arata Isosaki, has become expressively modern, particularly in Tokyo and especially with regard to the poetic deployment of functional forms, contemporary building technology and material finish. During much of the contemporary era in Hong Kong, a relatively unselfconscious attitude has been displayed towards architecture, ranging from straightforward articulation of modern building practices to a number of architecturally unusual and prominent modern commercial towers and infrastructural installations, usually with few if any references to local or East Asian cultural traditions. Recently, however, this laissez-faire attitude has begun to change somewhat, with attempts to use public architecture in a campaign to 'brand' Hong Kong as a gateway to the Orient and as a modern, some might say hyper-modern, city of commerce and tourism. Here, Norman Foster's recent proposal for the West Kowloon commercial and cultural centre development is a case in point, with its extensive 1-km-long, curvilinear roof structure, appearing to many to resemble the profile of the mountain range behind in the shape of the body of a mythical dragon (i.e., *long* or *loon* as in Kowloon). For many, Skidmore Owings and Merrill's slightly earlier concert hall complex, jutting out prominently into the harbour, has a similar symbolic connotation befitting the marine environment of Hong Kong, referred to with colloquial affection as 'the whale'. Elsewhere, in cities like Seoul, there has been a mixture of architecturally expressive approaches, although, as in Hong Kong, expedient modern construction and expression dominates Seoul's urban landscape, particularly through the extensive and rapid construction of satellite settlements and new towns, and strong local commitments to the progressiveness implied by modern apartment living.

One phenomenon immediately apparent in the early stages of architectural development of less-modernized East Asian cities was the construction of distinctive modern buildings with local expressive references and the deliberate acquisition of visible symbols of progress. An obvious example is the Jin Mao Tower of 1998, by Skidmore Owings and Merrill, rising 88 storeys above the Lujaizui financial district in Shanghai's Pudong New Area Development and, to date, China's tallest building. Designed to recall a historic Chinese pagoda form, with setbacks running its entire height, the finely wrought metal and glass curtain wall appears highly contemporary, yet intricately decorative in a traditional manner. The lower 50 storeys house commercial office space, while the upper 38 floors house a Grand Hyatt Hotel. With considerable symbolic resonance, when viewed from a distance, the tall spire has become a mecca for tourists visiting the city, as well as a leisure-time site for local people. Advanced structural engineering and intelligent integrated building sub-systems also point to China's advancement on the world stage, for those who want to look beyond the building's glitz and other obvious effects. As a part of the Lujaizui district, the Jin Mao Tower sits beside Century Avenue, a wide thoroughfare proposed by Jean-Marie Charpentier and his collaborators, apparently according to government wishes, in the manner of the Champs Elysées. Further to the east, this grand avenue terminates in a ceremonially disposed civic complex that includes a large contemporary science museum, by the American firm of RTKL, equally modern administrative offices for the local government, and a soon to be completed hyper-modern traditional arts and crafts centre, by Paul Andreu, as well as a nearby exhibition space, by von Gerkan, Marg and Partners. Continuing through this complex, in a pedestrian vein, to Century Park, the axial alignment of the avenue heightens the unusual, almost traditional monumentality of the urban ensemble, by sloping upwards to cross a passing thoroughfare. Also in Beijing, usually slower than Shanghai to open up to outside influences, state-sponsored projects like Paul Andreu's Opera House proposal of 1999–2000 – a large titanium-clad bubble-like form covering concert-hall pavilions near the commercial centre of the city – and Rem Koolhaas's proposed angular and twisting CCTV complex, as well as Jacques

37
Century Avenue, the Jin Mao building and Lujaizui, Shanghai, 2001.

Herzog and Pierre de Meuron's 'basket-weave' proposal for the Olympic stadium, deliberately combine the symbolism of hyper-modern architectural expression with what is intended to be a forward-looking, progressive spirit, befitting a nation that is arriving on the world stage in so many ways. Indeed, China's current embrace of the experimental in contemporary architecture, especially for state-sponsored projects, seems so complete that spectators in the future might be forgiven for labelling this form of hyper-modernism as a Chinese style. Only slightly more subdued, programmatically unexceptional, private-sector projects, like the Jian Wai SoHo residential and commercial complex in eastern-central Beijing, by Riken Yamamoto, appear likely to contribute to this future retrospective perception.

Undoubtedly, however, the most thoroughgoing inclination towards prestige architectural projects, with an overtly contemporary appearance, has occurred in the spate of airports, port and other infrastructural facilities recently constructed throughout East Asia, including Paul Andreu's Pudong airport in Shanghai, Renzo Piano's Kansai airport near Osaka, Norman Foster's Chek Lap Kok terminal in Hong Kong, Foreign Office Architects'

38
Paul Andreu's scheme for the Beijing Opera House, 1999.

139

Yokohama Passenger Ferry Terminal and Terry Farrell's tramway terminal on Pike's Peak in Hong Kong. Perhaps it is because they are the latest in infrastructure and on a scale largely novel to their respective cities that they take on such contemporary, high-tech forms. After all, it is difficult to recall an airport that was not modern in appearance, at least when it was built. Nevertheless, as literal gateways, again to their respective cities and often nations, deeper collusion between the symbolic aims of public authorities and the modern, even futuristic-looking, architecture cannot be discounted.

Apart from pursuing symbols of progress, prominent among the driving forces behind this architecturally expressive universalism are the extensive international practice and cross-cultural influence of modern design. If anything, the globalization of capital and commissions, as well as the presence of multinational corporations mentioned in chapter One, has increased the number of designers from one place producing projects somewhere else. Many well-known and sizeable American and European architectural firms now have projects and branch offices overseas, including in East Asia. Constant information sharing, over the Internet, or through internationally circulating design magazines and professional journals, together with the widespread adoption of Western building practices, almost ensures that any tendency towards parochialism is quickly overcome. Worldwide, architectural education is also dominated, by and large, by modern expressive approaches and even values. Moreover, in efforts to improve the quality and contemporary character of local building, it has become a not uncommon practice to attempt to transfer technological and architectural know-how through prestigious building projects.

During the 1970s and '80s, for instance, Singapore made a point of inviting internationally renowned modern architects to participate in rebuilding the commercial core and central areas of the city. Among those who participated were I. M. Pei, John Portman, Kenzo Tange and Paul Rudolph, practically all of whom designed high-rise commercial towers for banks, insurance companies and other commercial ventures, well beyond the scale of what was there before. Throughout this experience, Singaporean officials also insisted, when possible, on partnering with local design firms, in order to facilitate transfer of knowledge and relevant technology, as well as protecting local architects and engineers from outside competition for many other projects.[64] Outside design influences and expertise were used to help establish Singapore as a forward-looking modern city and to assist in accelerating the process of developing relevant local know-how. During subsequent years, this strategy has materially helped Singapore to reach quickly the high standards of modern building that it enjoys today, together with its own pattern of modern urban development. Similarly, with the opening up and accelerated modern urban development of Chinese cities, a similar formula is also often in play around major projects with foreign architects. Indeed, a number of smaller local practices in the hands of architects like Zhang Yonghe, Liu Jaikun, Ai Weiwei and Ma Qingyun, have begun to spring up, modelled in their strong design orientation after Western and Japanese counterparts, as a viable alternative to the large design institutes first formed as public enterprises during the earlier Communist era.

Working in the opposite expressive direction, a number of contemporary architects have attempted to incorporate traditional forms of architecture into their projects. Especially in China, as mentioned in chapter Two with regard to Chinese 'essence' and Western 'application', a prominent school of architectural thought has taken this approach for some time, perhaps most conspicuously during the Nationalist decade of the 1930s, and the expressive celebration of the architectural glories of China's past alongside a use of modern materials and structure. This stance was also prevalent during the 'big roof' phase of early Communist architecture (referring to the large gabled roofs, bracketing and other decorative elements often used on state projects, and some of the no less figural compositional principles that appeared to refer back to the massing of walls and large openings form the imperial period).[65] In the contemporary scheme of things, the work of Zhang Jinqiu in Xi'an pursues this line of expression. A pupil of Liang Sicheng, the father of modern historical and archaeological research into the origins of traditional Chinese architecture, her Shaanxi Museum of 1991 and immense central plaza and shopping centre project in the centre of Xi'an of 1996 are both overtly traditional despite the use of modern construction materials and the accommodation of modern programmes. The work of Wu Liangyong, a collaborator and professional colleague of Liang Sicheng, exhibits a similar orientation, though usually in a less effusive manner. His Ju'er Hutong housing project of 1983, for instance, in central Beijing, incorporates traditionally styled gable roofs, as well as window arrangements and other gateway motifs. The project's inclusion of courtyards, receding from the entry lane, although now serving several families, also attempts to recreate at least the circumstantial allure of the traditional *siheyuan*. Still more prominent is the huge Western Railroad Station in Beijing by Zhu Jialu (1996). Full of references to aspects of traditional Chinese building, like the immense opening at the centre of the station complex and the gate – *pailou* – motifs that span the base of the horizontal wall-like complex, the

39
A courtyard in
the Ju'er Hutong,
1983, by Wu
Liangyong. 1996.

station is crowned by a collection of gable-roofed pavilions intended to house a railroad museum. Outside China, an interest in traditional forms and motifs also persists, although to a lesser degree. Many public housing projects in Singapore, for instance, are crowned by traditional-appearing gable roofs, as are residential and commercial projects in Taipei. Chiang Kai-shek's mausoleum and surrounding complex of buildings (1977) almost appear to replicate imperial palaces of old in the mainland for symbolic reasons, in contrast to Mao Zedong's more modern, though traditionally inclined, final resting place

40
The Beijing West
railway station,
1996, by Zhu Jialu.
1997.

in Beijing's Tiananmen Square of much the same date. Mao's artistic idea of combining familiarity by way of reference to the past, yet presenting a sufficiently forward-looking interpretative challenge to knowledgeable members of society, is underlined by this example and seems to lurk, subconsciously or not, behind the work of many Chinese traditionalist architects.

Among recent attempts to assert a regional identity in otherwise modern developments in East Asia, two general problems have emerged. Sometimes there has been what might be called a misreading of the local tradition, especially from colonial periods. Extensive sections of both Dalian in northern China and Taipei in Taiwan, for instance, are defined by a Western-style, neo-Classical arrangement of streets and urban blocks. Mostly, this is a legacy from the Japanese occupation and a preference on the part of the Japanese at the time for the style, largely under the Meiji Restoration and Taishō eras. In Dalian, there was also a period of Russian occupation and, with it, strong Western urban-architectural influences, again in a northern European expressive mode. Today these distinctive urban landscapes are being transformed by modern skyscrapers and other individualistic architectural expressions which have little to do with either the style or the tradition of the original plan. In fact, in Dalian the present model seems to be more Houston than Paris or Vienna. Sometimes such cultural misreadings can produce provocative and enduring results. Unfortunately, however, many of the distinctive assets of the original plans can also be overwhelmed. In Dalian, for example, the well-shaped prominent plazas, squares and *rondpoints* of the neo-Classical plan are now in danger of being expressively undermined by indiscriminant high-rise developments.

The second problem arises when indigenous modern expression imitates prior architectural tradition too literally or inappropriately. The excessive pagoda-roof phenomenon in places like Beijing is understandable, perhaps, but frequently misplaced. Most problematic is the lack of any deeply felt cultural connection between the sign of past tradition and the reality of contemporary modern practice. In effect, the stereotype that emerges actively debases the host culture, symbolically speaking, and does nothing to temper or localize many otherwise banal and mundane modern buildings. Even accepting a certain inevitable separation between the 'form' and 'figure' of a building, to use rhetorical terminology for a moment, the sheer gap in comprehensibility between these two aspects is often too great to be taken seriously, or to avoid relegation to the realm of kitsch. Moreover, an apparent absence of deep understanding in the education and practice of many design professionals, particularly in China, either of architectural modernism or of traditional architecture, hampers progress towards a less problematic stance.[66]

Although superficially it may appear otherwise, the similarity in modern building design between one place and another need not mean that one culture is being converted to another. Certainly modern architectural expression began in the West. However, its ready adoption elsewhere may simply mean that it can be deployed both profitably and appropriately. It represents, in effect, an expansion of local cultural identity in a manner that suits the social, economic and material transformations taking place. Just as modern historians have been quick to point out the borrowing of indigenous non-Western traditions in the evaluation of the modern architecture of the West, so a converse flow of influences also appears to hold true. In other words, modern architectural expression is employed to enhance the evolution of local building practices and to continue local traditions. This is already obvious with regard to the accommodation of modern building programmes by traditional architectural forms of expression and construction. To put the argument another way, if it is assumed, as seems likely, that now is a period when the differences between civilizations and cultures are being actively sharpened, and not blurred, then acceptance of modern architecture, even with all its universal pretensions, must be seen as an acceptance of another way of building, without regarding it as rife with foreign cultural connotations. Wide acceptance of the English language as a means of communication among many different cultures for the conduct of international affairs is not a matter of ideology but of convenience and practicality. In fact, the proportion of people natively speaking English has apparently declined while expanding among those who converse at home in another tongue.[67]

As a practical matter there seems to be no reason to expect that non-Western nations should start afresh in devising a different expressive language for the architectural products of their modernization. Even if they did, there is no guarantee that the result would be materially different from what we see in many contemporary cities today. After all, modernization brings with it certain physical and technological imperatives, as described in chapters Two and Three. Even in a world of greater civilizational and cultural self-consciousness, and yet higher degrees of economic interaction and global communication, modern architecture – a little like the English language – becomes the mode of building, or lingua franca, necessary to accommodate the spatial exigencies of these communications and interactions in a direct, familiar and practical manner. It is not a case of Westernization but a matter of there being a comparatively limited number of ways of accomplishing something efficiently, with the result that things begin to look much the same. In contrast, in other areas of building, and when accommodating various functional programmes like housing and adaptive reuse of existing structures, indigenous cultures and architectural traditions tend to become more evident. Indeed, even in technologically advanced and modern nations like the United States, the shape and appearance of housing, judging from the ubiquitous neo-colonial single-family house, reflects traditional forms of building and a nostalgia for the past, far more than it does the contemporaneity of everyday life. Many other societies in the world seem to be similarly inclined in the strong local architectural reflection of religious and state authority. Even with the arbitrariness of architectural devices as symbols, form does seem to follow broad cultural function in a surprisingly consistent manner. Given all of this, however, one example where architectural modernism has been deployed effectively as a lingua franca, as well as a statement of national identity, is the Bank of China building by I. M. Pei in Hong Kong (1990). Arguably one of the most elegant modern skyscrapers of its time, the building has already become something of a symbol for China's financial enterprises and for its modern progress. The deliberate challenging of the *feng shui* tradition by Pei and, probably, by his clients, through the structural crossbracing expressively releases the architecture into the realm of technological advancement and prowess, while locating it in a particular cultural milieu. Though not without controversy because of its size and appearance, the building becomes at once recognizably modern, progressive and Chinese.[68]

In addition to Pei's masterpiece, there is a strong emerging interest in China and other parts of Asia in striking an appropriate balance between the local and universal expressive possibilities of modern architecture, sometimes referred to as a 'third way', as mergers, or still further as hybridization.[69] Returning to the 'big roofs' of China, two works in Shanghai that reinterpret this tradition in a thoroughly contemporary high-tech language are the Grand Theatre by Jean-Marie Charpentier in collaboration with the East China Architectural Design Institute (1998), and the Ministry of Construction's Shanghai Museum of Planning, built at much the same time. Both occupying prominent sites within People's Park, on either side of the municipal building in the centre of the city, each incorporates a transparent skeletal frame of steel and glass rising from a base, or podium in the case of the Grand Theatre like the *xumizuo* of old, capped by large roof elements. In the Grand Theatre the inverted, curved roof shape, adding to its scale, and the overall proportions and symmetries of the free-standing building, clearly invite a double reading – one in the manner of a traditional theatre pavilion and the other in the manner of a contemporary house of culture now found in other parts of the world. From the more traditional direction, the recent work of C. Y. Lee in Taipei and Taiwan, like the multistorey Hung Koo building, provocatively attempts to expand well-established Chinese cultural motifs to encompass modern programmes fully. Instead of accepting architectural modernism as the lingua franca for modern building, he sets out to reshape the local pre-modern

146

architectural tradition, through the use of a bold tapered silhouette in the manner of earlier mass-wall construction, capped and interspersed with over-sized detailing recalling the traditional scheme of roof bracketing and decoration around openings.

Also operating between local tradition and modernity in a hybrid manner, or even between traditions, is landscape architecture, a relative newcomer, at least as a profession in East Asia. Returning to Century Park in Shanghai, the British LUC Company's proposal merges strains of European and especially Anglo-American traditions of park-making with Chinese sensibilities towards the construction of landscapes. This is evident, on the European side of the ledger, with the creation of varied areas of landscape interest, reminiscent in scale and free-flowing integration of much earlier work by Joseph Paxton and Frederick Law Olmsted. In these regards, the immense upward-sloping lawn, the lakefront area, the sinuous treatment of pathways and treed areas, as well as the use of terraces, immediately come to mind. On the Chinese side there is the use of rock outcroppings, intricate interweaving of islands and water bodies, as well as the choice of numerous indigenous landscape materials and plant species. The overall effect, however, is less obviously separated than this brief description might convey, resulting in a comfortable merger between occidental and oriental garden arts. At 140.3 hectares in area, Century Park

43
Eastern and Western land-scape influences at Century Park, Shanghai, by the LUC Company. 2004.

is large and lined, especially on the southern side, by high-rise residential buildings, in the manner of New York's Central Park. Other recent major park installations in East Asian cities, like Kowloon Park in Hong Kong, also appear as mergers between Eastern and Western traditions, whereas those that grace Tokyo's and Beijing's urban landscapes, dating from earlier imperial eras, clearly do not.

Operating less vividly but no less consciously within the ambit of a spatial tradition, Fumihiko Maki in his Hillside Terrace project in Tokyo, spanning in phases 1973 to 1992, shies away from the issue of overall appearance in favour of a subtle and refined excursus on the formal arrangement of intermediate spaces, layering and relationships between inside and outside. Although rendered in a prototypically modern manner, involving exquisitely detailed elements of concrete, metal and glass, the ancient Japanese notion of *oku*, about which Maki also wrote, is clearly apparent.[70] Like the concept of *ma*, also present at Hillside Terrace, *oku* is a slippery concept, at least from a Western perspective. Conveying different ideas of relationship, depending on context and deployment, *oku* can refer to a sequential unfolding of built and natural elements, as one might find in an old temple complex set in the wilderness, or the successive layering and experiential unlayering of built and natural features common, for instance, as one moves up and down the hillsides of

44
Unabashed
modernity at
the Century
Park Metro and
Pudong adminis-
trative building.
2002.

45
Hillside terrace in
Tokyo, 1973–92,
by Fumihiko Maki.
1999.

Tokyo's inner-city neighbourhoods, with moments of occlusion and moments of
revelation. Not orchestrated in anywhere near the same singular or axial
manner as the perspectively organized ceremonial routes through ancient
Chinese tomb complexes, for instance, or in the prescribed unfolding of spaces
also common in the West, *oku* is far more circumstantial and operates without
the necessary presence of some overarching perceptual schema. At Hillside
Terrace, this concept can frequently be seen to come into play, when one moves

from the main street, through the centre of the linear arrangement of buildings, into courtyards and back alleys, as well as through the localized inflection of walls and occasional longer views encountered along the way. It is also apparent in the parallel movement of some entry sequences, in relationship to the street and buildings, as well as in the constant peeling back, so to speak, of delicately constructed and implied layers of both building material and space that one also encounters. The Danish Embassy complex, part of the overall ensemble, with its main structure set back from the street, approached through a gateway past an intermediate layer of lower buildings and courtyard gardens, appears to recall the preferred arrangement of much earlier *daimyō* estates. With nothing at all overbearing or conspicuously obvious in this interplay between traditional ideas about constructed space and contemporary architecture, the experience is nothing but delightful. Maki has clearly placed in evidence quite another way of being modern and local at the same time and one that relies on indigenous spatial, as distinct from formal and figural, architectural practices. Moreover, it is an approach that seems well suited to the contemporary period, with none of the obvious historically based disadvantages of mimicry and reinterpretation that lurks behind other forms of regionalism.

Also at work in Tokyo, as well as in other cities in Japan, is the flourishing of a kind of micro-urbanism, practised primarily by younger architects without the same access to larger commissions as firms and construction industry conglomerates in the thrall of the *zaibatsu*. Highly contingent on site-specific circumstances, largely with the barely buildable interstices prescribed by existing building and public rights-of-way, as well as on otherwise marginal sites, this kind of architectural production usually takes on the full range of difficult, expedient and overlooked conditions of habitation to be resolved, often producing stunningly innovative results. Specific architectural operations include unusual juxtapositions of programme, elaborate development of vertical sections through allowable building envelopes on tiny site footprints, and an intense interest in building materials and finishes, often involving unusual choices and juxtapositions. Examples include work by Jun Aoki, Ryue Nishizawa, Takaharu Tezuka and Yoshiharu Tsukamoto and Momoyo Kaijima, both of Atelier Bow-wow. Although not an organized architectural movement – in fact there is a wide variety of practices at work independently – a polite polemical quality has emerged, reinforced by the publication of small books documenting projects and drawing attention to inventive architectural propositions. Atelier Bow-wow's *Made in Tokyo* and *Pet Architecture*, for instance, are catalogues of ad-hoc urban conditions and responses for Tokyo, both rigorously serious and deliriously playful.[71] Overall, through a kind of hybridization that includes grafting on to parts of the urban landscape and insertion of small discrete elements, although with strong visual and programmatic reverberations beyond small and marginal sites, a palpable rearrangement of surrounding urbanization is deftly effected. On par, it is a rearrangement that enlivens, embellishes and makes more locally idiosyncratic what was there before, to the benefit of local inhabitants. Although more contingent and of the moment than Maki's timeless approach, again it is an interplay between local milieu and architectural possibilities, which is clearly part of a culture but eschews obvious formal and figural architectural references. Small design boutiques are also emerging in other East Asian cities, like Shanghai, with similar agendas and a relative absence of large-scale public or corporate backing. It is almost as if parallel universes of design are beginning to take hold with even less interplay, at least for now, than was and continues to be experienced across different scales and orientations of practice in the West.

Less Appreciable Middle Ground

Apart from particularities and peculiarities, one consistent feature of a closer encounter with modern urbanization in East Asian cities is the lack, or less appreciable existence, of a 'middle ground', certainly in the manner that might be expected in developed cities of the West. Institutionally, as discussed at some length, there is practically no local autonomy and not much by way of well-organized, bottom-up practices to counteract, respond to or give specific shape to, top-down master-planning practices. The undeniable fact that some semblance of earlier pre-modern patterns of urbanization has survived appears to have more to do with coping behaviour surrounding intense development, with little time, space and institutional wherewithal to respond adequately, other than by way of upward extrapolation, than it does to a self-conscious, well-defended traditional way of doing things. Most of the modern urbanization that has occurred in places like Singapore, Seoul, Taipei and Hong Kong has taken place as centrally induced new settlement development, well outside the ambit of tradition and according to expedient, readily available top-down blueprints. Certainly, in China, intermediate layers of municipal participation have been well and truly in train with higher authority, with the aim of constant replication of narrowly prescribed methods of community building. This is beginning to change, under freer market circumstances, although as yet there is little active tampering, outside the market, with more centrally administered procedures. As noted earlier, nowhere in East Asia do pro-active local interest groups, if they exist at all, have the same impact or access to participatory forms for placing pressure on municipal authorities in matters of urban design as in the United States or in Europe.

Expressively, the urban-architectural landscape of East Asian cities is predominantly modern and, outside of perhaps Tokyo, Hong Kong and Singapore, often ill-considered, banal and even garish, although with an increasing number of innovative and internationally prominent projects, usually by foreign architects. One aspect of sustained building booms, in footloose markets for architectural services, is a convergence, sooner or later, of international talent. There are, however, other reasons for the predominance of modernity and, on overall balance, little fertile cultural ground for the continuation of tradition in the architectural middle ground. First, there have been substantial ideological, as well as popular commitments, made to at least the nominal idea of urban and architectural modernism, as an antidote or progressive alternative to the squalor and dilapidation of former urban circumstances. This is clear in the outward expansions of Seoul, Singapore, Hong Kong and many Chinese cities. To be sure the idea of modernism is often vague and untutored, even among many in professional circles, where understanding has been circumstantially acquired rather than thoroughly learned. Nevertheless, a broad sense of contemporaneity and looking forward, in tune with similar individual and social aspirations, continues to be a powerful orientation, latching on to what appears to be modern in building along the way. Second, unlike the United States, where there has been an often contentious debate for some time over traditional or modern appearances in buildings and urban areas, with little expressive ground in between, nostalgia and respect for an architectural past do not run so deep in East Asia. Indeed, in China, where pride in the past has constantly impinged on architectural expression, recently there has been a backing away from resurrection and interpretation of tradition in favour of cutting-edge, contemporary architecture, in many public projects. Perhaps more profoundly, unlike many cities in Europe, where there is a constant display or palette of urban architecture on offer from other eras, far less well-conserved and reused residue remains in most East Asian cities, with the effect that differences between one period and another, or the continuities among them, cannot be directly appreciated. One upshot might be a real narrowing of preferences, another an undervaluation of urban-architectural authenticity as a meaningful and potentially useful category for debating, defining and expressively advancing cityscapes beyond the shrewdness of the marketplace. Third, the magnitude, speed, density and scale of much contemporary urban development in East Asia, a topic that will be taken up further in the next chapter, far outstripped traditional practices and could only be accommodated by resorting to modern building construction and mass production, often without much room for non-superficial further architectural embellishment.

Experientially, occupation and moving around East Asian cities also occurs with little by way of middle-ground reference in a direct and tangible sense. The contrast between the private realm of the domicile and the bustling public character of the city outside is often sudden and sharp, especially when compared to the gentler gradient, from private to semi-private and then through semi-public to public space, frequently experienced in the United States, with its strong suburban character. Even in analogous circumstances within East Asia, the compression experienced between the public and private realms is usually far from gradual, involves fewer spatial dimensions and, therefore, is distinctly more evident. When compared to European and other inner-city circumstances, categorical differences in the public–private gradient might be much the same, although the way in which they are spatially rendered typically provides far less of a pause or appreciable breathing room. In these regards and especially among neighbourhoods and sub-districts in the more traditional realms of East Asian cities, the sheer juxtaposition of the two worlds of lane life, with its village-like sentiments, and the neon-lit metropolitan environment beyond – for some one of the delights of East Asian cities – has an immediacy experienced far more rarely elsewhere.

In many respects, these compressions of spatial experience are due to the overall high density of East Asian cities, among the very highest in the world, but are often amplified by differences in relative scale and functional distribution. For example, residential space standards are low, whereas the overall external edifice of the city is usually quite the opposite – large, tall, compact and seemingly endless. Daily living, particularly in the case of Hong Kong, is often not highly self-contained, occupying the contrasting parts of both realms, with little opportunity in between. To some extent these observations are exaggerated and may change with higher standards of living. Certainly the charm of the *roji, hutong* and *lilong*, together with the streets beyond, seems to confirm the presence of an intermediate zone. However, it is either an extension of commerce or an extension of the domicile, appearing either as one place or the other, and leaving little ambiguity in between.

Finally, apart from the apparent bifurcation of the realms of daily experience, by way of spatial compression and lack of ambiguity, the indigenous intermediate spatial structure of East Asian cities is not particularly variegated nor organized in an immediately discernible hierarchical manner, with few middle-ground spatial devices to give emphasis, prominence, direction and other visual clues, as one might often find in the West. Indeed, the underlying spatial model appears to be both simpler and more organic. Often, it incorporates age-old principles of self-similarity that unify relationships between parts and wholes, rather than setting them apart and mediating them, compositionally, through a repertoire of other spatial devices like prominent axes, plazas, squares, avenues, esplanades, typically belonging to city-wide concepts of a Western hierarchical order. There are, of course, again notable exceptions. It is difficult to say that Beijing does not have a distinctive hierarchical spatial order, or that those in power do not continue to work on that order, as evidenced by the recent selection of the main site for the Olympic Games in 2008, on an axis to the north of the Forbidden City. Nevertheless, it is probably fair to say that the sheer presence and number of mediating spatial devices, which give many Western cities a highly discernible middle ground, is both less and fewer in East Asian cities, especially beyond the immediate realm of historical and modern sites of state power. During the 1950s and early '60s, for instance, when China had the opportunity to pursue its prolific urban district making and work-unit communities, along the lines of perimeter-block configurations with ample spatial modulation, variety and hierarchy, it swerved away, instead, into a dense, repetitive pattern of self-similar buildings and spaces in between.

In all this discussion of the absence of a middle ground, however, one also has to ask: so what? Or, to turn the question around, do East Asian cities suffer as a consequence of this absence? Institutionally, the answer may well be yes, although even with well-organized, highly articulated and active bottom-up and independent participatory processes to pressure governments into more and different municipal actions, it is not clear that the broad spatial results would suddenly change course. There is something to be said, after all, for a vacuum that can be occupied by many different ad-hoc arrangements. Expressively, the response might be mixed. There is also something to be said in favour of expressive cultural and, therefore, architectural continuity from one epoch to another by way of middle-ground positions, even if it is far from being a universal, time-independent category and, if anything, comes about during moments of doubt about the persistent expressive characteristics of one period into the next, as well as when cultural dynamics in one direction are strong enough to bridge over from one period to another. Certainly, many of the examples of modern architecture described earlier reflect one or other, or both, of these inclinations, at least to some degree. Nevertheless, after moments of substantial cultural rupture with the past, as occurred in East Asia, the justification of expressive transition and, therefore, a middle-ground position, might also be expected to lose a deeply felt relevance. Urbanistically, in terms of the shape, appearance, layout and experience of cities, the answer is probably no, particularly if East Asian cities have positive experiential traits, substituting and even defying Western categorizations through proclivities like juxtaposition and contraposition rather than by gradation and finely ordered harmony, or by constructing their urban environments through ideas of 'one in the many' rather than 'one and the many', or of resorting to properties of organism rather than those of stricter hierarchy. It is, after all, all in the eyes of the beholders and where they come from.

five

Urban Experience and Shaping the Space of a Time

It almost goes without saying that events mark the passage of time and especially those collective events involving human action and reflection define both widespread and individual experiences of time. Of course, the impact of events can vary from place to place, as will their experience. Nevertheless, the shared meanings that are conveyed shape views of the world, including perceptions and understandings of cities and the urban landscapes in which people live. With these perceptions and understandings, in turn, can come changes in preferences and orientations toward cities and, therefore, reasons to make them differently. Likewise, people's experience is often marked by the urban landscapes in which they live and, in turn, they make and remake those landscapes based on this spatial reaction, as well as the events that mark the passage of time. Then too, space and time interact directly in a simple descriptive manner, as well as through experience and in the creation of experience. For instance, it can be readily said that such and such a building was constructed in 1859 and observed, in much the same breath, that 1859 produced several hundred similar buildings. Less simply, a time can also become denotatively synonymous with experience and its surrounding urban circumstances. For example, the 'sixties' often implies liberal social change and urban reform in the United States, just as the 'fifties' points to the reverse. Similarly, an experience, including its spatial construction, can be so hegemonic as to become synonymous with a particular time. The word 'Victorian' can be used as a blanket term in contemporary circumstances to refer to certain values, attitudes towards the world, modes of living and styles of building. Furthermore, within an expressive manifold of space and time, one dimension can be manipulated with respect to the other to impart a particular meaning to either space or time. Projecting connotatively backwards in time usually involves deployment of recognizable elements of traditional architecture, whereas architectural modernism conveys a sense of time in the 'present-future', usually regardless of when it is actually built.

Sheer rates of change in urban space, with respect to time, can direct and even inhibit such wilful expressive manipulation, resulting in an amalgamation of what is most expedient. For example, strong pressures to build upwards in place, with little leeway to do otherwise, result in exactly that, upward construction in place. Furthermore, rapid and profound changes in ways of making constructed environments can render prior urban landscapes redundant. For instance, many early suburban malls in the United States are now well and truly outmoded by contemporary scale requirements and inclusion of entertainment amenities. Therefore, when viewing urbanization in one region of the world, such as East Asia, with respect to others, or when comparing places in the same region, it is useful to do so explicitly in terms of time, experience, space and their interactions. Again, some events and spatial conceptions have widespread reverberations, whereas others are more locally specific. The thirteenth-century Japanese Zen Buddhist sage Dōgen Kigen once said, in effect, that every being in the world is a separable time in one continuum and that man disposes himself and looks upon this disposition as the world, i.e., both being and man are time.[1] Useful distinctions and similarities, however, can be observed further removed from such singular personal experience. Indeed, the intent here is to pursue matters of time, urban space and their interaction in sufficient generality before such depictions become overwhelmed with too many particulars, as would almost surely happen upon ever closer scrutiny and consideration, as the sage predicted, and to probe further into the question as to whether there is a specific shape to the making of urban space in East Asian cities.

Eventful Experience of Time

From a Western perspective at least two broadly felt episodes have shaped the flux of urban space and time and its contemporary progress, with possibly a third in the offing. The first occurred roughly between the late 1960s and the early '70s. During this time, as noted in chapter Three, there was considerable social upheaval around issues of basic rights, justice and access to power, of which the events of May 1968 and subsequent anti-war demonstrations are probably most emblematic. There was also widespread social concern for issues regarding the continued sustainability of resources and limits to growth and modern expansion, perhaps best exemplified by Earth Day, the Environmental Movement and the Club of Rome. In addition, there was a wrenching condition in the marketplace, precipitated, among other events, by the Oil Embargo of 1973 and the onset of economic stagflation. At the risk of some oversimplification, arising from this concatenation of experience came widespread concerns for diversity, concomitant increases in social pluralism, environmentalism, some decline in business confidence, a certain loss of faith in government, and serious questioning of the hegemony of positivist interpretations of people and their worlds, at least in intellectual circles, giving way to more self-referential, hermeneutic attitudes and understandings. Of course, several aspects of this broad socio-cultural and political shift began developing much earlier in some places. A post-structuralist intellectual stance was already well entrenched, for instance, in continental European circles, as were analytical concerns for the environment, population and social equity in the Anglo-American academic world.[2] Moreover, the coming of age of the leading edge of the baby-boom, many of whom had enjoyed growing up in relative tranquillity and rising prosperity, probably had much to do with the turn of events, judging from the number of students on the front lines of confrontation and advocacy of alternative causes. Gender and issues of equality had also been playing a significant role for some time. Nevertheless, the scope and magnitude of convergence of all these events and experiences had certainly begun to reshape Western outlooks by the late 1960s and early '70s.

In the realm of urban affairs, again at the risk of a certain amount of caricature, what this episode brought down, or substantially weakened, was an era of big plans and governmental programmes, or at least their unquestioned ambition and strongly held beliefs in the possibility of social engineering and management. In a sense, for many, the idea of the 'modern city' came to an end, coinciding also with substantial real economic shifts in the direction of what some like to call 'post-Fordism', or an appreciable rise in tertiary sectors of production and reallocation of urban goods, services, buildings and infrastructure, usually along the decentralized and polynucleated lines described in chapter Two.[3] User and citizen participation in municipal and other related affairs increased significantly and civil society proliferated and extended its active reach, although there is some question about how widespread its communitarian interests were in many quarters, when one considers the concomitant rise of special interest groups, more highly localized autonomy and self-protection. For instance, tax caps and sentiments of 'not in my backyard', together with a general layering on of scrutiny of any public or private plans by local citizenry, became a new order of urban deliberation in the United States, if not elsewhere in the developed Western world.[4] Rapidly, the 'post-modern' city began to appear beyond its emerging economic profile. By the middle to late 1970s, in most urban-architectural academic circles, a post-modern turn was certainly evident in the reinstatement of a concern for history, alongside cultural theory, as well as replacement of comprehensive physical plans by more discrete projects. More generally, in professional, as well as lay circles, concerns for local context and the rise of contextualism as an appropriate rubric under which to shape urban environments also emerged, further particularizing the scope of urban activities. Often, larger-order public infrastructure projects, like freeway road extensions and the siting of urban services, ran foul of active local groups and interests. Unfortunately, while there is much to be said positively for local autonomy, continuity with the past, a modesty of building ambition, concern for sustainability, celebration of diversity, and so on, deeply structural problems of class, poverty, race and ethnicity persisted and, in some quarters, became amplified by an increased ability to set oneself off from a wider community in the protection of one's own interests.[5]

The second episode occurred around the end of the 1980s and into the early '90s. The demise of the Soviet Union and the symbolic collapse of the Berlin Wall in 1989 ended competition and confrontation between the two most distinctive modernizing regimes of the twentieth century, decidedly in favour of the West. A concomitant unravelling of the Bretton Woods and other accords, which had dictated the shape and flow of the world's economy for so long, gave way to a further opening up of free trade, commerce and resource availability.[6] The number and scope of multinational and transnational firms blossomed, and new instruments for financial and economic transaction were invented to suit and exploit business opportunities in the more liberal era, including those now more readily available for individuals. Advances in computers and information technology, symbolized by public access to the Internet and the World Wide Web around 1993, also made data-processing tasks possible that were previously only imaginable, and significantly increased the scope and density of communication and transaction, now in a comprehensible and ubiquitous virtual space. The rapid rise and proliferation of this technology into almost all walks of life brought with it its own economic sector and massive speculation on its future potential. Further empowerment of individual experience and action was made possible, at least in principle if not entirely in practice. Then, too, this was also a moment of privatization of public functions and a significant loosening of labour relations, as well as the emergence of many more non-governmental organizations, each pursuing wider community-based and international quasi-public functions. The period of the late 1980s and early '90s represents a palpable nexus of all these activities and reorganizations, rather than their onset of development. Once more, however, at least the highly developed Western world began to operate and conceive of itself differently, tending, if anything, to reinforce experiences and realizations of the prior era.

Amid all these geographic and modal expansions of transactional possibilities, as well as reductions of spatial frictions, the idea of the 'global city' emerged as a node in a far-flung network of communication and productive capacity that extended well beyond national borders. Products, for instance, were created in one place, parts manufactured and assembled in others, and orders and deliveries made almost anywhere. As command and control centres in this network, global cities, such as New York and London, took on added importance. Paradoxically perhaps, according to some observers, with increased possibilities, as well as practicalities for decentralized transactions, spatial agglomeration also occurred, as observed in chapter Two, around important nodes in networks and especially in global cities, caused by the sheer need for the compression of increasingly more numerous command and control functions, together with the face-to-face creative contact needed to keep abreast of these functions and to continue to invent different and better instruments and practices.[7] Wall Street, for example, always towards the centre of things in financial markets, became a veritable epicentre, at least for a time, spurred on by a burgeoning array of ancillary services and professional expertise. Similar agglomerations also occurred around areas fertile for high-tech industries, although there the role of sustained government interests and investment should not be overlooked. Silicon Valley, alongside other places, like Route 128 in Boston, leapt into the lexicon and experience of Americans and much of the well-developed world. Indeed, there has been a certain amount of triumphalism associated with the new Western, and particularly American, free-market democratic order, with the Soviet bloc effectively out of the way, and Japan entering into a deep and prolonged economic recession beginning in the early 1990s. With declined natural population growth rates, still rising affluence, at least for some, plenty of building on hand for an even more footloose society, with a wide range of lifestyle and environmental preferences, quite apart from more strongly entrenched attitudes toward conservation in their own locales, adaptive reuse of older urban structures, historic preservation, repair and reoccupation of abandoned or under-utilized sites, and even almost entire former settlements, occurred widely. Municipal attention about physical improvement frequently turned from matters of sheer supply to issues of increased local amenity, variety, creation of a particular identity, and rising competition for residents. Unfortunately, outstanding issues of equity and social justice remained, despite demonstrable rises in productivity, civic attention to local assets, less encumbered lifestyles, and access to communication and political participation.

Another episode, implying a further shift in outlook, may be in the making, depending on how one interprets recent events. The emergence of the 'Seattle people' and other populist anti-global blocs; increased concern for global warming, underdevelopment and the alleged culpability of corporate interests; 'September 11th' and the rising spectra of global terrorism; 'Empire'; financial scandals; mooted clashes of civilizations; recent strides towards the unification of Europe, and so on, if taken together, have the hallmarks of yet another broad socio-cultural and political reaction to what is in place.[8] Only time and further experience will tell. In essence, what has transpired in the West over the past 50 or so years, is a profound reshaping of the manner of collective experience of the strict timeline. Indeed, if one is willing to entertain this episodic presentation, there has been a shortening of the cycle of change. The first occurred after some twenty years, the second after another fifteen years and the third, if it comes about fully, in the space of the last ten years. It is not the case that each broad manner of collective experience has enjoyed plain sailing, or affected people equally, for it has not. There have been economic ups and downs and political about-faces, at more local and even national levels. Moreover, returning in the direction set out by the Sage Dogen, depending on who you are, what you are doing, how you are living, etc., shifts in experience may be more or less abrupt. Nor is it the case that influences in one period suddenly come to an end in the next. Going back to a point made in chapter Three, modernization and its experience is a cumulative process. However, for most there has been an opening-up of possible experience and participation, together with opportunities for local as well as global identity construction. Give people more choice and they choose more widely, or so it would seem. With regard to urbanization, the contemporary outlook has shifted from the 'modern city' to attributes of the 'post-modern city' and now to deliberations about the 'global city', even if the activity of most cities retains shapes, appearances, uses, regulations, etc., from prior periods.

In contrast, the course of events for those in East Asia over the same 50-year timeline, or even less, took a different turn. It is not that they were somehow unplugged from the rest of the world, even if the 'Bamboo Curtain' and protectionism were actively present in some quarters. At least at the beginning, however, East Asia was less significant in its outside influence, certainly by today's standards. As described in chapters Two and Three, all countries, in one way or another, were climbing out of similar crises of relative impoverishment, social and political disarray, as well as economic underdevelopment or extensive destruction. On the urban front, massive waves of either cross-border or internal immigration placed almost overwhelming pressure on inadequate services, infrastructure and housing. For the new political regimes in place throughout almost the entire region, the desire to modernize and to do so rapidly was imperative, not only to catch up and for some, like Japan, to regain their prominent position in the world, but to ensure the livelihood and longevity of their nascent political structures and emerging senses of nationalism. There were some exceptions, like the Crown Colony of Hong Kong, although even there the overwhelming shift in population and pent-up demand for a revised, independent entrepreneurial outlook began to exert a presence.

Without doubt, throughout the region, modernization, roughly along Western lines or, in the case of China early on, in synchrony with the Soviet Union, was a conscious choice. It proffered the one real hope of broad and basic societal benefits like the eradication of poverty, squalor and poor health. At the time it probably also seemed culturally malleable and politically neutral, given its procedural aspects and apparent high reliance on a technocratic outlook of ends and means. Of course, similar comments about recovery from destruction and political regime change could be made about European countries, like Germany and Italy during the post-World War II era. However, they were already fundamentally part of the West, with well if not deeply imbedded modern institutional structures and technical know-how. In post-war and post-colonial East Asia this was simply not the case, with the exception of Japan, and even there, as noted in chapter Three, the earlier movement towards thoroughgoing modernization had long come to an end, or had been substantially truncated towards militaristic objectives. On all fronts, modernization required importation and emulation of Western wherewithal to a considerable degree.

Contemporary modernization's first blush in East Asia occurred under strong centralized or authoritarian governments. At the risk of overgeneralization, it is as if the prospect of forming new societies required such a radical shift in experience as to require strong and relatively unquestioned leadership. In any event, there was little or no first-hand experience with alternatives. Modernization, especially at the high rates necessary to catch up with the more developed world, also required considerable degrees of social stability and cohesion; at least those in power saw it that way and promulgated ideas of people acting together in accord. As discussed earlier, the upshot for the maintenance of political power and forward modern progress – which became quickly intertwined – was development and propaganda around what amounted to broad 'social contracts', whereby those in power provided almost sole guidance and investment in return for a sufficiency of loyalty and social compliance with their central modernizing policies. The strength of the contract and the sufficiency of expected compliance varied from outright authoritarianism and state dictatorship in China, around the so-called iron rice bowl, to conformity according to various models of collective consumption from dictators and one-party rulers in Korea, Taiwan and Singapore, to Ikeda's promissory of income doubling in one-party and oligarchic Japan. In some places, perhaps most notably Singapore and Taipei, a crisis or siege mentality took over to spur things on, at least for a time and not without encouragement from the top.[9]

Essentially, what the social bargain hinged upon was enough growth in overall production for the income and living circumstances of those in society to improve constantly, or at least be guaranteed at acceptable levels. Concern for social equity played a role in most places, as demonstrated by the statistics presented in chapter Two, either as a matter of professed social ideology, or for fear that to do otherwise would encourage internal factionalism and social unrest, resulting in potentially serious challenges to political power and the ruin of the project of modernization. In effect, what was set in motion was a rather narrowly defined productionist mode of modernization, with emphasis on what amounted to growthism in particular economic quarters and the more obvious improvements in material benefits across society as a whole. Other simultaneous social institutional developments, expansion and strengthening of civil society, and a general opening-up in the manners of collective experience and participation, which occurred in the West, have either not happened or begun to happen slowly and often only recently.

In many respects, this description and explanation of what transpired in East Asia, during the contemporary period of nation building, is an overstatement. The course of events and their shaping of the passage of time varied from one place to another, often considerably and, as in the West, each place had its own internal episodic structure. China, for instance, after a post-Civil War period of enthusiastic reconstruction and economic development, fell into the tragic and debilitating grip of the 'Great Leap Forward', then into the 'Cultural Revolution' and its aftermath, followed by another period of

46
Rapid modern-
ization in Beijing,
1997

mounting stability during which the 'Bamboo Curtain' came almost all the way down, with the historic opening up to the rest of the world in 1978. The subsequent euphoric period – often referred to locally as the time of 'Culture Fever' – was then suddenly dashed by the events surrounding the Tiananmen Square incident in 1989, followed by the present period of sustained economic growth and development, as well as recent changes in political leadership.[10] As noted earlier, episodes of socio-political action and reaction often occurred elsewhere in the region. There was considerable civil unrest in Tokyo, for example in 1968 and 1969, followed by the confidence-shattering bursting of what turned out to be an 'economic bubble' in 1991, effectively closing down a sustained period of economic growth. Martial law finally came to an end in Taiwan in 1987, ushering in a period of democracy that shows signs of continued liberalization. Hong Kong made a reformatory about-face in 1971, as described in chapter Two, and then entered into an anxious period of uncertainty around the handing back to China in 1997. So one could go on.

166

Nevertheless, while there was certainly extraordinary change going on in various parts of the region, it was not, as events show, entirely tumultuous. Social attitudes and political sensibilities certainly shifted. However, on the whole they did not depart substantially from the broad social contracts and collective understandings already in place. Indeed, if anything, these episodes redoubled the efforts of those in power to sustain their productionist orientation and concomitant outlook on social welfare. Certainly this is a construction that can be placed on the aftermath of the Tiananmen incident, with Chinese authorities coming to understand more sharply the imperatives of continued and increased economic progress for the purposes of political stability. Reform occured in Japan after 1969, but well within the party framework of the governing regime. Even Akamatsu's metaphor of the 'closely following flying geese' described in chapter Two, belies a more introspective regional model – with Japan in the lead – than might otherwise be suspected amid the apparent outward orientation of export platforms, coveting of direct foreign investment, etc. In fact, the focus and collective experience never fell far outside the region, and despite local variations and imperfections, provided a relatively uniform *modus operandi* to be followed for top-down production-oriented modernization. In short, the broad social bargain, orientation and outlook on the world, struck during the initial episode of change towards contemporary modernization, still stands in East Asia. Much evolved, no doubt, and arrived at through different courses of events from one place to another, it nevertheless continues to be defined by a manner of collective experience through time that was substantially different from what occurred in the West.

Underlying the collective experience of time in East Asia, returning to several points again raised in chapter Two, there seems to be a neo-Confucian socio-cultural matrix of values and attitudes at work that contrasts particularly with the liberal-democratic matrix operative in the West. Traits of consensus-seeking and collectivism in East Asia, around social issues both big and small, appear to be ingrained and can be contrasted with habitual proclivities towards majority rule and individualism in the West. Both sets of traits seem to serve societies well, although both also have their downsides. Consensus, for instance, can require undue compromise and collectivism can lead to rote conformism, whereas majority rule and individualism can lead to divisiveness, factionalism and mistrust. Age, experience, inter-personal loyalties and social standing in East Asian communities might also be contrasted with the presence of meritocracy in the West. Again there are advantages and disadvantages to either stance. Relations without merit can be socially destructive, as can experiences of extreme inter-personal competition and disrespect. At root, however, there appears to be a substantial difference between an organic conception of society, built around constant application of hierarchical, though self-similar and closely nested relationships in East Asia, and the no less hierarchical, although more distinctly articulated set of relations built around principled balancing of many powers, interests and functions to be found in the West. From this distinction flow differences in proclivities towards toleration of narrow social exceptions in East Asia and a clamouring for pluralism and diversity in the West. This might go some way to explaining the relative weaknesses and strengths of well-organized civil society, between East Asia and the West, where civil society – largely a Western concept – has less of a role in organic, internally directed social arrangements than it does among more overtly and sharply differentiated powers, interests and functions. Without making too much of a point of it, maintenance of order through well-defined interpersonal relationships and expectations, arising from an organic social conception, might be seen to require less by way of abstract laws and guidance. The point is not to engage in debate between the pros and cons of the two systems, because both seem to be able to get the job done, at least within tolerable limits, and, no doubt, both require improvement. Moreover, in truth, most people live in between these overdrawn contrasts. It does, however, suggest that it is not only the presence of authority but requirements to reach broad collective social understandings in manners that are well orchestrated, agreed on and understood among members of society, that come into play in East Asia. It also suggests 'inward and exclusive' versus 'outward and inclusive' proclivities toward experiencing the passage of time and manners of being in the world.

Not surprisingly, the distinctions used to characterize concepts of the city over the last 50 years or so in the West do not apply with quite the same explanatory force in East Asia. 'Post-modernity', as outlined here, does not widely resonate culturally in East Asia, beyond perhaps casual labelling of some forms of architecture or other visual arts, or some strains of introspective literary work. There has been no effective indigenous groundswell towards the kind of epistemological shift, concern for 'differences' and ideas of pluralism that occurred in the West. If anything, 'post-industrial' tertiary functions have merged with, or matter-of-factly replaced, older urban functions, without the hubbub that accompanied these transitions in intellectual circles in the West. Nor, in spite of much rhetoric, are East Asian cities truly global. Tokyo may be hard to disregard in this respect but it is hardly cosmopolitan, and the aspirations of places like Shanghai appear at least as much in line with the longer-running state programme of modernization as with globalization per se. At present, Singapore and Hong Kong are probably better candidates in the all-around sense of being global. Rather, the concept of the city in East Asia seems to be more about all categories in one. It is again a more organic and less sequentially differentiated perspective than in the West. Of course, with modernization have come more and better buildings, infrastructure, public open space and other accoutrements of contemporary cities, including the introduction of novel features and forms of urbanity not previously experienced in East Asia. In fact, the transfer of modern city-building technologies, practices, regulations and management techniques, as described especially in chapters Two and Three, has been something of a one-way street from West to East, with moments of adaption and indigenization along the way, particularly in Japan, dating well back into the pre-modern era. Returning to an earlier point, it is more useful to speak of internationally available modern building technologies rather than simply Western technologies. Nevertheless, during the formative stages of contemporary modernization in East Asia, the prevalent style of top-down urban planning, regulation and management mostly coincided with internationally available models of the time, with origins in the West, and around the concept of the 'modern city'. As described in chapter Three, this style of planning, albeit with some modification, has fundamentally persisted, whereas outside the region it has gone by the board. This is a small wonder, given its efficiency in helping to promote and manage large programmes of expansive modernization along productionist lines without the fundamental challenges posed by changes in the manners of collective experience, and therefore resistance, that occurred in the West.

To summarize, again with a risk of oversimplification, in the West over the past 50 years, events and hence changes in collective experience and overall orientation to the affairs of the world were shaped by at least two, perhaps three, episodes of profound reaction to the intertwining of modernization with a predominantly well-established democratic socio-political and cultural structure. As a consequence, earlier, simpler and largely technocratic attitudes for addressing social issues became elaborated, embroidered and enriched with deeper and more diverse cultural purposes and meanings. For the processes of city making, this resulted in an expanded capacity to accommodate social pluralism, demands for a variety of community settings, concerns for growth and sustainability, as well as historic and other forms of conservation, and adaptive reuse of existing structures. It also resulted in a much more highly articulated and accessible managerial system of checks and balances.

In contrast, in East Asia, the overall orientation was shaped by a single profound reaction, at the outset of the same period, to widespread devastation, underdevelopment, poverty and squalor, through the arrival of new political regimes, whose centralized and often authoritarian structures meshed with pre-modern and longstanding neo-Confucian traits and outlooks on life. Quickly availing themselves of available international technologies, largely of Western origin, those in power pressed forward, often in concert, with rapid, incremental forms of production-oriented modernization. As a consequence, economies grew and, given the paltry baselines, often at astonishing rates; material standards of living also improved, as did those of public health, education and other forms of welfare. This push towards progress, together with a cultural background tending toward collectivism, the value of relationships and an organic conception of society, framed a broad social compact that fell in line with the overall objectives of modernization and remained intact, in spite of sporadic and even substantial internal social reactions. City building followed suit. Indeed, the comprehensive character of international planning techniques, rife at the time, conformed well with the prevailing top-down sense of social organization and, without encountering too much resistance, has persisted. The result is a relatively unarticulated centralized system of urban construction and management still married to production-oriented objectives and far less open to participation and multiple courses of action than in the West. Exceptions lie in highly developed cities, like Tokyo and Singapore, but even there urban management and improvement, often of a very high quality, takes place from the top, on behalf of constituents and remains well within long-established planning practice. Like the characters living together in the old fable, it is as if the West took after the fox in knowing many things and being capable of pursuing many different objectives, and East Asia took after the hedgehog in knowing only one thing but pursuing it persistently.

Broad Urban Transformations

One way of viewing the spatial effects of the passage of time, collective experiences and resulting outlooks towards city building is to consider them as aspects of a process of urban territorialization involving the simultaneous presence of 'deterritorializing' and 'reterritorializing' phenomena.[11] Under this rubric, effective deterritorialization occurs at moments when enough pressure is brought to bear on the existing territorial order so as to eliminate existing distinctions, socio-political power relations, or ways of doing things, to the extent that aspects of the prior regime collapse on the way to becoming something else. Reterritorialization is the process that takes up in new and different ways, then, with the elimination of prior distinctions, relations, ways of doing things, etc., or, rather, with the forces behind them, resulting in a different territorial order, and so the process of urban territorialization continues to unfold. Historically, clear examples of deterritorializing influences can be found among the technological and managerial means governing production and consumption in an urbanizing territory, such as those described earlier in conjunction with East Asia, like shifts from agriculture to manufacturing and then on to service industries. Changes in power relations among segments of populations, through revolution or reform, again very present in East Asia, usually have profound effects on urbanizing territories. Furthermore, natural events, like the Kantō earthquake in Tokyo, or the massive migrations discussed earlier, are often powerful deterritorializing influences. Reterritorialization is not automatic, other than perhaps coping behaviour, nor necessarily rational in the sense of following predictably from what has gone before. Competing interests and cultural politics often get in the way and sometimes, in hindsight, can be out of step with an otherwise perceived need for reterritorialization, as in the case of China's slavish following of Soviet practices during the early days of the Communist regime. Nor does either influence act, as it were, across the board. Birds still sing, for instance, and gravity remains in effect. Nevertheless, the shifts that occur in transportation, availability of building technologies, means of production, power relations, and so on, are significant in ways that change patterns of urbanization and territorialization or, conversely, occur when simple extrapolation of prior urban territorialization fails to take full advantage of the new regime. For example, the dispersal and then reconcentration of urban functions, which began occurring in metropolitan areas of the United States during the 1970s, as described in chapter Two, was a response to limits in access to traditional central locations and the footloose characteristics of commercial, institutional and other enterprises, aided and abetted by improved metropolitan-wide automobile access.

With these phenomena in mind, physical aspects of urban territorialization can be observed, albeit in broad abstract terms, through three basic

and often simultaneous spatio-temporal movements and outcomes. They are: 1) expansion, or the spreading out of urbanization into a territory; 2) intensification, or the concentration and reconcentration of activities within an urban territory; and 3) deconcentration, or even evacuation, of certain urbanized areas. Over the past 50 years, in the Lower Changjiang Delta region of China, for instance, outward expansion of Shanghai is very noticeable, as is concentration of activities in earlier relatively vacant land, like the Lujaizui financial district in Pudong opposite the Bund, as well as reconcentration of activity towards the periphery, as described for expanding smaller cities like Suzhou. Deconcentration of overcrowded and dilapidated urban areas is also pronounced, especially among the region's major cities and towns. However, evacuation of territory is less evident, given the region's expanding population, although concentration of surplus agricultural labour and population in nearby larger townships, and away from smaller towns and villages, is noticeable. Furthermore, although all three different movements often act in combination, taken together they can usually be seen to produce a net effect through an identifiable urban spatial pattern, at least for a period of time. For example, as described in chapter Three, the post-war rebuilding of Tokyo resulted in substantial outward expansion of suburban development, reconcentration of commercial activity in more closely centred locations like Shinjuku and Shibuya, and yet a prevailing dominant focus on central Tokyo for most inhabitants' lifestyles.

However, once the distinctive underlying characteristics and relationships that define and promote a particular combination of the three basic spatio-temporal movements change or dissipate (i.e., urban deterritorialization takes place), then a different spatial pattern emerges under a different combination of urban expansion, reconcentration and deconcentration. For example, returning to Shanghai, the recent location of the expressway in the lower Changjiang Delta leading to Nanjing and to Hangzhou generated appreciably different conditions of relative transportation access that contributed strongly to the polarization and agglomeration of local urban settlement. Analytically, identification of this kind of urban spatial regime change can be observed through the relative displacement of measures of all three spatio-temporal operations taken together, over time and, hence, the net rearrangement of the urban territory that has taken place. Abrupt changes in successive relative displacements signal moments in which territorialization fails to follow prior behaviour and, therefore, moments when deterritorialization comes into effect, leading to further reterritorialization.

Pursuit of this conceptual framework, aided by the use of empirical data, reveals, perhaps not surprisingly, reasonably strong conformity with the broad societal changes and shifts in outlook towards city building discussed in the last section.[12] In the United States, for example, three periods of urban deterritorialization and subsequent reterritorialization are obvious. First, as noted in chapter Two, was the post-World War II suburban boom, occasioned among other things by prolific highway construction, municipal complicity and even advocacy, as well as federal and other governmental support, that effectively completed the modern version of the American city beginning as far back as 1920. Second, from the 1970s, there was a period of dispersal and multiple concentration of urban activities – sometimes referred to as 'bundled deconcentration' – including severe depopulation of some inner cities, resulting in a polynucleated form of urban territory, similar to the model described in chapter Two – the so-called post-modern city. Shifts in this direction coincided with the initial episode of broad socio-cultural reaction, as well as alterations in modes of production. Third is the current period, stemming from the 1990s, involving dual processes of ex-urban development and simultaneous reconcentration in many inner-city areas, due, among other factors, to an increased capacity for people to make changes in their urban environments, especially around various stages of their life-cycles, as well as by increasing levels of communication. The onset of this period appears to coincide with the second episode of social change described earlier. Similarly, although for ostensibly different local reasons, three periods can be seen to have emerged in the case of Italy – to pick a European example – but again coinciding in time around similar broadly felt episodes of shifting social consciousness.[13] The first was the period of post-World War II peripheral development, especially in larger cities, due mainly to superior employment opportunities and involving massive in-migration from outlying areas and from southern to northern Italy. The second followed on the heels of greater local and regional autonomy in the early 1970s, bringing shifts in government expenditure and institutional programmes largely favouring smaller cities at the expense of larger ones, together with completion of major national infrastructure programmes and networked economic development. A third period occurred in the early 1990s, coinciding with the advent of the Second Republic, substantial privatization, as well as other institutional reforms, and involved further decentralization of urban populations, coupled with expansion in the size of well-placed smaller cities. For China, after an initial episode of prolonged deterritorialization and urban reterritorialization, the observable course of urban territorialization

48
Development
around the
Shanghai–Nanjing
expressway. 1997.

has been steady, though expansive, at least with regard to the combined effect of the three spatio-temporal movements specified above. It began with the post-Civil War developments and heavy industrial programmes of the Maoist era, and included a substantial swing in initial policy through the early, relatively prosperous years on to the disastrous 'Great Leap Forward' and the 'Cultural Revolution', which resulted in some expansion, though massive overcrowding and substantial population growth in the countryside. Then followed a sustained period of generally accelerating new development, resulting in extensive urban expansion and considerable intensification, after the historic opening to the outside world and the transition from a centrally planned economy, through a socialist market economy into a fuller-fledged market economy. Although unique in the specifics of its history, China was not alone among East Asian nations in the general trajectory of its rapid forward urban development, once the calamitous interlude of the late 1950s and '60s went into abeyance.

What this kind of depiction seems to suggest is, first, that cycles of pronounced deterritorialization in conjunction with concomitant urban reterritorialization have occurred differently in East Asia, compared to those in the West, and certainly between, say, China and the United States. Second, these cycles also coincide reasonably well with the broad underlying shifts in collective experiences, social outlooks and attitudes to city building outlined in the preceding section. Third, although urbanizing and urbanized areas in East Asia may have been subject to massive territorial expansion, given the population explosions that have taken place there, they have also exhibited less of a proclivity towards cycles of fundamental spatial change and fragmentation, once their urbanizing operations got up and were fully running. This might also explain the often relentless, even monotonous, character of much of the urbanization that has taken place. It may, however, also be partly due to the relatively immature systems of modern urbanization, particularly in places like China, where the proportion of overall urbanization is still very low, or in Korea, where it is high and yet has come with a rush under the hegemony of a sustained singular outlook on city building. In contrast, mature systems and ones that are more inclusive, like those to be found in the well-developed West – returning to the metaphor of the fox and the hedgehog – have stronger tendencies towards internal change and transformation, under pressure of continued urbanization, in some cases even without further expansive territorialization. The results in both contexts may be big cities, tied to extensive hinterlands, more or less plugged into the same available technologies and building methods, but with very different underlying forces at play, and very different internal dynamics of urban change and territorialization at work.

A second way of looking at spatial qualities of the passage of time in developing urban circumstances is to examine the relative effects of different rates of urbanization. Commonsensically, when rates are low, little spatial expansion might be expected, whereas when they are high, considerable expansion might be anticipated. However, two other less obvious conditions might also

49
A new scale of
projects in
Roppongi, Tokyo.
2004.

become apparent. First, slow rates of urbanization may result in relatively sudden incidences of spatial transformation, by allowing sufficient time to pass for otherwise stable physical settings to need to adapt to gradual but persistent changes in urban living. For example, adaptive reuse of older urban structures usually takes place incrementally in less than highly pressurized conditions, but can also occur momentarily once certain thresholds of demand are reached. Declining rates of urbanization might also push communities into moments when they try to cope with the decline by actively making spatial changes to their physical environment. In fact, recent successful and unsuccessful applications of 'enterprise zones' and 'main streets programs' in smaller US towns seem to fit this last condition.[14] Second, rapid rates of urbanization, returning to the point made earlier about territorialization, although hugely expansive, may result in little radical spatial transformation of certain fundamental aspects of urban form, by allowing little time, or, indeed, immediately felt necessity, for more thoroughgoing adaption to take place. Many of the vertical building extrapolations of small property holdings, discussed for several East Asian cities in chapter Four, are clear cases in point. Only now, for instance, in Tokyo's much cooler real-estate climate, are substantial efforts being made to create more rational and comprehensive changes to many urban block structures in strategic locations, in order to make them compatible with the wide building footprints, large amounts of rentable space and integrated facilities demanded by contemporary international competition for commerce. More straightforwardly, the rote production of urban building, often associated with high rates of urbanization, produces little in the way of spatial transformation, once such a process is underway. In short, while the rate effect of urbanization certainly influences spatial expansion in a more or less symmetrical and direct manner – it goes up and more is constructed – arguably it does not necessarily have the same relatively uniform influence on the kind of spatial transformation that involves thoroughgoing change in the shape, size and other aspects of the physical structure of urban districts, blocks and buildings.

As described in chapter Two, rates of urbanization in East Asia during the past 50 years, or less, have been uniformly high, at times very high, by way of broader international comparisons. This was the case particularly in the larger East Asian cities. To reiterate, 8 of the top 20 most populous cities are now in East Asia and sustained rates of economic production, diversification and corresponding urbanization have been high to very high. South Korea's population, for example, leapt from being just 50 per cent urban in 1970 to around 81 per cent today and even more highly developed Japan achieved a jump of similar proportions between 1950 and the 1980s. Throughout, urbanization has been massively expansive, especially in comparison to former times, across virtually every indicator – population, land area, building volume, extent of infrastructure networks, etc. The result of this process generally conformed to a relatively steeply inclined growth curve of urban development and production over time, beginning and ending, in most cases, as rates of contemporary urbanization began to get underway and as the overall proportion of urban population tends to become asymptotic around 75 to 80 per cent. The exceptions in this last respect were Hong Kong and Singapore where, arguably, as city states the proportion of urban population was always high, and in China, which is still evolving, although rapidly. Furthermore, spatial change to many aspects of East Asia's prior urban scene was also rapid during the initial stages of contemporary urban development, especially under the technical wherewithal and focus that could be brought to bear in stronger doses than during the much early stages of modern urbanization in the developed West. These changes were mainly manifested in construction of high-rise structures, wholesale demolition of dilapidated areas from pre-modern times, and extensive introduction of contemporary transportation and other forms of public infrastructure. In most places, however, once this initial and often protracted period of urban spatial change together with expansion had occurred, the rate of thoroughgoing transformation of the spatial order of urbanization slowed down, even as urban expansion continued, often massively. Put another way, once adequate means for continued reproduction of modern urbanization had been achieved, it was broadly applied, with relatively little modification. Returning to the examples of Hong Kong's, Seoul's and Singapore's prolific construction of housing estates and new-town communities described in chapters Three and Four, once satisfactory prototypes had been created, the rate of deployment and replication predominated over slower and only marginal changes in general urban and building configurations. The same may be said, although with more caution, of Tokyo's explosive suburban development, where rote reproduction was certainly a dominant characteristic. Generally, then, the result of this process appears to conform to spatial transformation over time, as distinct from expansion that rose rapidly before levelling off.

If the rate of change of urban development, or throughput, over time is compared to the rate of spatial transformation, also over time, a distinctive pattern emerges. It is one in which urbanization's sheer throughput effect appears to become dominant, after an initial as well as short intermediate periods during which the rate of spatial transformation is highly visible, before tending towards relatively consistent changes in both rates and at lesser levels. Further, this tendency, or trajectory, is significant, as it appears to move in a different direction, or lag behind, similar interactions encountered in the developed West, over much the same period. There, after an early period when the rate of urbanization was relatively strong in comparison to spatial transformation, the reverse seems to have occurred. In the United States, for instance, the post-war suburban boom saw proliferation of a particular pattern of settlement – the low-density automobile suburb – to be followed by adjustments in this spatial distribution and later by a widening variety of patterns, as pluralistic adaption to changing local and lifestyle circumstances became registered on the urban landscape through new developments and extensive redevelopment. Consequently, although in both cases spatial transformation and expansion, seen in relationship to sheer urban development throughput,

50
A small variety of
building types in
contemporary
Shanghai. 1995.

may reach some kind of steady-state condition in which both processes contribute to the shaping of urban environments in a more or less equal manner,
the prior dynamics of the interaction of the two processes is markedly different.
In addition, the results in urban shape, appearance, monotony, variety and so
on, reflect these differences, with East Asia having more of the same and being
locked in, as it were, to the moment of prototype formation, and developed
Western circumstances probably exhibiting more substantial variety, while
operating under less unifying constraints.

   This kind of analysis throws observations made in chapter Four regarding
the apparent influence of local customs and patterns on settlement into a
different light. It suggests that, rather than being the result of some kind of
indigenous resistance to, or preferential shaping of, the high rates and throughput effects of urbanization, the distinctive and apparently traditionally based

conformity of these environments was more a matter of incompletion of spatial transformations potentially on offer and a kind of path of least resistance in the dash to reurbanize in the most expedient manner possible – the coping behaviour mentioned earlier. Indeed, most of the 'upward extensions of inherited patterns of settlement', 'contemporary labyrinths' and transportation infrastructure improvements described in chapter Four seem to have this underlying spatial logic. Basically, it stems from the fact that urban form is rarely completely mutable, or that not all of its aspects are totally necessary in moving from one stage of urban development to the next. So long as certain thresholds of performance are met – in East Asian cities largely concerning sufficient increases in available building volume and direct access – wholesale reconfiguration of urban block and building arrangements is superfluous, especially if it means the severe disruption of the interests of those already involved in more or less self-beneficial unison.

A third way of considering spatial qualities of the passage of time, in relationship to urban territorial development, is to examine centralizing and decentralizing influences of urban areas on their broader hinterlands. It has long been recognized that the scope of influence of large urban centres, especially in East Asia, extends across broad regions, composed of sub-regions and smaller urban centres. The relationship between Hong Kong and adjacent towns and cities in Guangdong Province is a clear example of this kind of influence. In some quarters, terms like 'mega-city' and 'primate city' provide a kind of short-hand reference for urban conurbations that extend well beyond concentrations around large centres, into hinterlands of interdependent communities of regional scale, scope and significance.[15] According to observations on the spatial distribution of various urban activities, urban regions in the United States, like the greater Los Angeles region, are usually dominated by a very large concentration that acts economically and otherwise, well beyond the region itself, followed some distance away in a generally urbanized landscape by semi-autonomous urban centres not closely integrated with each other, suggesting sub-regionalization, and then areas with a relatively high dependence on the centres of nearby, lower-ranked urban areas, by way of population size and the mix of economic and cultural activity. This loose confederation of adjacent urbanized territories, often with strong internal interdependencies among the smaller communities of which they are composed, along with large dominant and outward-oriented centres, was not always the case. It is an arrangement that has evolved, largely after World War II, as suggested by the dominant model of modernization presented in chapter Two, with the emergence of Los Angeles as a truly major international city. Prior to that time, many of today's communities either did not exist or were centred on larger communities, according to relative population size, and ultimately on the City of Los Angeles itself. Current trends suggest further prominence for larger centres and further concentration and diversification of activities around today's smaller and more localized centres. Areas of Orange County, for instance, located to the south of Los Angeles proper, are beginning to enjoy the benefits of a decentralization of cultural institutions and activities that begins to rival those in the central city. In short, the urbanized territory has not only expanded dramatically but has also become distinctly more mosaic-like in its once relatively uniform spatial qualities, and more congealed around local centres of intensifying and diversifying activity, serving surrounding communities in a more continuous and more complete fashion.[16]

In contrast, returning to a European example, in a country like Italy, known for so long as the 'nation of 100 cities and their hinterlands', the larger cities and towns of its major urban territories have consistently been lower in size than might be predicted according to a straightforward hierarchical rank ordering. Further down in scale this is often followed by reasonable-to-high integration among smaller centres, often economically reflecting a spatially networked configuration of small-enterprise activities in a particular territory – the so-called industrial districts, for instance, of the Po River Valley. In effect, concentration of population and economic activity has occurred, but only up to a point, before giving way to the exploitation of unions of municipalities and transactional networks among otherwise distinct and separate towns. This may be changing, however. In Romagna, for instance, part of the broader and economically important Emilia-Romagna region to the north of Italy, increased polarization of both activity and population seems to be occurring around its two major centres of Forlì and Cesena, whereas towns in the adjacent, inland sub-regional area have lost population and economic activity. This is probably due to the exigencies and needs of enterprises now operating at larger scales and the increased presence of major institutions, like universities. It is also due to improved networking capacities provided by improved infrastructure along a corridor stretching from Bologna in the north to Rimini in the south, and including both Forlì and Cesena.[17] More generally, what seems to be occurring in many of Italy's urbanizing territories is a bare maintenance in size of larger cities, but increases in the size of some well-located smaller cities and some diminution in population of outlying towns. In other words, Italy's centralizing urban tendency involves dispersal and reconcentration, although never at a very large scale of agglomeration. While direct comparison with the American condition would clearly produce nothing but anomalies, for they are two different urbanizing conditions, they share one aspect in common, to be found elsewhere in the developed West. This is a general dispersal of the pattern of centralization and concentration of population, as well as economic and other activity, through the passage of time, across broad urban and urbanizing regions. If anything, this tendency may be becoming more pronounced, producing a kind of further 'lumpiness' in future urban spatial distributions.

Once again the ways of the world seem to operate the other way around in East Asia. While there have certainly been attempts to decentralize functions within the region's larger cities, as described in chapter Three, they have been less than successful, with the upshot that a singular centralizing tendency still persists in most places. Tokyo and Seoul are prime examples, with similar pressures mounting, day by day, in Beijing and Shanghai, despite government programmes intended to keep a proverbial lid on runaway concentrated urban development. Smaller cities, like Hong Kong and Singapore, through their well-linked satellite towns, may have been more successful. However, in Hong Kong's case, the outward push into the surrounding territory seems to coincide with the sheer saturation of central areas, although with Kowloon now enjoying a building boom upward in scale, centralized reconcentration seems likely to reassert itself. One exception is Taipei, which continues its pattern of dispersal of local concentrations across the urbanizing territory of the Taipei Basin.

As discussed in chapter Three, behind this tendency toward singular concentration have been overwhelmingly strong pressures for urbanization – the dominant throughput effects discussed in the preceding section – and a comparative failure to display enough varietal functional order and locational incentives elsewhere, once the contemporary centralizing tendency was well underway. The failure to complete timely and thoroughgoing spatial transformation, as well as the exaggerated degree of the paths of least resistance discussed earlier, also seems to have played a role. If nothing else, these functions influenced rote production in central locations of an extensive urban fabric that was sufficient to become self-reinforcing over time. One other consequence has been density and, as described earlier, urban density in many places of a largely unprecedented degree. Not only that, but, especially in a place like Hong Kong, although elsewhere in East Asia, a workable urban density was produced, which once again seems to have had a self-reinforcing

51
Verticality and
workable density
in Central, Hong
Kong. 2003.

effect, by encouraging singular centralization, or at least not deterring it. In contrast, one of the factors shaping the American city was an adverse reaction to density, not only because of demands for individual property ownership, but also due to a lack of experience in making high density workable in comparison to the easier pursuit of horizontal mobility and propinquity. During their formative years most contemporary East Asian cities did not have this alternative at their disposal, other than through mass transit systems, which in themselves encourage high densities of urban concentration. Even the elevated automobile expressway systems that snake their way through Tokyo and now through other places like Shanghai are designed and constructed in a manner that does not deter close by high-density urban development, and where the underside street level remains inhabitable and well used.

Finally, a fourth way of looking at the interaction between urban space and time is through expressive aspects of a city's urban architecture. This is often a complicated representational issue involving both denotative and connotative components, as suggested in the introductory paragraph of this chapter. Basically, if buildings (architecture) are regarded, at least symbolically, as spatio-temporal objects, then cultural perceptions of certain configurations of these objects can carry with them certain widely recognizable meanings. For example, the neo-colonial house in the United States is strongly associated with ideas of tradition, even if constructed recently. This is because the temporal framework of the mode and style of building is deliberately oriented backwards in historical time, through the choice of particular volumetric, material and ornamental elements that sufficiently emulate what was actually built in the past. This present-day reflection, as it were, is traditional in so far as it coincides with broadly held cultural perceptions of the colonial era at the very start of the nation, during the revolutionary period, in a manner that was somehow essential, pioneering and heroic.[18] Other related meanings may become evident to many, including acquisition of a certain level of social status on the part of the occupants and maybe a middle-of-the-road viewpoint on matters of community concern. Some observers in the same cultural context might see the house as a symbol of a self-satisfied, middle-class and conservative lifestyle, eschewing the pioneering and heroic references as being nostalgic and maudlin. While such differences in perception demonstrate the slipperiness of many signs and symbols, the fact remains that the house does represent a connection with a past, regardless of how that might be interpreted in the present. In other words, a building, as a particular spatio-temporal object, can be made with a deliberate construal backwards in time. Conversely, buildings can be made to look futuristic, so long as there is sufficient cultural agreement as to what shapes, forms and materials will broadly convey such an impression. Many of the Case Study Houses, built in the Los Angeles hills during the 1950s and '60s, came across to most observers as being at least contemporary, if not about downright future prospects for the single-family home.[19] Over time, this perception may also have altered to one of a certain kind of contemporaneity that belonged in the past, again pointing up a slipperiness of meanings, although this time in the direction of changing meanings. Up to a point, then, it is possible to shape the spatial aspects of building in a particular historico-temporal direction ranging from, say, traditionalism, through eclecticism and modernism to futurism. Moreover, cultures tend to give to buildings such meanings, even if the implications might be debated and the meanings eventually changed.

Another aspect of variation among buildings, and in architecture, is the coherence of the spatial artefact itself in expressive terms. For example, in widely recognized great works of architecture, spatial expressive coherence, almost by definition, is very high. In contrast, in the case of an extreme reduction of almost any expressive content, as happened in the makeshift building of the 'Cultural Revolution' in China, spatial expressive coherence was very low. It is not that buildings don't stand up, or don't have walls, floors, roofs and other necessary appurtenances. It is more a case of something like the Vitruvian triad of 'firmness', 'commodity' and 'delight', which, bundled together, made for good and proper architecture. First, coherence requires thoroughgoing qualities of 'thingness' about buildings that are somehow internally consistent. Many of the Case Study Houses were composed of narrow steel frames, large panes of glass, cantilevered decks and flat roofs that were entirely consistent with inherent ideas about lightness, transparency between inside and outside, as well as a certain kind of phenomenal levity with respect to site surroundings. Second, coherence embodies social aspirations about basic spatial qualities such as adequate size, functionality and convenience. Third, coherence requires a capacity to arrest the mind's eye in a manner that provokes contemplation and aids understanding in the pursuit of non-trivial meaning. Exercise of these stipulations may well vary from one observer and potential user to others. Clearly, the last requirement of what constitutes 'non-trivial meaning' undoubtedly begs considerable latitude, depending on taste, connoisseurship and architectural background, as does the first. Nevertheless, the opposites of these stipulations are probably recognizable without too much debate. For instance, a building that is poorly constructed in a hodge-podge of a materials and construction methods is inadequate in its functional layout, and is gussied up in an excessive pastiche, or is of an unfathomable idiosyncrasy in appearance, cannot be said to have a positive spatially expressive coherence, at least to a broad audience.

With these two properties in mind (i.e., expressive temporal outlook and expressive spatial coherence) a simple two-space can be imagined, with expressive spatial coherence running from positive to negative along one axis and expressive temporal outlook running from forward-looking in one direction to backward-looking in the other, along the other axis. Within this space 'modernism', for example, would be placed in a zone qualified by a forward-looking orientation and, if done well, a high degree of spatial coherence. 'Traditionalism', however, would be found in another zone, characterized by being backward-looking in time, even if of a high degree of spatial coherence. Vernacular forms of expression would be located nearby, although probably with a slightly less high degree of spatial coherence. 'Pastiche', in contrast, might be located in yet another zone, with still less spatial coherence and a backward-looking orientation, whereas reductivist forms of building and expression, like those mentioned in conjunction with China's 'Cultural Revolution', would be located in the fourth zone, spatially incoherent but, if anything, with something of a forward-looking orientation, and so one could go on. What is more important than locating particular stylistic labels is the trajectory that contemporary urban-architecture makes in expressively constituting a city.

At the risk of overgeneralization, what occurred in the United States after World War II was a moment of contemporary expressive commitment in both office building and construction of substantial aspects of the domestic environment. This was followed by a relative breakdown in spatial coherence, as suburbs burgeoned and as commercial speculative developments became more expedient, resulting in buildings of reduced architectural quality, finally culminating in widespread post-modern reaction, during the 1970s and '80s, clearly with a backward-looking orientation and varying degrees of expressive spatial coherence.[20] Today, the cultural landscape seems to be split among proponents of traditionalism and those in the vanguard of cutting-edge modernism. In many parts of Europe there was a similar kind of trajectory, especially during the post-war boom, although the dramatic opposition among traditionalists and modernists was never quite so strong and broader attention was paid to context in a more relaxed and inclusive manner. Again at the risk of oversimplification, for there are many exceptions, an expressive path can be charted, during contemporary city building, in roughly one direction through the imaginary two-space.

In the case of East Asia, however, the trajectory was again different, at least in most places, moving roughly in the opposite direction. In China, for example, most post-Civil War urban architecture, at least with an official stamp on it, made conscious reference to tradition, involving horizontal forms, prominent gabled roofs and ornamental detailing, combined with modern building technology.[21] It was in some sense a continuation of the stylistic proclivity of the pre-war Nationalists, although, as explained in chapter Four, from a different motivation and line of aesthetic argument, which aimed at familiarity and cultural continuity rather than aggrandizement of the past. Expressive matters quickly came to a head, however, with the 'Big Roof' controversy in the 1950s and the official realization that more parsimonious and strictly functional use of material would be required if China was to meet its building needs. Some continued attempts to sinify buildings persisted, before most urban construction fell into a bare minimum of acceptable standards and a kind of crude modern functionalism. During China's recent recovery, most aspects of spatial coherence have improved and the dominant temporal outlook is forward-looking and modern, although a traditionalist strain persists. In fact, recently there was controversy in official circles over appropriate style of buildings and how sinified aspects might be best expressed. Judging from the results, however, including the Beijing Opera House, the city's planned Olympic facilities and cctv complex, the Shanghai Grand Theatre and major airports, described in chapter Four, Chinese officialdom seems to favour high-tech contemporary architecture and subtler references to local culture, as well as more extreme forms of hyper-modernism. Indeed, with most major institutional building projects in major cities likely to be undertaken over the next decade or so, the conflation of hyper-modernism with a Chinese style of architecture, again mentioned in chapter Four, may be even more likely.

Japanese architects also made early forays into traditional themes during post-war construction, although they quickly turned in a modernist and contemporary direction. Again, during boom times, a substantial amount of building was thrown together quickly, without the generally high level of spatial coherence for which the Japanese construction industry is notable. South Korea made strong, almost ideological, commitments to architectural modernism during the formative years of cities like Seoul's rapid growth, as did Hong Kong, although without the same self-consciousness. In both cases, there were also periods during which cost constraints were severe, and resulting spatial coherence in urban construction was at a low ebb. Finally, overall changes in Singapore's urban-architectural expression shifted in a different direction, more, although not entirely, consistent with the American trajectory. After an initial period which saw widespread construction of simple modern building complexes, like the early, relatively large-scale efforts of the Housing Development Board, attention was directed towards commercial building of an internationally prominent ilk, primarily in the hands of foreign architects. During recent phases of development, increasing attention has been paid to historic preservation and to incorporation of allegedly local architectural

52
Tropical land-
scape and infra-
structure,
Singapore, 2000.

references in the form of gabled roofs, screened window openings and more use of colour. In this regard, renovations of early modern housing complexes, like Queenstown, are clear cases in point. Sounder use has also been made of the lush tropical landscape that now graces much of Singapore's major streets, expressways and other large-scale infrastructural improvements. Together with simultaneous architectural projection of tradition and contemporaneity, this tactic lends further explicit support to the more or less official idea of a 'glocal city' – one that is both global and local in its expressive orientation. Far from being unique to Singapore, however, this orientation is now deployed widely elsewhere in the world, especially when one thinks of recent construction in cities like Barcelona, Bilbao and Berlin. In its particular urban-architectural results, this approach undermines claims by anti-globalists of undue uniformity and overwhelming commodification in contemporary urban construction, even if the overall expressive strategy seems to be much the same.

To summarize, fundamental interactions between urban space making and the passage of time underlying the conformation of most East Asian cities over the past 50 years, or less, appear to have been considerably different from those encountered during much the same period in the developed West. First, moments of deterritorialization followed by periods of urban reterritorialization in East Asia have taken different cycles, consistent once again with broad shifts in collective social experience, resulting in sustained and massive urban territorialization without substantial changes in underlying spatial models once the process was really underway. Second, this lack of much mediating or arresting intermediate spatial transformation appears to be due, as much as anything, to coping with the high rate of change in urban throughput with little respite. Third, there has been a strong tendency towards centralization, over time, in singular urban concentrations and mega cities, with workable high density as a by-product. Fourth, expressive aspects of urban-architectural production have generally taken a different turn, with a widespread outcome of appearing to be modern in a commonplace manner. Consequently, most East Asian cities, in addition to having pockets of local colour and variation, appear to be different from their counterparts in the developed West, although not those in, say, Latin America where there seem to be some similar underlying trends. On the whole, more urbanization has been constructed relatively recently and its urban expanse is very large. Extensive tracts of urban development appear to be much the same and primarily modern in line with the moments in which they were constructed, but with a general upward escalation in building scale and size. Finally, the density of concentration of habitation and other aspects of life is unusually high. No doubt all this might be placed at the feet of rapid regional development, as in the Gulf States during the oil boom and the recent boom in services. However, amid the flux of urban space, time and events, the size, scale and sheer muscularity of urban development is largely unprecedented and, more important, took particular turns in the predominant orientation of shape-making and appearance.

Differences in Degree and Kind

Finally, returning more squarely to the two questions posed at the beginning of the book, with regard to the first, concerning how well East Asia generally follows dominant concepts of modernization, particularly with respect to urbanization, the answer is that, by and large, it does conform. The strong relationship between modernization and industrialization followed by expanding development of tertiary functions transpired, often with remarkable speed and comprehensiveness. As described in chapter Two, labour and other forms of human activity have become increasingly more specialized. Advances in overall economic production and per capita wealth have increased substantially throughout the region, certainly in relative terms. Material standards of living have risen for many, as have the benefits of better health and welfare. The proportions of populations now living in urban conditions has also risen, or are well on the way to rising to locally unprecedented levels, comparable with most well-developed circumstances elsewhere in the world. Big cities have emerged in larger numbers and, at least in broad outline, the introduction of modern planning strategies, land-use zoning legislation, building codes and public improvements have emulated or paralleled those to be found in the West. Even negative effects, like environmental impacts and disparities in income, have emerged in a characteristically modern urban fashion, shared in many other places. Certainly, there are many differences from place to place in East Asia, depending upon specific historical circumstances, what was there before contemporary modernization really took off, comparative progress with the project of modernization itself, and substantial sub-regional differences in climate, geography and the bountifulness of natural and human resources. Nevertheless, the same or broadly similar trends towards rapid and relatively complete modernization in material urban terms are there for all to see.

Guidance of modernization, however, conforms less well to dominant Western practices, as described in chapters Two and Three, often despite apparently similar institutional trappings and planning organizations based on Western precedents. Largely, it has involved revolution from the top; substantial rounds of collective consumption and deep public involvement; proliferation of viable export platforms and special economic zones and capitalization on local assets, ranging from well-entrenched conglomerates in Japan and South Korea to small business networks in Taiwan, and in China state-owned industries and township-village enterprises. A distinctive, although not unique feature, has been the step-by-step emulation by one nation of the practices of others in the region that were slightly better off, with Japan very much in the lead. Contrary to the success, if not prevalence, enjoyed by liberal-democratic socio-political and culture regimes in the West, people in East Asia, especially those in power, have been selective in adopting Western traits and values. For the most part, modernization has occurred under one-party systems, non-representative governments and downright dictatorships. Civil society, strong in the West, is almost uniformly weak and a bifurcated view was often taken in pursuit of Westernized practical applications alongside indigenous socio-cultural biases and practices that often stressed collectivism, consensus and the interests of relations, clans, companies and other circumscribed politico-economic groups. Secularism is widespread, although recent expressions over deep-seated differences in values between East Asia and elsewhere are not unknown, especially when fending off outside influences. Wider adoption of Western intellectual, social and political attitudes may yet occur. There are certainly signs of this in Taiwan, Singapore and in the Hong Kong populace's stance on 'Article 23' – the anti-subversion law – as well as in South Korea's recent crackdown on corruption and special interests, together with Japan's professed reforms and the promise of lasting departure from the '1955 Agreement' that occurred during the 2003 elections.

In China, the rising star in the region, gradual though relatively sustained loosening of Marxist hegemony can also be detected in the post-Maoist era. Some commentators have suggested nationalism in itself, without prefixes, as a plausible long-term trajectory of historical events, reaching back to Kang Youwei's 'Great Unity' of the late nineteenth century.[22] Even during Mao's earlier period, the resurrection of China as a nation appears to have been uppermost in his mind, as he pushed for a United Front with the despised Nationalists and fought off the Japanese, and it remained a persistent feature of his subsequent rule. Later, Deng Xiaoping's pragmatic leanings effectively pushed China towards the right, tipping the thrust and balance of modernization towards emerging, cosmopolitan urban areas. Jiang Zemin, his successor, basically continued this trend, despite often proclaiming a leftist cultural line.[23] The present regime, under Hu Jintao, seems likely to continue a reasonably open pragmatic approach, while actively attempting to redress the urban–rural imbalance and the economic disparity among regions.

Apart from these disparities, China's central government is also trying to manoeuvre an overheated and under-regulated economy into a soft landing and to eradicate corruption. With something like 30 per cent of the world's iron ore consumption, 27 per cent of its steel, and growing volumes of oil at stake, a sudden slowdown, as occurred in 1994, could have a strong adverse effect on international commodity markets, not to mention more localized negative impacts on the economies of other nations and multinational enterprises tied up with China's recent economic boom.[24] Control of where the money goes will continue to be crucial. China is already flooded with foreign capital and, as noted, has relatively weak financial controls and poor banking practices, with non-performing loans in some sectors running at 40 to 45 per cent. Insider business dealings, especially at local levels, remain high, despite recent crackdowns begun by Zhu Rongji, among others, and there is mounting pressure for upward valuation of the yuan, potentially affecting future exports on which China's economy has become dependent. There is, however, still ample room for stronger and more thoroughgoing institutional reform, without resorting entirely to non-oligarchic Western practices. Nevertheless, what the next ten to fifteen years hold will be critical to China's longer-term future. If all goes well, at lower more sustainable rates of economic expansion, China could draw roughly level, over this period, with some other developed economies in the region, if not in the world. Urbanization, at current rates of about a 1 per cent shift from non-urban to urban populations, will probably reach the 50 per cent mark, again during this vital period, before rising to more well-developed levels, around 60 per cent or more, by 2035. The cultural impacts of this flip-flop in population distribution alone on inter-personal relations and lifestyles, in roughly a generation or under, are likely to be substantial, continuing to produce more cosmopolitan and consumer-oriented segments of society. Recent widespread emergence of a so-called grey culture, which is essentially apolitical, ironic and, at times, cynical, appears to signal an effective change in an otherwise tightly held cultural climate.[25] So far, however, a thoroughgoing conversion to Western attitudes has not occurred and may well not in the future. It is not clear, for instance, that collective, consensus-based conceptions of society – albeit modified – will be broken up in favour of Western proclivities towards individualism and pluralism.

In response to the second question about the extent to which East Asian cities collectively describe, or represent, a particular regional urban identity, different in kind as well as degree, again the answer seems to be affirmative, the very real differences among the region's cities notwithstanding. Certainly, the collective social experience of action and reaction to urbanization was orchestrated in a particular manner, varying from place to place within the region, but also in a manner very different from experience in the West. Moreover, the underlying socio-cultural matrix – the neo-Confucian scheme mentioned earlier – seems distinctive enough and intact enough to continue to promote an orientation towards city making that stresses comprehensive top-down planning and management, with little bottom-up, or middle-level, local involvement and autonomy. The lack of a middle ground comes through, rather literally, in other ways as well. As discussed, there is often a very different ambiguity between public and private realms in East Asian cities. There are few intermediate spatial devices and visual frames of reference giving emphasis, direction and continuity among parts of the city and between those parts and the whole. Individual buildings give off much the same evidence of many different operators and property owners at work as they do elsewhere in the world, with much the same levels of urban-architectural consistency and idiosyncrasy. However, deeply rooted cultural concepts about organic relations and self-similarity among parts and wholes seem to be at work, effectively ruling out sharper distinctions among buildings by way of a broader contrivance of their intermediate environment, or 'middle ground', in relation to the city at large. East Asian cities are very dense, even in non-overcrowded conditions, and with that density has come a potentially different way of urban life and perception of urban space, especially in exaggerated circumstances like the high-rise environments of Hong Kong and, more recently, in Shanghai. In addition, very particular environments have been maintained or recreated among historical enclaves and among inherited patterns of urban settlement, including the 'spaces in between' described in chapter Four, although probably less as a function of a persuasive role for tradition than by ad-hoc local responses, coping behaviour and the incomplete spatial transformation of urban pressures described earlier in this chapter. There remains, particularly in cities like Tokyo, Shanghai, Beijing and parts of Singapore, an unusual and often sharp juxtaposition of a sense of village life within the hustle and bustle of the modern city, again with little spatial mediation in between. Commercial streets and districts, ablaze with colour and signage, have always been a part of East Asian cities, but under contemporary pressures of spatial compression, upward extension in height, and the free-for-all interplay of neon and other visual media, they have reached new levels of brilliance and visual excitement. Architecturally, modernism and even neo-modernism has become the lingua franca, even if mostly in a rather commonplace and often mundane manner, with some exceptional work in between. Traditional forms of expression, especially in the figuration and ornamentation of buildings, have been fighting a rearguard action, if anything, as a less-specific cultural confidence in contemporary architecture has been mounting. In this regard, it seems likely that formal adherence to longstanding local architectural patterns of spatial organization is likely to be more enduring and meaningful than figural and ornamental expressions and, therefore, a more fertile ground for further exploration and explicit grounding of urban architecture in local conditions.

In the end, however, one also has to ask just how different the urban form of contemporary cities can become, particularly when they must incorporate similar demands for building programme, transportation access and public open space, as well as being constructed using similar available technologies and management practices. Picking up on the discussion in chapters Three and Four, the answer is probably not very different, especially at one end of the urban spatial spectrum, seen largely from high altitude and concerned with aggregate volumes, lengths, areas and key relationships among various functional parts, and also at the other end, when contemplating specific contemporary building from a stationary pedestrian vantage point. Nevertheless, depending on how urban spatial and temporal processes have interacted, contradicted each other, unfolded and even provided entry into new realms of practical urban experience, differences among cities around the world, especially from the middle-ground perspective of a helicopter flight or a drive by, have become quite pronounced. Despite obvious individual distinctions among them, it is primarily in this last regard that East Asian cities have given a varied though particular and, so far, unique shape to the recent and contemporary space of time, returning to the idea of a nexus in the flux of demands and flows mentioned at the beginning of chapter Two.

Future Urban Prospects and Choices

Yet again, what the future holds for the shape of East Asian cities is difficult to predict fully. It may be that closer alignment with urban considerations being undertaken elsewhere will occur once the rapid, contemporary large-scale and centralizing phases of urban development have abated, or begin to abate, and if and when the East Asian hedgehog becomes more fox-like. To be sure, much of this 'first-round' urban development has been moving in the opposite direction to recent, predominantly 'second-round' urban redistribution, redevelopment, conservation, revitalization, and so on, that has taken place in well-developed cities in the West. However, rates of urbanization in East Asia are already beginning to slow down, with the conspicuous exception of China, not without a fair amount of introspective reconsideration about the quality and long-lasting relevance of what was built, often dictated by mounting environmental concerns, worries about international competitiveness and social pressures for better and more varied living conditions from, by now, much more affluent populaces. Even in China, these trends are becoming apparent, especially in several fairly well-modernized urban areas. Certainly, the public and private sectors in many East Asian cities already appear to be hard at work, beginning to modify and repair past, and even relatively recent, urban projects. More specifically, from city to city, stances are altering, or everyday concerns mounting, to the point that different attitudes towards urbanization almost seem to be inevitable. This is particularly evident among the seven major cities that have been the primary focus of this text.

In Beijing and Shanghai, for instance, China's two most prominent and trendsetting cities, plans are in the works to redress problems either left unattended or arising from the urban boom of the late 1980s and '90s. Despite massive construction activity, Shanghai has been comparatively well served by recent comprehensive plans and remains a relatively compact city, with a metro area covering around 690 km^2 and a further 520 km^2 of as yet to be completed development in Pudong. This compares favourably with Singapore, which occupies an area of 648 km^2, with about a third the population. Consequently, metro Shanghai is one of the densest cities in the world, although, as in its southern neighbour Hong Kong, the density seems to be workable. In particular, transit continues to be pursued aggressively, with completion of the first subway line in 1995, three lines totalling 30 km in length by 2003, and a further seventeen lines to be installed by 2020 for from 300 to 540 km of service, depending upon the rate of construction. Concerted efforts to build self-contained satellite communities on the metro area's periphery are also underway, although their success in limiting Shanghai's outward sprawl from the centre remains to be seen. Less compact, Beijing is now being subjected to a new round of comprehensive planning activity, especially to the north and east – in conjunction with nearby Tianjin on the coast

– that appears likely to break with the prior planning orthodoxy of creating successive urban rings around the city, and to take pressure off the central city by more actively promoting strong multiple nuclei of development and employment. This strategy, coupled with more active conservation in the old city, and a more nuanced approach towards adaptive reuse of existing structures and well-scaled urban infill projects, has at least a fair chance of preserving the overall horizontal spatial character and *feng mao*, or visual environment, of the city and much of what is left of its cultural heritage. As noted in chapter Four, public green open-space provision is also high on both cities' urban agendas, with a number of successful projects already completed. Nevertheless, Beijing, with relatively low automobile ownership, is beginning to choke on its own exhaust fumes and frustrating commutes, well behind the pace of public transit improvements necessary to breathe easily. Basic resources like water and energy are now becoming scarcer, as noted earlier, requiring expensive, large-scale infrastructural investments to sustain the future of the city, as well as massive reforestation programmes in the north and west to combat air pollution problems. Shanghai, better served on the transit front, continues to expand, potentially running up against confrontation with high concentrations of nearby peasantry, many of whom are less well equipped, or supported, than their urban counterparts to mainstream into modern life. In addition, environmental problems, like land-surface subsidence and surface-water pollutions linger, requiring timely attention, if Shanghai is going to be all that it can be. Both cities, like many elsewhere in China, must also deal with potentially severe problems of future social stratification, as discussed in chapter Two and in the preceding section of this chapter.

Tokyo now appears to be counteracting earlier decisions about urban development and the resulting monotony and blandness of many urban environments, through a ground swell of programmes and initiatives. From the top comes the recent urban renewal policy of 2002 and 2003, with its emphasis on Urgent Improvement Zones to make Tokyo physically and functionally more attractive and internationally competitive. Designated at the *ku* or municipal level, enablement of these improvement zones essentially bypasses the once all-powerful metropolitan government, but also offers a far more streamlined process for private sector engagement and inducement. However, while this approach to urban regeneration appears to give local stakeholders greater freedom of expression, certainly on the private-sector side, it remains to be seen whether it might also erode the longstanding social contract, alluded to several times in this book, of protections in favour of parity and egalitarianism. Other signs of a weakening of top-down metropolitan rule and management are becoming visible through pressures for local municipal autonomy, more favourable ratios for returning taxes and other local revenues back to the local level, local planning initiatives to particularize specific environments even in advance of the Urgent Improvement Zones, and private ventures aimed, independently, at broader public amenity and engagement. There is also the recent emergence of 'townscape' as an issue of discussion by local review boards, reflecting a new concern for urban design and conservation of physical character, much like the concept of *feng mao*, in conjunction with Beijing and other Chinese cities. Strong and laudable though many of these local efforts might be, Tokyo continues to face growth management and urban servicing issues on a metropolitan scale. Furthermore, local-level planning capacities are often weak, and it remains to be seen whether Tokyo can successfully attend to potentially enlivening local interests yet still maintain its excellent track record in overall urban management.

In Singapore, a rising and more sophisticated middle class is already pressing – albeit politely – for greater variety and some slackening of paternalism from its lifelong one-party government. Quite apart from socio-political pressures, there is a more profound interest in the island state's urban-architectural past – shunned for so long – in addition to interests in more substantial housing choice and higher variety and scope for leisure-time and recreational activities and amenities. Singapore's recent Green-Blue Plan, mentioned in chapter Three, with its emphasis on environmental conservation and natural amenities, may go part way to meeting these interests, as will privatization of public housing and providing for a more footloose population through greater private-sector domestic involvement. However, there remains an underlying inherent paradox and even tension between 'father knows best' and a loosening of the socio-political strictures necessary to promote indigenous institutional strength, both inside and outside of government, and to foster the independent and yet often chaotic entrepreneurial and cultural spirit necessary to move creatively, for instance, into potentially vital and fast-breaking areas of the tertiary industrial sector.

Hong Kong, not hampered by quite the same social strictures, is not yet comfortable with its role and place in China and is clearly feeling the proverbial 'heat' from Shanghai in its quest to remain a global city. Whether or not this really should be a concern, for China is a vast country probably with room for several financial and commercial meccas, Hong Kong has embarked upon a 'branding' exercise, as noted in chapters Three and Four, including substantial public–private projects with an emphasis on expansion of mainstream cultural venues, more leisure-time facilities and more general engagement with active recreation. With pollution mounting, often to alarming levels, there is also a new-found emphasis on clean-up programmes and environmental amenity, especially in association with the city's extensive and, at times, magnificent waterfront, cut off for so long from inviting public access and enjoyment. Readjustment of the historic relationship with Guandong Province and other parts of Southern China seems to be in order and appears to be partially occurring through several planned major roadway and rail infrastructure projects, needed for Hong Kong and the region to maintain its competitive advantage. No doubt these infrastructure improvements will usher in further rearrangement of the sub-region's economic geography and settlement patterns, probably emphasizing strong corridors of potential development, with burgeoning centres at transit points, around the major hubs of Hong Kong, Shenzhen and Guangzhou.

Seoul, having taken on the modern juggernaut and remade itself in that image, must continue to deal with the growth management conditions of its own success as the primate city in South Korea, but also find ways of offering more to a more sophisticated and affluent populace. The prospect of reorienting urban development to the north – denied by the demilitarized zone – is now becoming more real. However, such a prospect will almost surely force strong debate over the appropriate scale and arrangement of further urban development, in the face of strong pressures to preserve much of the area for environmental conservation. In Seoul itself, recovery of the past and traditional identity is also underway. For instance, plans are already being drawn up to uncover the stream described in chapter Three, running east–west through its centre, which formed a significant component of the cosmic force field behind the city's original cartographic formation. Proposals are also afoot to 'green' several significant major thoroughfares, especially in the south of the city, in a manner that reflects traditional expressive motifs and manners of using the landscape.

Meanwhile, Taipei, although bustling with new-found freedoms and the vivacity that goes with such a discovery, must continue to wrestle with profound issues of identity, physical coherence and standing in the world. Tensions with mainland China have again increased of late, unsettling the climate for investment and economic development, quite apart from placing those on the island in a difficult position from which to imagine an independent future.

At more mundane levels, traffic congestion and an overdependence on private automobile use continues literally to cloud Taipei's attempts to offer a pristine urban environment. Several ill-fated transit projects have not helped in this regard. Nevertheless, now that the pressures for outright expansion have subsided, the sprawling laissez-faire style of urban development described in chapter Three has begun to settle into a more legible and sensible pattern of multiple centres and surrounding communities, each with their own character and much in keeping with the mosaic of Taipei's three original settlements.

In short, many East Asian cities now seem to be entering into the tasks of redevelopment, reconversion, revitalization and expanding the physical terms of reference of their rather narrowly defined and production-oriented urban environments, as happened earlier in many developing Western cities. Moreover, while the urban boom continues, especially in China, it is certainly not clear that those in East Asian cities, with a capacity to do something about it, must repeat the mistakes and missed opportunities that occurred in Western cities during their boom periods of urban growth. For one thing, many of the issues at stake are generally more apparent, for those wishing to acknowledge them, without the same costs of discovery. For another, the scope and number of means for tackling urban preservation, conservation, redevelopment and revitalization, again for those wishing to avail themselves of them, is much broader and more numerous than it has been in the past. Furthermore, enough is generally now known to contemplate an orientation towards mixed modes for producing urban space that prevent constantly putting the proverbial foot of urban development, per se, in front of the other concerned with no less consequential qualitative considerations of redevelopment. Nevertheless, even if this turn from 'first-round' to 'second-round' development is undertaken and undertaken soon, as it appears it might be, all that is already different about East Asian modern urbanism will also be in play, forming the broad background for what occurs ahead and probably ensuring a unique physical urban identity for the region. After all, elsewhere and in the relatively recent past, it was the broad modern foundations that set the tone and counted most, both in terms of what had to be overturned and what had to be continued.

References

one Introduction

1 The Economist, *Pocket World in Figures* (London, 2002), p. 18; Irene Lee, ed., 'Dossier Hong Kong', *Spazio Societá*, 79 (1997), p. 81, and Roger Simmonds and Gary Hack, eds, *Global City Regions: Their Emerging Forms* (New York, 2000), p. 19.

two Relationships and Urbanizing Trajectories

1 Samuel P. Huntington, *The Clash of Civilizations and the Remaking of World Order* (New York, 1996), pp. 40–78, and V. S. Naipul, 'Our Universal Civilization', *New York Review of Books*, 10 (1990), p. 20.
2 US Census, *Labor Statistics* (Washington, DC, 1950–2000).
3 Peter G. Rowe, *Making a Middle Landscape* (Cambridge, MA, 1991), pp. 3–34.
4 Saskia Sassen, *The Global City: New York, London and Tokyo* (Princeton, NJ, 1991), pp. 168–9.
5 The Economist, *Pocket World in Figures* (London, 2002), p. 222, and US Census, *Labor Statistics*, p. 37.
6 The Economist, *Pocket World in Figures*, p. 106.
7 Philippe Legrain, *Open World: The Truth About Globalization* (London, 2002), pp. 6–7 and 80–117.
8 Naomi Klein, 'The Tyranny of the Brands', *New Statesman*, January 2000, p. 24.
9 Ezra Vogel, *The Four Little Dragons: The Spread of Industrialization in East Asia* (Cambridge, MA, 1991).
10 Steven Radelet and Jeffrey Sachs, 'Asia's Reemergence', *Foreign Affairs* (November–December 1997), p. 44.
11 Huntington, *Clash of Civilizations*, p. 46.
12 Based on data drawn from the Japan Institute for Social and Economic Affairs, *Korea Statistical Yearbooks*, ROC *Statistical Yearbooks*, *Singapore Yearbooks* and the Hong Kong Census and Statistic Department and World Bank, *World Development Indicators – Electronic Resource* (July 2003).
13 Radelet and Sachs, 'Asia's Reemergence', p. 49, and Stevel Radelet, Jeffrey Sachs and Jong-Wha Lee, 'Economic Growth in Asia', *Harvard Institute of International Development*, Discussion Paper 609 (1997), pp. 57–61.

14 The Economist, *Pocket World in Figures*, pp. 124, 196, 204, 212, 146, 162 and 222.

15 At present there is some debate about Japan's second-place standing, with China ranked second to the US in the purchasing power parity of goods and services produced – a four-fold increase over the past 25 years.

16 Based on the World Bank, *Development Indicators – Electronic Resource* and the Groningen Growth and Development Centre and the Conference Board, *Total Economy Database* (July 2003), http://www.ggdc.net. Purchasing Power Parity (PPP) adjusts GDP rates according to cost of living differences defined by equalized prices for a standard 'basket' of goods and services.

17 Keizai Koho Centre, *Japan 2000: An International Comparison* (Tokyo, 2000), p. 40.

18 Based on ROC *Statistical Yearbooks, 1956–2000, Korea Statistical Yearbooks, 1980–2000,* and Joochul Kim and Sang-Chuel Choe, *Seoul: The Making of a Metropolis* (New York, 1997), pp. 43–52.

19 Drawn from The Economist, *Pocket World in Figures*, pp. 146 and 196; Hong Kong Census and Statistics Department; *Singapore Yearbook of Statistics, 2000*; and the World Bank, *Development Indicators – Electronic Resource*.

20 The Economist, *Pocket World in Figures*, p. 222, and Asian Development Bank, *Asian Development Outlook* (London, 1996), p. 6 and pp. 20–30.

21 Drawn from *China Statistical Yearbook, 2000*; The Economist, *Pocket World in Figures*, p. 124; Wu Liangyong, Weijia Wu and Jian Lin, *Recent Urbanization in China* (Beijing, 1998), p. 33; and Asian Development Bank, *Asian Development Outlook*, pp. 40–45.

22 Vogel, *The Four Little Dragons*, pp. 13–41.

23 Manuel Castells, Lee Goh and R. Yin-Wang Kwok, *The Shek Kip Mei Syndrome: Economic Development and Public Housing in Hong Kong and Singapore* (London, 1990), pp. 329–33.

24 Radelet and Sachs, 'Asia's Reemergence', p. 52.

25 Radelet, Sachs and Lee, 'Economic Growth in Asia', pp. 34–40, and Vogel, *The Four Little Dragons*, pp. 83–112.

26 Drawn from the UN *Common Database*, the ROC *Statistical Yearbooks*, Fu-Chen Lo and Yue-Man Yeung, *Emerging World Cities in Pacific Asia* (New York, 1996), pp. 20–25; World Bank, *World Development Report* (New York, 1993), pp. 10–15, and Guohang Zhu, 'Urbanization and the Problem of Population in China's Big Cities', in *The Renewal of Redevelopment in Shanghai*, ed. Zheng Shiling (Shanghai, 1994), p. 18.

27 The Economist, *Pocket World in Figures*, pp. 160, 220 and 106, respectively.

28 Based on cohort-survival projections using data from *Population Statistical Yearbooks of China*. See also Institute of Population Research of China, *Papers in Population Research* (Beijing, 1995 and 1996).

29 Data drawn from the US Census Bureau, *China Statistical Yearbooks, Korea Statistical Yearbooks, Singapore Yearbook of Statistics,* Japan Institute for Social and Economic Affairs, Roger Mark Selya, *Taipei* (New York, 1995), p. 91, and World Bank, *Urbanization Selected Working Papers* (Washington, DC, 1972).

30 Calculated based on data from The Economist, *Pocket World in Figures*, pp. 18, 104, 140 and 220.

31 Richard Robison and David S. G. Goodman, *The New Rich in Asia: Mobile Phones, McDonalds and Middle-class Revolution* (London, 1996), pp. 1–18.

32 E. G. Pryor, *Housing in Hong Kong* (Hong Kong, 1983), p. 24; Brian Sullivan and Ke Chen, 'Design for Tenant Fitout: A Critical Review of Public Housing Flat Design in Hong Kong', *Habitat International*, V (1997), p. 2; Lü Junhua, Peter G. Rowe and Jie Zhang, eds, *Modern*

Urban Housing in China, 1840–2000 (Munich, 2001), p. 22; Kim and Choe, *Seoul*, p. 108; and Selya, *Taipei*, p. 188.

33   Minoru Mori, *Urban New Deal Policy: Striving to Recover from the Largest Crisis of the Post War Era* (Tokyo, 1999), p. 5; A. K. Wong and S.H.K. Yeh, eds, *Housing a Nation: Twenty-five Years of Public Housing in Singapore* (Singapore, 1985), p. 15; and Castells, Goh and Kwok, *The Shek Kip Mei Syndrome*, p. 266.

34   The Economist, *Pocket World in Figures*, p. 19, and Peter G. Rowe, 'A Difference of Degree or a Difference in Kind: Hyperdensity in Hong Kong', in *Hong Kong: Defining the Edge*, ed. Elizabeth Mossop and Richard Marshall (Cambridge, MA, 2001), pp. 14–39.

35   The World Bank, *The East-Asian Miracle: Economic Growth and Public Policy* (New York, 1993) p. 173; The World Bank, *World Development Report* (Washington, DC, 1996), pp. 196–7; United Nations Center for Human Settlements, *Cities in a Globalizing World: Global Report on Human Settlements* (London, 2001), p. 18.

36   Wenhui Shan, *Reconfiguration of Urban Communities in a Transitional Era* (Cambridge, MA, 2003), pp. 25–30, and Qiang Li, *About the Investigation of Social Structure* (Beijing, 1996), p. 29.

37   Roger Simmonds and Gary Hack, *Global City Regions: The Emerging Forms* (London, 2000), p. 21; Robinson and Goodman, *The New Rich in Asia*, pp. 17, 161, 182, 206 and 223; and 'A Reality Check on the American Dream', *Financial Times*, 6 September 2001, p. 5.

38   Patrick Smith, *Japan: A Reinterpretation* (New York, 1998), pp. 24–5 and 255.

39   The Economist, *Pocket World in Figures*, p. 29.

40   Peter D. Rogers, Kazi F. Jalal, Bindu N. Lohani, et al., *Measuring Environment Quality in Asia* (Cambridge, MA, 1997), pp. 76–82.

41   The Economist, *Pocket World in Figures*, p. 98.

42   X. Chen and Y. Zong, 'Major Impacts of Sea Level Rise on Agriculture in the Yangtze Delta Area around Shanghai', *Applied Geography*, XIX (1999), p. 32.

43   Duncan McCargo, *Contemporary Japan* (New York, 2000), pp. 145–6, and Theodore C. Bestor, *Neighborhood Tokyo* (New York, 1989), pp. 46–81.

44   McCargo, *Contemporary Japan*, pp. 69–70, and Smith, *Japan*, pp. 264–80.

45   T. R. Reid, *Confucius Lives Next Door: What Living in the East Teaches Us About Living in the West* (New York, 1999), and Alex Kerr, *Dogs and Demons: Tales from the Dark Side of Japan* (New York, 2001).

46   Kim and Choe, *Seoul*, pp. 99–150, and Kun-Hyuck Ahn and Yeong-Te Ohn, *Recent Urbanization in South Korea and its Policy Responses* (Seoul, 1997), pp. 8–9.

47   Jinnai Hidenobu, *Tokyo: A Spatial Anthropology* (Los Angeles, 1995).

48   J. Blain Bonham, Jr, Gerri Spilka and Darl Rastorfer, *Old Cities–Green Cities: Communities Transform Unmanaged Land* (Washington, DC, 2002), pp. 4–5.

49   Yuichi Takeuchi, 'The Tokyo Region', in *Global City Regions*, ed. Simmonds and Hack, pp. 153–9.

50   Norton Ginsburg, Bruce Koppel and T. G. McGee, eds, *The Extended Metropolis: Settlement Transition in Asia* (Honolulu, 1991), pp. 3–27.

51   Radelet, Sachs and Lee, 'Economic Growth in Asia', pp. 58–9.

52   The Economist, 'The Weakest Link: A Survey of Asian Finance', *The Economist*, 8 February 2003, p. 17, and Radelet, Sachs and Lee, 'Economic Growth in Asia', p. 45.

53   Personal communication with Keimi Harada, Mayor of Minato-ku, March 2002.

54   Paul Krugman, 'The Myth of Asia's Miracle', *Foreign Affairs*, LXXIII (December 1994), pp. 62–78.

55   Weidong Ma, 'A Comparison of Major Social and Economic Indicators between Beijing

and Shanghai, 2002', *Architecture and Urbanism*, XII (2003), p. 17.
56 The Economist, 'Cost of Living Index', *The Economist*, 9 August 2003, p. 82; the Economist, *Pocket World in Figures*, pp. 22–3.
57 Rogers, Jalal and Lohani, *Measuring Environmental Quality*, pp. 83–102.
58 Mori, *Urban New Deal Policy*, p. 3.

three Outside Influences and Urban Patterns

1 Richard L. Bernstein, *The Restructuring of Social and Political Theory* (New York, 1976), pp. 5–15.
2 Wong Lin Ken, 'The Strategic Significance of Singapore in Modern History', in *A History of Singapore*, ed. Ernest C. T. Chew and Edwin Lee (London, 1991), pp. 18–31.
3 Nicholas Tarling, *Imperial Britain in South-East Asia* (Kuala Lumpur, 1975), pp. 7–30.
4 Martin Perry, Lily Kong and Brenda Yeoh, *Singapore: A Developmental City State* (New York, 1997), pp. 25–30.
5 Arthur Lim Joo-Jock, 'Geographical Setting', in *A History of Singapore*, ed. Chew and Lee, pp. 3–14.
6 Frank Welsh, A *History of Hong Kong* (London, 1993), pp. 101–31.
7 Welsh, *A History of Hong Kong*, p. 1.
8 Linda Cooke Johnson, *Shanghai: From Market Town to Treaty Port, 1074–1858* (Stanford, CA, 1995), pp. 184–5.
9 F. L. Hawks Pott, *A Short History of Shanghai* (Shanghai, 1928), pp. 10–41.
10 Johnson, *Shanghai*, pp. 78–83, and Jen Yuwen, *The Taiping Revolutionary Movement* (New Haven, CT, 1973), pp. 153–60.
11 Milton W. Meyer, *Japan: A Concise History* (Lanham, MD, 1993), p. 121.
12 Meyer, *Japan*, pp. 97–105, and Richard Storry, *A History of Modern Japan* (London, 1982), pp. 70–93.
13 Edward Seidensticker, *Low City, High City: Tokyo from Edo to the Earthquake* (Cambridge, MA, 1991), pp. 25–89.
14 Roman Cybriwsky, *Tokyo* (London, 1991), pp. 54–7.
15 H. D. Smith, 'Tokyo and London: Comparative Conceptions of the City', in *Japan: A Comparative View*, ed. A. M. Craig (Princeton, NJ, 1979), p. 51.
16 Bruce Cummings, *Korea's Place in the Sun: A Modern History* (New York, 1997), pp. 86–138.
17 Murray A. Rubinstein, *Taiwan: A New History* (Armonk, 1999), pp. 209–12.
18 Roger Mark Selya, *Taipei* (New York, 1995), pp. 19–22, and C.-S. Chen, *The City of Taipei* (Taipei, 1956).
19 Joochul Kim and Sang-Chuel Choe, *Seoul: The Making of a Metropolis* (New York, 1997), p. 9.
20 Kim and Choe, *Seoul*, pp. 7–8, and Jong-Soon Yoon, *Seoul* (Seoul, 1999), pp. 52–106.
21 Peter G. Rowe and Seng Kuan, *Architectural Encounters with Essence and Form in Modern China* (Cambridge, MA, 2002), pp. 2–22.
22 Madeleine Yue Dong, 'Defining Beiping under Reconstruction and National Identity, 1928–1936', in *Remaking the Chinese City: Modernity and National Identity, 1900–1950*, ed. Joseph W. Esherick (Honolulu, 2000), pp. 121–38.
23 Nancy Shatzman Steinhardt, *Chinese Imperial City Planning* (Honolulu, 1990), pp. 20–26, and Victor F. S. Sit, *Beijing: The Nature and Planning of a Chinese Capital City* (New York, 1995), pp. 54–81.

24 Perry, Kong and Yeoh, *Singapore*, p. 43.
25 G. B. Endacott, *A History of Hong Kong* (New York, 1964), pp. 243–59; Jan Morris, *Hong Kong* (London, 1997), p. 139, and Welsh, *A History of Hong Kong*, pp. 313–45.
26 Pott, *A Short History of Shanghai*, pp. 109–17.
27 Dong, 'Defining Beiping', p. 127.
28 Seidensticker, *Low City, High City*, pp. 59–73.
29 Cybriwsky, *Tokyo*, p. 74.
30 Yun-Ming Chuang, *Taipei Lao Cheh* (Taipei, 1991), p. 7; Yu-Yuan Hwang, *Taipei Shih Fa Chan Shih* (Taipei, 1983), pp. 10–25; and Selya, *Taipei*, pp. 23–4.
31 Storry, *A History of Modern Japan*, p. 123.
32 Pott, *A Short History of Shanghai*, p. 133.
33 Marie-Claire Bergère, *The Golden Age of the Chinese Bourgeoisie, 1911–1937* (New York, 1989), p. 22.
34 Pan Ling, *In Search of Old Shanghai* (Hong Kong, 1982), pp. 31–49.
35 Wong Lin Ken, 'Commercial Growth before the Second World War', in *A History of Singapore*, ed. Chew and Lee, pp. 41–63, and S. H. Saw 'Population Trends in Singapore, 1819–1967', *Journal of Southeast Asian History*, x (1969), pp. 36–49.
36 Welsh, *A History of Hong Kong*, p. 389.
37 Cybriwsky, *Tokyo*, p. 81, and Baron Shimpei Goto 'Greater Tokyo Plan for 7,000,000 Population', *Trans-Pacific*, ii/1 (1921), pp. 45–54.
38 Edward Seidensticker, *Tokyo Rising: The City since the Great Earthquake* (Cambridge, MA, 1991), pp. 3–20, and Kohei Okamoto, 'Suburbanization of Tokyo', in *The Japanese City*, ed. P. P. Karan and Kristin Stapleton (Lexington, KY, 1997), pp. 79–105.
39 Perry, Kong and Yeoh, *Singapore*, p. 43.
40 Dong, 'Defining Beiping', p.122.
41 Pott, *A Short History of Shanghai*, p. 299.
42 Brian Hook, ed., *Shanghai and the Yangtze Delta: A City Reborn* (New York, 1998), pp. 12 and 32; Parks M. Coble, Jr, *The Shanghai Capitalists and the Nationalist Government, 1927–1937* (Cambridge, MA, 1980), pp. 29–52, and John King Fairbank, *China: A New History* (Cambridge, MA, 1992), p. 288.
43 Rowe and Kuan, *Architectural Encounters*, pp. 72–4.
44 Pott, *A Short History of Shanghai*, pp. 286–7.
45 Welsh, *A History of Hong Kong*, pp. 335–6.
46 Seidensticker, *Tokyo Rising*, pp. 10–12.
47 Rowe and Kuan, *Architectural Encounters*, pp. 4–8.
48 Fairbank, *China*, p. 217.
49 Sun Yat-sen, 'The Three Stages of Revolution', in *Sources of Chinese Tradition*, vol. 2, ed. William Theodore de Bary, Wing-tsit Chan and Chester Tan (New York, 1964), p. 119.
50 Chiang Kai-shek, *Outline the New Life Movement* (Nanjing, 1934), pp. 1–3.
51 Storry, *A History of Modern Japan*, pp. 182–213.
52 Welsh, *A History of Hong Kong*, pp. 405–40, and Eunice Thio, 'The Syonan Years, 1942–1945', in *A History of Singapore*, ed. Chew and Lee, pp. 95–114.
53 G. Daniels, 'The Great Tokyo Air Raid, 9–10 March 1945', in *Modern Japan: Aspects of History, Literature and Society*, ed. W. G. Beasley (Los Angeles, 1975), pp. 113–31.
54 Manuel Castells, Lee Goh and Ri Yin-Wang Kwok, *The Shek Kip Mei Syndrome: Economic Development and Public Housing in Hong Kong and Singapore* (London, 1990), p. 225.
55 Castells, Goh and Kwok, *The Shek Kip Mei Syndrome*, pp. 15–18.

56 Ezra F. Vogel, *The Four Little Dragons: The Spread of Industrialization in East Asia* (Cambridge, MA, 1991), p. 17.

57 Kim and Choe, *Seoul*, p. 10.

58 Cybriwsky, *Tokyo*, pp. 93–7.

59 Chan Heng Hee, 'Political Developments, 1965–1979', in *A History of Singapore*, ed. Chew and Lee, pp. 157–9.

60 Lee Kuan Yew, *The Singapore Story* (Singapore, 1998), pp. 290–95.

61 Castells, Goh and Kwok, *The Shek Kip Mei Syndrome*, p. 232.

62 Robert F. Ash and Luo Qi, 'Economic Development', in *Shanghai*, ed. Hook, pp. 165–73.

63 China Architecture and Building Press, *Shanghai Lujaizui* (Shanghai, 1999), vols I–V.

64 Gao Shangquan and Chi Fulin, *Several Issues Arising during the Retracking of the Chinese Economy* (Beijing, 1997), pp. 1–61.

65 Personal observation, February 1997; Wu Liangyong, Wu Weijia and Liu Jian, *Recent Urbanization in China* (Beijing, 1997), p. 56, and Godfrey Linge, *China's New Spatial Economy: Heading towards 2020* (New York, 1997), pp. 24–45.

66 Wu, Wu and Liu, *Recent Urbanization in China*, p. 33.

67 Welsh, *A History of Hong Kong*, pp. 474–7.

68 James Hayes, *Tsuen Wan: Growth of a New Town and its People* (Hong Kong, 1993); George Pryor and Shin-hung Pau, 'The Growth of the City: A Historical Review', in *Hong Kong: The Aesthetics of Density*, ed. Vittorio Magnago Lampugnani (Munich, 1993), pp. 111–16.

69 William H. Overholt, *China: The Next Economic Superpower* (London, 1993), pp. 118–64.

70 Patrick Smith, *Japan: A Reinterpretation* (New York, 1997), pp. 3–36.

71 Duncan McCargo, *Contemporary Japan* (New York, 2000), p. 35; Smith, *Japan*, p. 11, and David J. Lu, *Japan: A Documentary History* (Armonk, 1997), pp. 509–12.

72 Smith, *Japan*, p. 12, and Lu, *Japan*, p. 506.

73 Hiromichi Ishizuka and Yorifusa Ishida, *Tokyo: Urban Growth and Planning, 1868–1988* (Tokyo, 1988), p. 56, and Tokyo Metropolitan Government, *A Hundred Years of Tokyo City Planning* (Tokyo, 1994), p. 48.

74 Ishizuka and Ishida, *Tokyo*, p. 59; Tokyo Metropolitan Government, *A Hundred Years*, p. 56, and Masanori Kobayashi, *Alternative Models for Planning a Metropolitan Region: Challenges for the Tokyo Metropolitan Region* (Cambridge, MA, 2001), pp. 14–21.

75 Ishizuka and Ishida, *Tokyo*, p. 63, and Kobayashi, *Alternative Models*, pp. 21–9.

76 David L. Callies, 'Urban Land Use and Control in the Japanese City', in *The Japanese City*, ed. Karan and Stapleton, p. 137, and Ishizuka and Ishida, *Tokyo*, p. 64.

77 Minoru Mori, *Urban New Deal Policy: Striving to Recover from the Largest Crisis of the Post-War Era* (Tokyo, 1999), pp. 1–2.

78 Heijin Kwak, *A Turning Point in Korea's Modern Urbanization* (Cambridge, MA, 2002), p. 95.

79 Kim and Choe, *Seoul*, pp. 115–17.

80 Thomas A. Reiner and Robert H. Wilson, 'Planning and Decision-Making in the Soviet City: Rent, Land and Urban Form', in *The Socialist City: Spatial Structure and Urban Policy*, ed. Ian Hamilton and Tony French (New York, 1979), pp. 57–68.

81 Castells, Goh and Kwok, *The Shek Kip Mei Syndrome*, p. 216.

82 Perry, Kong and Yeoh, *Singapore*, pp. 196–8.

83 Urban Redevelopment Authority, *Living the Next Lap* (Singapore, 1991), pp. 14–19.

84 Based on Castells, Goh and Kwok, *The Shek Kip Mei Syndrome*, p. 2, and data from the Department of Census and Statistics, *Hong Kong Annual Digest of Statistics* (Hong Kong, 1995), p. 25.

85 James R. Richardson and Jeffrey W. Cody, 'Sha Tin New Town, 1975–1997', in 'Dossier Hong Kong', ed. Irene Lee, *Spazio Societá*, 79 (1997), pp. 97–9.

86 Kim and Choe, *Seoul*, pp. 155–7.

87 Hyung Min Pai, 'Modernism, Development and the "Transformation" of Seoul: A Study of Sewoon Sangga and Yoido', in *Culture and the City in East Asia*, ed. Kim Won Bue (New York, 1997), p. 55, and Inha Jung, *The Architecture of Kim Soo Geun* (Seoul, 1996).

88 Kun-Hyuck Ahn and Yeong-Te Ohn, *Recent Urbanization in South Korea and Its Policy Responses* (Seoul, 1997), p. 15.

89 Kim and Choe, *Seoul*, pp. 156–8.

90 Ahn and Ohn, *Recent Urbanization in South Korea*, pp. 30–32, and Korea Land Development Corporation, *Bundang New Town* (Seoul, 1992).

91 Ishizuka and Ishida, *Tokyo*, p. 59, and Cybriwski, *Tokyo*, p. 200.

92 Yuichi Takeuchi, 'The Tokyo Region', in *Global City Regions: The Emerging Forms*, ed. Roger Simmonds and Gary Hack (London, 2000), p. 160.

93 Ishizuka and Ishida, *Tokyo*, p. 60.

94 Ishizuka and Ishida, *Tokyo*, p. 62.

95 Cybriwsky, *Tokyo*, pp. 203–6.

96 Tokyo Metropolitan Government, *Vision 2000 Plan: Vitalizing Greater Tokyo* (Tokyo, 2000).

97 Pertinent standards are gathered under circular GBJ 137-90, *Urban Land Use Types and Land-Use Planning Criteria* and circular GB50180-93, *Urban Residential District Planning and Design Regulation*, all under the Urban Planning Law of the People's Republic of China.

98 City of Wuhan, *Wuhan Statistical Yearbook* (Wuhan, 2003), pp. 10–12.

99 Lin Yangchun and Hao Gangyi, *Old Wuhan* (Wuhan, 1999).

100 Peter G. Rowe and Hashim Sarkis, *Yi-Ti-Liang-Yi Zhi Jian: Redevelopment in Suzhou, China* (Cambridge, MA, 1997), pp. 18–42, and Yinong Xu, *The Chinese City in Space and Time: The Development of Urban Form in Suzhou* (Honolulu, 2000), pp. 11–15.

101 Zhu Xiao Di, Huang Lei and Zhang Xinsheng, 'Housing and Economic Development in Suzhou, China: A New Approach To Deal With the Inseparable Issues', *Joint Center for Housing Studies, Harvard University*, Working Paper (2000), pp. 7–17.

102 City of Suzhou, *1996–2010 Masterplan* (Suzhou, 1997).

103 Suzhou Industrial Park Administrative Committees, *Suzhou Industrial Park* (Suzhou, 1997), pp. 10–17.

104 Suzhou New District Administrative Committee, *Suzhou New District* (Suzhou, 1997), pp. 15–16.

105 Personal communication with Suzhou Industrial Park officials, March 1997.

106 T. G. McGee, 'The Emergence of Desakota Regions in Asia: Expanding a Hypothesis', in *The Extended Metropolis: Settlement Transition in Asia*, ed. Norton Ginsburg, Bruce Koppel and T. G. McGee (Honolulu, 1991), pp. 3–26.

107 Peter G. Rowe, Alex Krieger, John Driscoll and Lei Huang, *Urbanization and Urban-Regional Management in North-Eastern Asia* (Cambridge, MA, 1998), pp. 95–105.

108 Peter G. Rowe and Lei Huang, 'Realignments of Urban Development in China', *Harvard China Review*, III/1 (2002), pp. 5–9.

109 For instance, David Harvey, *The Condition of Postmodernity* (London, 1989), pp. 66–98.

1 Chris Luebkeman, 'Pencil Towers', in 'Dossier Hong Kong', ed. Irene Lee, *Spazio Societá*, 79 (1997), pp. 95–7.
2 Discussion with officials of Hong Kong's Town Planning Department, March 2002.
3 Tunney Lee, 'Hong Kong: Hyper-Dense City', in 'Dossier Hong Kong', ed. Lee, p. 91.
4 Edward Seidensticker, *Low City, High City: Tokyo from Edo to the Earthquake* (Cambridge, MA, 1983), p. 11, and S. Longstreet and E. Longstreet, *Yoshiwara: The Pleasure Quarters of Old Tokyo* (Tokyo, 1988).
5 Derived from Jinnai Hidenobu, *Tokyo: A Spatial Anthropology* (Berkeley, CA, 1995), p. 40, 49, 52 and 61, as well as measurement from nineteenth-century maps of Edo–Tokyo.
6 Theodore C. Bestor, *Neighborhood Tokyo* (Tokyo, 1989), p. 13.
7 Hiroto Kobayashi, *Chō: A Persistent Neighborhood Unity Maintaining Microculture in Japanese Cities* (Cambridge, MA, 2003), pp. 21–36.
8 Seidensticker, *Low City, High City*, pp. 59 and 68.
9 Edward Seidensticker, *Tokyo Rising: The City Since the Great Earthquake* (Cambridge, MA, 1991), p. 24.
10 Roman Cybriwsky, *Tokyo* (London, 1991), p. 160.
11 Hidenobu, *Tokyo*, pp. 22–39.
12 T. Gill, 'Sanbancho's Last Stand', *Tokyo Journal*, 11 September 1990, pp. 82–6. Groups under the name *jageya* or, literally, 'land raisers'.
13 Seidensticker, *Low City, High City*, pp. 75–9.
14 Roman Cybriwsky, 'From Castle Town to Manhattan Town', in *The Japanese City*, ed. P. P. Karan and Kristin Stapleton (Lexington, KY, 1997), pp. 66–71.
15 Tokyo Convention and Visitors Bureau, *The Official Guide to Tokyo* (Tokyo, 2001), p. 13.
16 Personal communications, Planning Department of Sumida-ku, October 2001.
17 Seidensticker, *Low City, High City*, pp. 185–251.
18 Roger Mark Selya, *Taipei* (New York, 1995), pp. 19–49.
19 Bingjian Ma, *The Architecture of the Quadrangle in Beijing* (Beijing, 1999).
20 Bing Lu, 'The Lilong of Shanghai', in *The Vast Vanishing Shanghai Lanes*, ed. Mao Xichang (Shanghai, 1996), p. 119.
21 Beijing Municipal Institute of City Planning and Design, *Beijing: Striding Forward to the 21st Century* (Beijing, 1992), p. 13, and Beijing Municipal Planning Commission, *Conservation Planning of 25 Historic Areas in Beijing's Old City* (Beijing, 2002).
22 Gretchen Lin, *Pastel Portraits: Singapore's Architectural Heritage* (Singapore, 1984), pp. 97 and 99–105.
23 Jeannie Meejin Yoon, *Hybrid Cartographies: Seoul's Consuming Spaces* (Seoul, 1998), p. 4.
24 Yoon, *Hybrid Cartographies*, p. 6.
25 Jonathan D. Spence, *To Change China: Western Advisors in China, 1620–1960* (Boston, MA, 1969), pp. 282–3.
26 Jie Zhang and Tao Wong, 'Housing Development in the Socialist Planned Economy from 1949 to 1978', in *Modern Urban Housing in China, 1840–2000*, ed. Junhua Lü, Peter G. Rowe and Jie Zhang (Munich, 2001), pp. 103–70.
27 Peter G. Rowe and Seng Kuan, *Architectural Encounters with Essence and Form in Modern China* (Cambridge, MA, 2002), p. 111.
28 Jie Zhang and Tao Wang, 'Housing Development in the Socialist Planned Economy', p. 117. Also, on Soviet models, see Barry Naughton, 'Cities in the Chinese Economic System:

Changing Roles and Conditions for Autonomy', in *Urban Spaces in Contemporary China*, ed. Barry Naughton (New York, 1993).

29 Peter G. Rowe, 'Housing Density, Type and Urban Life in Contemporary China', *Harvard Design Magazine* (Summer 1999), pp. 40–45.

30 Yuxue Shi, *Housing in Shanghai* (Shanghai, 1998), pp. 81–5.

31 People's Republic of China, *Urban Residential District Planning and Design Regulation*, GB50180-93 (Beijing, 1993).

32 Ebenezer Howard, *Garden Cities of To-Morrow* (London, 1945), p. 42.

33 Jie Zhang and Tao Wang, 'Housing Development in the Socialist Planned Economy', pp. 124–7.

34 Jie Zhang and Tao Wang, 'Housing Development in the Socialist Planned Economy', pp. 180–81.

35 Peter G. Rowe and Yue Wu, *Shan-Shui City: Urban Development in Wenzhou, China* (Cambridge, MA, 2002), pp. 36–42.

36 Manuel Castells, Lee Goh and R. Yin-Wang Kwok, *The Shek Kip Mei Syndrome: Economic Development and Public Housing in Hong Kong and Singapore* (London, 1990), pp. 226–9.

37 Castells, Goh and Kwok, *The Shek Kip Mei Syndrome*, pp. 323–9.

38 B. Y. Sullivan, 'Hong Kong's High Density Housing', in 'Dossier Hong Kong', ed. Lee, p. 108.

39 The Shek Kip Mei Squatter Settlement, in Northern Kowloon, was devastated by fire on Chrismas Eve 1953, see Castells, Goh and Kwok, *The Shek Kip Mei Syndrome*, p. 18. Also Sullivan, 'Hong Kong's High Density Housing', p. 106.

40 Sullivan, 'Hong Kong's High Density Housing', p. 109.

41 D. Drakakis-Smith, *Housing Provision in Metropolitan Hong Kong* (Hong Kong, 1979), p. 52, and Sullivan, 'Hong Kong's High Density Housing', p. 109.

42 Sullivan, 'Hong Kong's High Density Housing', p. 110.

43 Brian Sullivan and K. E. Chen, 'Design for Tenant Fitout: A Critical Review of Public Housing Flat Design in Hong Kong', *Habitat*, 242 (1997), pp. 1–13.

44 Hong Kong Housing Authority, *New Standard Rental Block: The Harmony Series* (Hong Kong, 1989).

45 Hong Kong Housing Authority, *Concord Blocks: Report on Public Consultation on the Concord Block* (Hong Kong, 1988), and Sullivan and Chen, 'Design for Tenant Fitout', pp. 10–11.

46 Peter G. Rowe, 'A Difference of Degree of a Difference in Kind: Hyperdensity in Hong Kong', in *Hong Kong: Defining the Edge*, ed. Elizabeth Mossop and Richard Marshall (Cambridge, MA, 2001), p. 30.

47 Rowe, 'A Difference of Degree', p. 32.

48 Ken Tadashi Oshima, 'Denenchōfu: Building the Garden City in Japan', *Journal of the Society of Architectural Historians*, LV/2 (1996), p. 141.

49 Oshima, 'Denenchōfu', p. 142.

50 Oshima, 'Denenchōfu', p. 143.

51 Hiroto Kobayashi, *Chō*, p. 38.

52 Arata Isozaki, 'Ma: Japanese Space-Time', in *Ma*, ed. Musée des Arts Décoratifs (Paris, 1978), and Fred and Babro Thompson, 'Unity of Time and Space', *Ma* (Helsinki, 1981), pp. 68–70.

53 Xiaowei Luo, 'Shanghai Longtang, Shanghai People and Shanghai Culture', in *Shanghai Longtang*, ed. Zhende Zhou (Shanghai, 1997), pp. 2–18; Mao Xichang, ed., *The Vast Vanishing Shanghai Lanes* (Shanghai, 1996), and Shouyi Zhang and Ying Tan, 'Early Development of Urban Housing in the Semifeudal and Semicolonial Period from 1840 to

1949', in *Modern Urban Housing in China*, ed. Junhua, Rowe and Zhang, pp. 41–7. Also, the terms *nong, nontang* and *longtang* are mainly used in Shanghai, as different expressions of 'lane' or 'alley', instead of *xiang* in Southern China and *hutong* in the north.

54 Mao, *The Vast Vanishing Lanes*, p. 123, and Zhang and Tan, 'Early Development of Urban Housing', p. 64.

55 Zhang and Tan, 'Early Development of Urban Housing', pp. 64–72.

56 Victor F. S. Sit, *Beijing: The Nature and Planning of a Chinese Capital City* (New York, 1995), pp. 265–6.

57 Joochul Kim and Sang-Chuel Choe, *Seoul: The Making of a Metropolis* (New York, 1997), pp. 191 and 211–12.

58 Rowe, 'Housing Density', pp. 32–5.

59 See, for instance, Lynn Pan, *Shanghai: A Century of Change in Photographs, 1843–1949* (Hong Kong, 1994), and Pan Junxiang, *The Vicissitudes of Shanghai Folk Style and Features* (Shanghai, 1998).

60 William T. Rowe, *Hankow: Commerce and Society in a Chinese City, 1796–1839* (Stanford, CA, 1984), pp. 69 and 75; Yoon, *Hybrid Cartographies*, pp. 5–6, and Bruce Cummings, *Korea's Place in the Sun: A Modern History* (New York, 1997), p. 81.

61 Alan Balfour and Zheng Shiling, eds, *World Cities: Shanghai* (New York, 2002), pp. 156–7.

62 Seidensticker, *Low City, High City*, pp. 158–9 and 207–8.

63 Peter G. Rowe and Seng Kuan, *Architectural Encounters with Essence and Form in Modern China* (Cambridge, MA, 2002), pp. 161–99.

64 Personal communication with the Urban Redevelopment Authority of Singapore, March 1996.

65 Rowe and Kuan, *Architectural Encounters*, pp. 87–106.

66 Rowe and Kuan, *Architectural Encounters*, pp. 171–5.

67 Joshua A. Fishman, Robert L. Cooper and Andrew W. Conrad, *The Spread of English: The Sociology of English as an Additional Language* (Rowley, MA, 1977), p. 89.

68 Christina Cheng Min Bing, 'Resurgent Chinese Power in Postmodern Disguise: The New Bank of China Buildings in Hong Kong and Macan', in *Hong Kong: An Anthropology of a Chinese Metropolis*, ed. Grant Evans and Maria Tam Sin-Mi (Richmond, Surrey, 1997), pp. 102–23.

69 Peter G. Rowe, *L'Asia e il Moderno: le città asiatiche* (Ancona, 1998), pp. 49–52.

70 Fumihiko Maki, 'Japanese City Spaces and the Concept of *Oku*', *Japan Architect*, V (1979), pp. 51–63.

71 Momoyo Kaijima, Junzo Kuroda and Yoshihara Tsukamoto, *Made in Tokyo* (Tokyo, 2001), and Tokyo Institute of Technology Tsukamoto Architectural Lab and Atelier Bow-wow, *Pet Architecture* (Tokyo, 2000).

five Urban Experience and Shaping the Space of a Time

1 Roshi Philip Kapleau, *The Three Pillars of Zen* (New York, 1989), pp. 307–11.

2 For instance, as explored in Richard L. Bernstein, *Beyond Objectivism and Relativism: Science, Hermeneutics and Praxis* (Philadelphia, PA, 1983) and as expressed by H. W. Helfrich, Jr, ed., *The Environmental Crisis: Man's Struggle to Live with Himself* (New Haven, CT, 1970).

3 David Harvey, *The Condition of Post-modernity* (London, 1989), pp. 141–72.

4 Myron Orfied, *American Metropolitics: The New Suburban Reality* (Washington, DC, 2002), pp. 85–110 and 174. See also, Alan Altshuler, William Morrill, Harold Wolman and Faith

Mitchell, eds, *Governance and Opportunity in Metropolitan America* (Washington, DC, 1999).

5   Richard Sennett, *Respect* (New York, 2003).

6   Philippe Legrain, *Open World: The Truth About Globalization* (London, 2002), p. 140.

7   Saskia Sassen, *The Global City: New York, London and Tokyo* (Princeton, NJ, 1991), pp. 168–9.

8   Michael Hardt and Antonio Negri, *Empire* (Cambridge, MA, 2000), pp. 93–113 and 183–204.

9   Beng-Huat Chua, *Communitarian Ideology and Democracy in Singapore* (New York, 1995), pp. 17–20, and Ezra F. Vogel, *The Four Little Dragons: The Spread of Industrialization in East Asia* (Cambridge, MA, 1991), pp. 38–41.

10   Xudong Zhang, *Chinese Modernism in the Era of Reforms: Culture Fever, Avant-Garde Fiction and the New Chinese Cinema* (Durham, NC, 1997), pp. 37–68.

11   Based on terminology from Gilles Deleuze and Felix Guattari, *A Thousand Plateaus: Capitalism and Schizophrenia* (London, 1987), pp. 508–10.

12   Empirical data from comparative study were drawn from land area and population data for the United States, China and Italy, covering the period from 1950 to 2000. Sources were US Census Bureau, *China Statistical Yearbooks* and the Instituto Statistica di Italia.

13   Giancarlo Storto, *Rapporto sulla condizione abitativa in Italia* (Rome, 1996), pp. 157–60.

14   Keith R. Ihlanfeldt, 'The Geography of Economic and Social Opportunity in Metropolitan Areas', in *Governance and Opportunity*, ed. Altshuler, Morrill, Wolman and Mitchell, pp. 230–33.

15   Roger Simmonds and Gary Hack, eds, *Global City Regions: Their Emerging Forms* (London, 2000), pp. 3–22.

16   Robert M. Fogelson, *The Fragmented Metropolis: Los Angeles, 1850–1930* (Berkeley, CA, 1993), pp. 137–63, and M. Gottdiener and George Kephant, 'The Multinucleated Metropolitan Region: A Comparative Analysis', in *Postmodern California: The Transformation of Orange County since World War II*, ed. Rob Kling, Spencer Olin and Mark Poster (Berkeley, CA, 1991), pp. 31–54.

17   Peter G. Rowe and Roberto Pasini, eds, *Urban Territorialization in Romagna, Italy* (Cambridge, MA, 2004).

18   Peter G. Rowe, *Making a Middle Landscape* (Cambridge, MA, 1991), pp. 67–107.

19   Esther McCoy, ed., *Case Study Houses, 1945–1962* (Los Angeles, 1977).

20   Rowe, *Making a Middle Landscape*, pp. 143–6.

21   Peter G. Rowe and Seng Kuan, *Architectural Encounters with Essence and Form in Modern China* (Cambridge, MA, 2002), pp. 87–106.

22   Ross Terrill, *Mao: A Biography* (Stanford, CA, 1999), pp. 487–8.

23   Terrill, *Mao*, pp. 483–4.

24   The Economist Intelligence Unit, *China Hand* (London, 2004), pp. 9–13, 73–80.

25   Orville Schell, *Mandate of Heaven: A New Generation of Entrepreneurs, Dissidents, Bohemians and Technocrats Lay Claim to China's Future* (New York, 1994).

Bibliography

Abbas, Ackbar, *Hong Kong: Culture and the Politics of Disappearance* (London, 1997)
Adams, Edward Ben, *Palaces of Seoul: Yi Dynasty Palaces in Korea's Capital City* (Seoul, 1985)
Ashihara, Yoshinobu, *The Aesthetic Townscape* (Cambridge, MA, 1983)
—, *The Hidden Order: Tokyo Through the Twentieth Century* (New York, 1992)
Arlington, L.C., and W. Lewisohn, *In Search of Old Peking* (Hong Kong, 1987)
Balfour, Alan and Shiling Zheng, *Shanghai* (London, 2002)
Barclay, George W., *Colonial Development and Population in Taiwan* (Princeton, NJ, 1954)
Beamish, Jane, *A History of Singapore Architecture: The Making of a City* (Singapore, 1985)
Bergère, Marie-Claire, *The Golden Age of the Chinese Bourgeoisie, 1911–37* (New York, 1989)
Bestor, Theodore C., *Neighborhood Tokyo* (Tokyo, 1989)
Boyd, Andrew, *Chinese Architecture and Town Planning, 1500 BC – AD 1911* (Chicago, 1962.
Breen, Michael, *The Koreans* (London, 1998)
Brook, Timothy, and B. Michael Frolic, eds, *Civil Society in China* (Armonk, NJ, 1997)
Bristow, M. Roger, *Hong Kong's New Towns: A Selective Review* (New York, 1989)
Buruma, Ian, *A Japanese Mirror: Heroes and Villains in Japanese Culture* (London, 1984)
—, *Inventing Japan: 1853–1964* (New York, 2003)
Cameron, Nigel and Brian Blake, *Peking: A Tale of Three Cities* (New York, 1965)
—, *Hong Kong: The Cultured Pearl* (New York, 1978)
Castells, Manuel, L. Goh and R. Y-W. Kwok, *The Shek Kip Mei Syndrome: Economic Development and Public Housing in Hong Kong and Singapore* (London, 1990)
Chan, Kam Wing, *Cities With Invisible Walls: Reinterpreting Urbanization in Post-1949 China* (Hong Kong, 1994)
Chance, Norman A., *China's Urban Villagers: Changing Life in A Beijing Suburb* (Fort Worth, TX, 1991)
Chen, Cheng-siang, *The City of Taipei* (Taipei, 1956)
Cheung, Peter T.Y., Jae Ho Chung and Zhimin Lin, eds, *Provincial Strategies of Economic Reform in Post-Mao China* (London, 1998)
Chew, Ernest C.T. and Edwin Lee, eds., *A History of Singapore* (New York, 1991)
Chew, Sock Foon, *Ethnicity and Nationality in Singapore* (Athens, OH, 1987)
Ching, Frank, ed., *China in Transition: Towards the New Millennium* (Hong Kong, 1997)
Chiu, T.N., and C.L. So, eds, *A Geography of Hong Kong* (Hong Kong, 1983)
Christianson, Flemming, and Junzuo Zhang, eds, *Village Inc.: Chinese Rural Society in the 1990s* (Honolulu, HI, 1998)

Chua, Beng-Huat, *Communitarian Ideology and Democracy in Singapore* (London, 1995)

Clark, Allen D., and Donald N. Clark, *Seoul: Past and Present* (Seoul, 1969)

Clifford, Mark L., *Troubled Tiger* (Armonk, NY, 1994)

Cody, Jeffrey W., *Building in China: Henry K. Murphy's 'Adaptive Architecture,' 1914–1935* (Seattle, WA, 2001)

Cummings, Bruce, *Korea's Place in the Sun: A Modern History* (New York, 1997)

Cybriwsky, Roman A., *Tokyo: The Changing Profile of an Urban Giant* (London, 1991)

Davidson, Cynthia C., ed., *Anywise* (Cambridge, MA, 1996)

Davis, Deborah, and Stevan Harrell, eds, *Chinese Families in the Post-Mao Era* (Berkeley, CA, 1993)

— and Richard Kraus, eds, *Urban Spaces in Contemporary China: The Potential for Autonomy and Community in Post-Mao China* (New York, 1995)

Drakakis-Smith, D. W., *High Society: Housing Provision in Metropolitan Hong Kong, 1954–79* (Hong Kong, 1979)

—, *Urbanization, Housing and the Development Process* (New York, 1980)

Dutton, Michael, ed., *Street Life in China* (New York, 1998)

Edwards, Norman, *The Singapore House and Residential Life, 1819–1939* (New York, 1990)

Elvin, Mark, and G. William Skinner, eds, *The Chinese City Between Two Worlds* (Stanford, CA, 1974)

Endacott, G. B., *A History of Hong Kong* (New York, 1964)

Esherick, Joseph W., ed., *Remaking the Chinese City: Modernity and National Identity, 1900–50* (Honolulu, HI, 2000)

Fairbank, John King, *China: A New History* (Cambridge, MA, 1992)

Grasso, June, Jay Corria and Michael Kort, *Modernization and Revolution in China* (Armonk, NY, 1997)

Huang, Ray, *China: A Macro History* (Armonk, NY, 1997)

Ikels, Charlotte, *The Return of the God of Wealth: The Transition to a Market Economy in Urban China* (Stanford, CA 1996)

Johnson, Linda Cooke, *Shanghai: From Market Town to Treaty Port, 1074–1858* (Stanford, CA, 1995)

Ka, Chih-ming, *Japanese Colonialism in Taiwan: Land Tenure, Development and Dependency, 1895–1945* (Boulder, CO, 1995)

Karan, P. P., and Kristin Stapleton, eds, *The Japanese City* (Lexington, MA, 1997)

Kent, Ann, *Between Freedom and Subsistence: China and Human Rights* (New York, 1993)

Kerr, Alex, *Dogs and Demons* (New York, 2001)

Khoo, Joo Ee, *The Straits Chinese: A Cultural History* (Amsterdam, 1996)

Kim, Chewon, *Seoul* (Tokyo, 1969)

Kim, Joochul, and Sang-Chuel Choe, *Seoul* (New York, 1996)

Kim, Won Bae, Mike Douglas, Sang-Chuel and Kong Chong Ho, eds, *Culture and the City in East Asia* (New York, 1997)

Klintworth, Gary, *New Taiwan, New China: Taiwan's Changing Role in the Asian-Pacific Region* (New York, 1995)

Knapp, Ronald G., *China's Living Houses: Folk Beliefs, Symbols and Household Ornamentation* (Honolulu, HI, 1999)

Kuan, Seng and Peter G. Rowe, eds, *Shanghai: Architecture and Urbanism for Modern China* (Munich, 2004)

Kyong-hee, Lee, *Korean Culture: Legacies and Lore* (Seoul, 1994)

Lampugnani, Vittorio Magnago, ed., *Hong Kong Architecture: Aesthetics of Density* (Munich, 1993)

Lee, Leo Ou-Jan, *Shanghai Modern: The Flowering of a New Urban Culture in China, 1930–45* (Cambridge, MA, 1999)

Lee, Yok-shiu F., and Alvin Y. So, eds, *Asia's Environmental Movements: Comparative Perspectives* (London, 1999)

Legrain, Phillippe, *Open World: The Truth About Globalization* (London, 2002)

Lin, Lee Kim, *The Singapore House: 1819–1942* (Singapore, 1995)

Lin, Zhiling, and Thomas W. Robinson, eds, *The Chinese and Their Future: Beijing, Taipei and Hong Kong* (Washington, DC, 1996)

Ling, Pan, *In Search of Old Shanghai* (Hong Kong, 1992)

Linge, Godfrey, ed., *China's New Spatial Economy: Heading Towards 2020* (New York, 1997)

Lu, Hanchao, *Beyond the Neon Lights: Everyday Shanghai in the Early Twentieth Century* (Berkeley, CA, 1999)

Lu, David J., *Japan: A Documentary History* (London, 1997)

Lü, Junhua, Peter G. Rowe and Zhang Jie, eds, *Modern Urban Housing in China: 1840–2000* (Munich, 2001)

Lü, Xiaobo, and Elizabeth J. Perry, eds, *Danwei: The Changing Chinese Workplace in Historical and Comparative Perspective* (London, 1997)

Ma, Lawrence J. C., and Edward W. Hanteu, *Urban Development in Modern China* (Boulder, CO, 1981)

Malaysian Branch of the Royal Asiatic Society, *Singapore: 150 Years* (Singapore, 1982)

Marsh, Robert, *The Great Transformation: Social Change in Taipei, Taiwan Since the 1960s* (Armonk, NY, 1996)

McCargo, Duncan, *Contemporary Japan* (New York, 2000)

Min, Kyong-Hyun, *Korean Gardens* (Seoul, 1992)

Morris, Jan, *Hong Kong* (New York, 1989)

Murray, Geoffrey, and Audrey Perera, *Singapore: The Global City State* (New York, 1996)

Nakane, Chie, *Japanese Society* (Berkeley, CA, 1970)

Nouet, Noel, *The Shogun's City: A History of Tokyo* (Folkestone, 1990)

Overholt, William H., *China: The Next Economic Superpower* (London, 1993)

—, *The Rise of China: How Economic Reform is Creating a New Superpower* (New York, 1993)

Patten, Christopher, *East and West* (New York, 1998)

Perry Martin, Lily Kong and Brenda Yeoh, *Singapore: A Developmental City State* (New York, 1997)

Phillips, David R., and Anthony G. O. Yeh, *New Towns in South-East Asia: Planning and Development* (Hong Kong, 1987)

Popham, Peter, *Tokyo: The City at the End of the World* (New York, 1985)

Pott, F. L. Hawks, *A Short History of Shanghai* (Hong Kong, 1928)

Qi, Fang, and Jiran Qi, *Old Peking: The City and Its People* (Hong Kong, 1993)

Rafferty, Kevin, *City on the Rocks: Hong Kong's Uncertain Future* (London, 1989)

Reid, T.R., *Confucius Lives Next Door: What Living in the East Teaches Us About Living in the West* (New York, 1999)

Rho, Yung Hee, and Myong Chan Hwang, *Metropolitan Planning: Issues and Policies* (Seoul, 1979)

Robinson, Richard and David S. G. Goodman, eds, *The New Rich in Asia: Mobile Phones, McDonalds and Middle-Class Revolution* (New York, 1996)

Rogers, Peter, ed., *Measuring environmental Quality in Asia* (Cambridge, MA, 1997)

Rowe, Peter, and Seng Kuan, *Architectural Encounters With Essence and Form in Modern China* (Cambridge, MA, 2002)

Rubinstein, Murray A., ed., *The Other Taiwan: 1945 to the Present* (London, 1994)
—, *Taiwan: A New History* (London, 1999)
Sassen, Saskia, *The Global City: New York, London, Tokyo* (Princeton, NJ, 1991)
Schell, Orville, *Mandate of Heaven* (New York, 1994)
Schoenhals, Michael, ed., *China's Cultural Revolution: Not a Dinner Party* (Armonk, NY, 1996)
Seidensticker, Edward, *Low City, High City: Tokyo from Edo to the Earthquake* (New York, 1983)
—, *Tokyo Rising: The City Since the Great Earthquake* (Cambridge, MA, 1991)
Selya, Roger Mark, *Taipei* (New York, 1995)
Sergeant, Harriet, *Shanghai* (London, 1991)
Sit, Victor F.S., ed., *Chinese Cities: The Growth of the Metropolis Since 1949* (New York, 1985)
—, *Beijing: The Nature and Planning of a Chinese Capital City* (New York, 1995)
Simmonds, Roger, and Gary Hack, eds, *Global City Regions: Their Emerging Forms* (London, 2000)
Simon, Denis Fred, ed., *The Emerging Technological Trajectory of the Pacific Rim* (Armonk, NY, 1995)
Smil, Vaclav, *China's Environmental Crisis: An Inquiry into the Limits of National Development* (Armonk, NY, 1993)
Smith, Patrick, *Japan: A Reinterpretation* (New York, 1998)
Spence, Jonathan D., *The Search for Modern China* (New York, 1990)
Steinhardt, Nancy Shatzman, *Chinese Imperial Planning* (Honolulu, 1990)
Storry, Richard, *A History of Modern Japan* (London, 1982)
Tan, S.H., *Singapore Chinese* (Petaling, Jaya, 1985)
Tamney, Joseph B., *The Struggle Over Singapore's Soul: Western Modernization and Asian Culture* (New York, 1996)
Terrill, Ross, *Mao: A Biography* (Stanford, CA, 1999)
Tokyo Metropolitan Government, *A Hundred Years of Tokyo City Planning* (Tokyo, 1994)
Turnbull, Constance Mary, *A History of Singapore: 1819–1988* (New York, 1989)
United Nations Center for Human Settlements, *Cities in a Globalizing World: Global Report on Human Settlements* (London, 2001)
Vervoorn, Aat, *Re orient: Change in Asian Societies* (New York, 1998)
Vines, Stephen, *Hong Kong: China's New Colony* (London, 1998)
Vogel, Ezra F., *One Step Ahead in China: Guangdong Under Reform* (Cambridge, MA, 1989)
—, *The Four Little Dragons: The Spread of Industrialization in East Asia* (Cambridge, MA, 1991)
Wakeman, Frederic Jr., and Wen Hsiu, eds, *Shanghai Sojourners* (Berkeley, CA, 1992)
Waley, Paul, *Tokyo: City of Stories* (New York, 1991)
Walker, Anthony, *Land Property and Construction in the People's Republic of China* (Hong Kong, 1991)
Welsh, Frank, *A History of Hong Kong* (London, 1993)
Wu, Dingbo and Patrick D. Murphy, eds., *Handbook of Chinese Popular Culture* (Westport, CT, 1994)
Wu, Liangyong, *Rehabilitating the Old City of Beijing* (Vancouver, 1999)
Xu, Yinong, *The Chinese City in Space and Time: The Development of Urban Form in Suzhou* (Honolulu, HI, 2000)
Yahuda, Michael, *The International Politics of the Asia-Pacific, 1945–95* (New York, 1996)
Yatsko, Pamela, *New Shanghai: The Rocky Rebirth of China's Legendary City* (New York, 2001)
Yeung, Yue-man, *Changing Cities of Pacific Asia: A Scholarly Interpretation* (Hong Kong, 1990)

—, and Xu-wei Hu, eds, *China's Coastal Cities: Catalysts for Modernization* (Honolulu, HI, 1992)

—, and Sung Yun-Wing, *Shanghai: Transformation and Modernization Under China's Open Policy* (Hong Kong, 1996)

Yew, Lee Kuan, *The Singapore Story* (New York, 1998)

Zha, Jianying, *China Pop* (New York, 1995)

Zhang, Xudong, *Chinese Modernism in the Era of Reforms* (Durham, 1997)

Zhang Yingjin, *The City in Modern Chinese Literature and Film: Configurations of Space, Time and Gender* (Stanford, CA, 1996)

Zheng, Shiling, ed., *The Evolution of Shanghai Architecture in Modern Times* (Shanghai, 1999)

Zhu, Jainfei, *Chinese Spatial Strategies: Imperial Beijing 1420–1911* (London, 2004)

Acknowledgements

Knowledge of East Asian urbanization, at least for me, required patient and prolonged orientation. Luckily, I had many willing guides and mentors. To the following, I owe considerable gratitude for their forbearance, instruction and special knowledge of their cities: Teo Ah-Khing, Kun-Hyuck Ahn, the late Yoshinobu Ashihara, Shigeru Ban, Nelson Chen, Feng Shao, Huang Yan, Mikiko Ishikawa, Michael Koh, Tunney Lee, David Lie, Lü Jinhua, Ronald Lu, Fumihiko Maki, Sohn-Joo Minn, Milton Tan, Tan Ying, Yoshio Taniguchi, Paul and C. F. Tao, Sidney Ting, Wu Jiang, Wu Liangyong, Andrew Yang, Yang Weifang, Zhang Jinqiu and Zheng Shiling. Others were also involved in my education, including Zhang Xinsheng and Wu Xidi, now in their ministerial positions, and three fine mayors: Keimi Harada, Li Xiansheng and Qian Xinzhong. Very particular graduate students, at Harvard, also come to mind in these regards, including Cheng Yan, Sandy Chung, Huang Lei, Heui-Jeong Kwak, Hiroto Kobayashi, Hiroshe Koike, Shan Wenhui, Shen Yahong, Zhao Liang and Zhu Bing. Throughout, I have shared a special bond with Masami Kobayashi, Seng Kuan, Wang Bing, Wu Yue and Zhang Jie. They have kept me from coming completely off the rails, at least some of the time, and to all five I owe an enormous debt of gratitude. Close to home, I have also had the benefit of advice and encouragement from several colleagues including Toshiko Mori, Alex Krieger and Richard Marshall. Finally, in the important technical realm of things, I would like to express my appreciation to Michael Sweeney and to Maria Moran, my most valued assistant in so many ways.

Photo Acknowledgements

The author and publishers wish to express their thanks to the following sources of illustrative material and/or permission to reproduce it:

Photos by the author: 2, 4, 6, 10, 11, 13, 14, 16, 18, 19, 20, 21, 23, 24, 25, 26, 30, 32, 33, 34, 35, 36, 39, 40, 41, 42, 43, 44, 45, 51, 52; from the collection of the author: 9; photo AXYZ: 38; photo Beijing Arts and Photography Publishing House: 46; photo Beijing Municipal Institute of City Planning and Design: 31; photo Deke Erh: 22; computer simulation by Hiroto Kobayashi: 7; photo Housing Development Board, Singapore: 12; photo Lands Department of Hong Kong: 28; photo Mori Building Co., Ltd: 49; photo from city model at the Mori Building Co. Headquarters, Roppongi: 19; photo Planning Commission of Beijing: 8; photo Guido Alberto Rossi: 5; photo L. G. Rowe: 27; photo Information Office, Shanghai Municipal People's Government: 48; photos Shanghaishi Yingxiang Ditju: 37, 47; Planning Bureau, City of Suzhou: 17; Tokyo Metropolitan Government: 3, 15, 29; photo Urban Redevelopment authority of Singapore: 1; photo Xu Yugen: 50.

Index

Illustration numbers are indicated by *italics*.

Abercrombie, Patrick 83
Aberdeen 28
Abrams, Charles 79
agriculture 11, 15, 16
Ai Weiwei 141
Ainu 31
Airport Core Program 37
Akamatsu, Kaname 22, 28, 167
Akasaka 58, *19*
Ando, Tadao 136
Andreu, Paul 35, 137, *38*, 139
Ang Mo Kio 79
Anglo-Chinese War 49
Anglo-Dutch Treaty 47
Anju 113
anko-gawa 98, 102
Aoki, Jun 152
architectural education 140
Argentina 16, 26
Arrow War 51
Asakusa 85, 98, 135
Atelier Bow-wow 152
Australia 16, 18, 24, 25

Bank of China Building 35, 146, *41*
Beard, Charles 61
Beijing, 7, 10, 16, 25, 55, *8*, 65, 87, 91, 103, 110, 112, 144, 156, *46*, 183, 194
architectural expressions 137–8, *38*, 144, 188
environmental issues 29, 43
Forbidden City 56, 57
future prospects 196–7
historical underpinnings 55–7
hutongs 103, 106, 124–5, *31*, 126, 141, *39*
modern prefaces 58
open spaces 133, 135
pedestrian environments 135
siheyuan 103, 105, 113, *31*, 125, 126
Beijing Olympic Stadium 139, 188
Beijing Opera House 137, *38*, 188
Beiping 56, 65, 66
Bilbao 190
Bishan 79

Bohai Bay Region 72
Boston 35
Britain 18, 60, 61, 78
Buenos Aires 16, 26
Bund 9, 60, 133
Bundang 82
burakumin 31

Canada 18, 29
Caoyangxincun 111
CCTV complex 137, 188
Century Avenue 134, 137, *37*
Century Park 133, 134, 137, 148, *43*
Century Park Metro Station *44*
chaebols 77, 82
Changjiang Delta 42, 60, 72, 87, 91, 173
Charpentier, Jean-Marie 134, 137, 146, *42*
Chek Lap Kok 7, 35, 97, 139
Chen Hsin-chu 54
Chen Nei 54, 103
Chen Yi, General 66
Chiang Kai-shek 56, 61, 64, 66, 142
China 7, 8, 9, 10, 18, 38, 40, 44, 46, 49, 63, 64, 67, 91, 117, 119, 153, 164, 165, 166, 171, 174, 176, 187, 188
architectural traditionalism 144–8
Cultural Revolution 67, 165, 175, 186, 187
economic factors 19, 21, 27–8, 193
economic reforms 72–4
environmental sustainability 29, 42, 74
further urbanization 91–2
future trajectories 193
Great Leap Forward 22, 165, 175
iron rice bowl compact 28
managing urban growth 43
modern planning, 85–90
political regimes 30, 31
population 24, 25
residential districts 109–13
residential space standards 26
Self-Strengthening Movement 31, 55, 64
treaty ports 50–51, 58, 60, 63, 87
chō 99
chōnaikai 31
Chosun dynasty 54, 55, 126
civil society 12, 31, 38, 93, 192

Club of Rome 160
Constitutional Movement 56
collective consumption 22, 68, 70, 74
collective experience of time 159–70
  East-Asian episodic structures 165–7
  East-Asian underlying cultural matrix 167–8
  effects on East Asian urbanization 168, 169
  experiential differences 169, 170
  Western episodes 159–60, 161–2, 163
  Western urban affairs 160–61, 162–3
Conder, Josiah 58
Confucianism 28
  neo-Confucianism 28, 167, 168
  principles of propriety 57
  traits and values 64, 170, 194
Convention of Beijing 51
Crawfurd, John 47
Cultural norms and values 16, 18, 30, 31, 32, 39, 43, 174, 192, 194
Cultural Revolution 67, 117, 165, 175, 186, 187
Cyberport 42

Da Bei 72
daimyō 52, 58
  estates 98, *19*, 100, 121, 152
Dalian 26, 51, 72, 144
danyuanlou 88, 110, *25*, 111
De Meuron, Pierre 139
Denenchōfu 119–21, *29*
Deng Xiaoping 67, 72, 88, 112, 192
dependency ratios 39, 40
desakota regions 91
Detroit 35
dirigisme 22
Dōgen Kigen 159, 163
Dongdaemun 108
Dong Dayou 62
Doosan Tower 109
Dutch East Indies 47

Earth Day 160
East China Architectural Design Institute 146
East India Company 47
Economic Freedom Index 28
EDAW 133
Edo 34, *7*, 52, 63, 99, 101, 121, 135
Elliot, Captain 49
Emerald Hill 108, *24*
Emilia-Romagna 182
entrepôts 23, 60, 63
environmental sustainability 28–9, 42, 43
export processing zones 22

Farrell, Terry 140
feng shui 54, 146
Finland 29
'flying geese formation' 22, 28, 167
Forbidden City 56, 57, 106, 156
Foreign Office Architects 139
Foster, Norman 134, 136, 139
France 16, 61

Garden City Movement 112, 119
von Gerkan, Marg and Partners 137
Gini Index 27–8
Ginza 99, 100, 130
Ginza Brick Quarter 58, 99
Globalization 8, 16, 162–3
  branding 17
  capital 16
  spatial distinctions 17
Great East Asia Co-prosperity Sphere 65
Greater London Plan 83
Great Leap Forward 22, 165, 175
Gregotti, Vittorio 133
Germany 21, 51, 78, 164
Gross Domestic Product (GDP) 7, 18, 28, 29, 40
  per capita 8, 39
  growth 18–20, 41, 73
Guangdong Province 72, 75, 181
Guangzhou 10, 43, 49, 58, 60, 63, 75
Guomindang 30, 64, 66

Hainan 72, 73
Han River 82
Hanyang 54
Hangzhou 87, 173
Hankou *16*, 87, 135
hanok 125, 126, *32*
hatamoto 52, 121
Herzog, Jacques 139
Hillside Terrace 149–52, *45*
historic preservation 34, 38
Hong Kong 9, 10, 18, 23, 33, 34, 35, 39, 43, 44, 6, 55, 63, 64, 65, 67, 92, 113, 118, 136, 153, 154, 155, 166, 169, 178, 181, 183, 192, *51*, 194
  Airport Core Program 37
  architectural expression 136, 137, *41*
  collective consumption 74
  contemporary labyrinths 126–9, *33*
  Crown colony 30, 51, 66, 164
  density 27, 117–19
  economic factors 19, 21, 28
  environmental sustainability 29
  future prospects 198
  historic underpinnings 49
  Maclehose reforms 67, 74
  modern prefaces 58, 60
  neon environments 129–33
  new towns 75, *14*, 81
  public housing 22, 74, 75, 114–17, *27*, *28*
  residential space standards 26, 114–17
  Special Administrative Region 30, 81, 97
  tall buildings 95–7, *18*
  urban population 24
Hong Kong Cultural Center 134
Hong Kong-Guangdong Joint Venture 75
hottog 124
Houston 126
Howard, Ebenezer 112, 119, 120
Hu Jintao 193
Huang Fu Xiang 133
Huang Hui 35

220

Huangpu River 50, 60, 133
Hubei Province 72
Hundred Days Reform 56
Hung Koo building 146
hutong 56, 103, 106, 124, 125, 155
Hyongsedo cartography 54
hyperdensity 27

Ikebukuro 84, 85, 126, 129
Ikeda's income doubling plan 28, 67, 76, 165
Imperial Diet 52, 58
India 47
Indigenization 8
Indonesia 9, 47
industrialization 11, 42
    export processing zones 22, 23
    import substitution 21
    modernization 13, 15-16, 18
    state involvement 22
    technological developments 22, 24
    urbanization 11, 13–15, 38
Industrial Revolution 18, 45, 58, 60
infrastructure 3, 34, 38, 39, 41
Insadong 125
International Financial Centre 97
Isosaki, Arata 136
Islan 82
Istanbul 16
Italy 50, 164, 174, 182

Jackson, Lieutenant 47, 106
Jamsil 82
Japan 7, 8, 9, 37, 38, 39, 53, 58, 60, 64, 67, 136, 162, 164,
    167, 178
    Dark Valley Decade 65
    economic factors 19, 20, 21, 28
    Edo period 34
        see also Edo
    environmental sustainability 28
    Ikeda's income doubling plan 28, 67, 165
    oyabun-kobon relations 32
    Meiji Restoration 18
        see also Meiji Restoration
    modern developments 75, 76, 77
    political regimes 31
    rule of law 30
    Taishō period 31
        see also Taishō period
    urban population 24–5
    zaibatsu 23, 59, 75
Japan–US Security Treaty 76
Jian Wai SoHo complex 139
Jiang Zemin 192
Jin Mao building 35, 4, 137, 37
Jinqiao Export Processing Zone 72
Joongdong 82
Ju'er Hutong 141, 39
Junk Bay 81
Jurong 7, 22, 2, 69, 89

Kaijima, Momoyo 152
Kales, Frances 10
Kang Youwei 192
Kangman 82
Kansai Airport 37, 139
Kantō earthquake 61, 97, 119, 120
Kasumigaseki Building 84
Keelung 54
keiretsu 22, 75
Keopyong Freya 108
Khubilai Khan 57
Kim Hyun-ok 77
Kim Soo Geun 82
Kobe, Susume 79
Koenigsberger, Otto 79
Koolhaas, Rem 137
Korea (South Korea) 18, 19, 23, 39, 43, 63, 77, 165, 176,
    178, 192
    economic factors 19, 20, 21, 27, 28, 42
    Japanese influence 53, 82
    public housing 22
    urban population 24, 25
Korean Housing Corporation 78
Korean War 19, 67
Kowloon 51, 58, 81, 95, 97, 130, 34, 136
Kowloon Park 133, 149
Kyongbok palace 55, 126
Kyongsong 54

labour 11, 22
    productivity 13
    specialization 11, 13–16, 20–21
Lee, C. Y. 146
Lee Kuan Yew 65, 68
Liang Sicheng 141
Liaodong Peninsular 53
liberal democracy 12, 30, 32, 68, 192
lilong 103, 22, 105, 23, 106, 123–4, 155
Liu Jaikun 141
Lo, Vincent 106
London 11, 25, 26, 162
Lorange, E. E. 79
Los Angeles 181, 182, 185
LUC Company 148, 43
Lujaizui 13, 72, 73
Lyon 16

ma 123, 149
Ma Qingyun 141
Macao 49
Maclehose, Governor 67, 74
Magdok 82
MAGLEV 7
Majapahit empire 49
Maki, Fumihiko 136, 149, 150, 45, 152, 153
Malacca 47
Malacca Straits 47
Malacca Sultanate 49
Malay *kampong* 47
Malay Federation 68
Malay Forum 65

Malay Peninsula 47, 60, 65, 66
Malayan Communist Party 65
Malaysia 9, 68
Manchuria 53, 55, 67
Mao Zedong 110, 142, 143, 175, 192
Marunouchi *15*, 100
Mauritius 47
May 4th Movement 64
mega-city 25, 181
Meiji Restoration 18, 52, 53, 54, 101, 144
Mengchia 54, 103
Mexico 26
Mexico City 26
Ming dynasty 51, 54, 56, 57, 133
Minneapolis 126
modern city 160, 163, 169
modernism 17, 33, 78
modernization 8, 9
    cumulative processes, 45–6, 163
    markets 12
    resistance to 62–5
    scenarios 43–4
    standard interpretations 11–18, 29–30
    technological advancements 12, 17
    trajectories 8, 18–24, 35
    two distinct forms 12
    urbanization 13–16
    universalizing tendencies 33
    western practices 12, 44, 159–63
monocentric model of the city 14
Mori, Minoru 100
Municipal Council of Shanghai 51, 58

Namdaemun market 108
Nanjing 56, 61, 73, 87, 134, 173
Nanjing Road 134, 135, *36*
Nanshi 50
Nanyang 47
Nathan Road 130
Nationalists 56, 61, 63, 64, 141, 187
New Life Movement 64
New Territories 58, 75, 81
New York 11, 25, 26, 34, 42, 130, 149, 162
Netherlands 29
New Zealand 18
Nihonbashi 134
Nishizawa, Ryue 152

Oil Embargo of 1973 160
Olmsted, Frederick Law 148
Olympic Games
    (1998) 82
    (2008) 156
Olympic Green 133
oku 150–52
Orange County 182
oranglaut 49
Orchard Road 106, 108, 130, *34*
Organization for Economic Cooperation and
    Development 19–20
Osaka 10, 37

Osaki 84

Padang *5*
Palladianism 47
Palmerston, Lord 49
Paris 11, 25, 26
Paxton, Joseph 148
Peak Residence Ordinance 58
Pearl River 49
Pei, I. M., 35, 140, 146, *41*
Pelli, Cesar 97
Penang Island 47
pencil buildings 33, 95, *18*, 132
People's Action Party 30, 65, 68
Perry, Commodore 52
Philadelphia 35
Phillipines 9
Piano, Renzo 100, 139
Pinjiang 87, 88
planning 37, 40
    'bottom-up' capacity 41, 93
    early ordinances 57, 58
    land use zoning 61, 78, 191
    legislation 76–7
    master planning 40
    spatial aspects 78–90
    'top-down' procedures 37, 68–78
pluralism 30, 31
polycentric model of the city 14, 160
population 7
    concentrations 25
    demographic trends 39
    density 7, 26, 38
    urban proportions 15–16, 24–6
Portman, John 140
post-Enlightenment 13, 45
post-Fordism 160–68
postmodern city 92, 160, 161, 163, 168
Pudong 7, 37, 72, 73, 113, *26*, 133, 134, 137
Pudong administrative building *44*
Pudong airport 139
Puxi 50
Pyunchon 82

Qianmen Daijie 112
Qingdao 51
Qing dynasty 49, 55, 56, 57, 87
Queenstown 190

Raffles, Thomas Stamford 47
Rahman, Tunku Abdul 65, 68
Rainbow Town 85
Renmin Park 133, 134
Republican period 56, 58
roji 121–3, *30*, 124, 155
Rome 16
Roppongi 130, *49*
Roppongi Hills 100
Route 128, 162
RTKL 137

Rudolph, Paul 140
Russia 51, 53
Ryōunbaku 58

Saitama Prefecture 61
San Domingo 54
Sanbon 82
sankin kōtai 52, 58
Sanlinyuan 26
Sasaki and Associates 133
Self-Strengthening Movement 31, 55, 64
Seoul, 10, 25, 34, 43, 63, 67, 91, 108, 118, 130, 134, 137, 153, 154, 183, 188
 apartments 33
 density 27
 future prospects 199
 hanok 125–6, 32
 historical beginnings 54–5
 Japanese influence 82
 land adjustment 41, 61
 marketplaces 106–7
 modern development 77, 78, 81–3
 'moon villages' 11, 67
Seven Years War 47
Sewoon Sangga 82
Shaanxi Museum 141
Shanghai 7, 10, 25, 33, 34, 35, 41, 55, 9, 13, 87, 89, 91, 92, 113, 26, 130, 153, 47, 173, 48, 185
 architectural expression 137, 37
 Chinese settlement 51, 58, 60
 environmental issues 29, 43
 foreign concessions 50–51, 58, 60, 63
 future prospects 196, 197
 high-rise building 33, 50
 historical underpinnings 49–51
 lilong 103, 22, 105, 23, 106, 123–4
 modern development 72, 73
 modern prefaces 58, 59
 open spaces 133–5
 pedestrian environments 134, 135, 36
 residential space standards 26
 social stratification 27, 28
Shanghai Grand Theatre 146, 42, 188
Shanghai Museum of Planning 146
Shanghai Science Museum 137
Sha Tin 75, 14, 81
Shenzhen 10, 26, 72
Shibusawa Eiichi, 120
Shibuya 61, 84, 85, 126, 173
shikumen 123
Shilla and Koryo kingdoms 54
Shimpei Gotō 53, 60
Shinbashi 52
Shinjuku 61, 83, 84, 15, 85, 101, 31, 126, 129, 130, 173
Shitamachi 52, 53, 63, 97
siheyuan 56, 103, 105, 113
Silicon Valley 162
Singapore 7, 8, 9, 10, 15, 18, 34, 37, 39, 41, 44, 5, 64, 65, 66, 12, 74, 92, 24, 130, 153, 154, 165, 169, 170, 178, 179, 183, 52, 190, 194
 architectural expression 140

contemporary developments 106–8
 early plan 47
 early planning 61
 Economic Development Board 23–4, 26, 69, 70
 economic factors 19, 21, 22, 28, 40, 42
 environmental sustainability 29
 future prospects 188, 198
 historical underpinnings 47–9
 Housing Development Board 69, 70, 113, 188
 Modern development 68–71
 modern prefaces 57, 60
 National Ideological Commison 31
 neon environments 129–33, 34
 new plans 80
 new towns 79
 public housing 70, 113
 residential space standards 26
 Ring Concept Plan 79, 80
 shophouses 108
 urban population 24
 Urban Redevelopment Authority 70, 89
Singapore Amendment 68
Singapore River 47
Sino-Japanese War 30, 65
Skidmore, Owings and Merrill 35, 4, 136, 137
Smithson, Peter and Allison 82
socio-economic relations 10
 Economic Freedom Index 28
 guanxi 32
 income disparities 27, 28
 oyabun-kobun 32
South-East Asian currency crisis 19
Southern Manchurian Railroad 53
Soviet Union 18, 67, 79, 85, 110, 112, 162, 164, 171
Srivijaya empire 47
St Louis 35
state-owned enterprises 73
Sumida River 52, 59, 101
Sun Yat-sen 64
Sunda Straits 47
Sunshine City 129
Suzhou 87, 88, 89, 17, 92, 25, 173
 Industrial Park 89
 New District 89
Suzhou Creek 50, 133

Tai Po 75, 81
Tiananmen 58, 135, 143, 166
Tianjin 27, 51
Taipei 10, 25, 33, 43, 66, 21, 130, 142, 146, 153, 165, 183
 future prospects 199, 200
 historical underpinnings 54
 Japanese influence 53, 144
 land adjustment 61
 modern prefaces 58
 residential space standards 26
 upward extensions 103, 21
Taipei 101 Building 7
Taiping Rebellion 51
Taishō period 31, 53, 54, 144
Taiwan 9, 18, 23, 39, 44, 55, 165, 166

collective consumption 74
economic factors 19, 20, 21, 28
Japanese influence 53, 74
political regimes 30
urban population 24, 25
Tamshui River 54
Tange, Kenzo 84, 101, 136, 140
Taniguchi, Yoshio 136
Tao Payou 79
Ta-tao-chen 54, 103
Team 10 82
Temasek 47, 49
Temengong 47, 49
Tezuka, Takaharu 152
Thailand 9
Tin Shui Wai 81
Tokyo 7, 8, 10, 25, *3*, 33, 34, 41, 42, 43, *7*, *15*, 53, 90, 92, 95,
    19, *31*, 119, 121, 152, 154, 166, 170, 173, *49*, 178, 179,
    183, 185, 194
    allied bombing 65
    architectural expression 136, *45*, 188
    contemporary labyrinths 126–9
    declining competitiveness 77
    density 27
    districts 97–103, *29*
    future prospects 197, 198
    historical underpinnings 52, 53
    housing 67
    modern plans 83–5
    modern prefaces 58, 59, 60
    new plans 85
    pedestrian environments 135
    planning legislation 41, 76–7, 84–5
    post-war recovery 76
    residential space standards 26
    roji 121–3, *30*
Tokyo Bay 52, 59
Tokyo Bay Plan 84
Tokyo Metropolitan Government 76–7, 85, 101, *31*
Tokugawa 52
    Shogun Ieyasu 52
    Shogunate 58, 97, 100
transportation 13, 14, *1*, 34, 35, 37, 97
Treaty of Nanjing 49, 50
Treaty of Portsmouth 53
Treaty of Shimonoseki 30, 53
Treaty of Vienna 47
Tsuen Wan 75
Tsukamoto, Yoshiharu 152
Tsukuba Campus City 83
Tuen Mun 75
Turkey 16

United Malay National Organization 65
United Nations 79
United States 13, 15, 18, 19, 21, 25, 27, 28, 29, 38, 60, 61,
    64, 66, 78, 91, 92, 145, 154, 155, 159, 161, 176, 181,
    185, 187
urban architectural expression 34–7, 136–53
    haphazard 34
    hybridization 146

monumentality 137
symbols of progress 34, 140
universalism and localism 38, 136, 141–3
western influence 144–5
urban qualities of life 24, 25–32
urban spatial transformations, 7, 170, 171–195
    centralization and decentralization, 181–5
    deterritorialization and reterritorialization, 171–3, *47*
    different expressive outcomes 187–91
    differences in degree and kind 191–5
    different territorial outcomes 174–6
    effects of rates of change 176–81

Vietnam 9, 55

Waigaoqiao Free Trade Zone 72, 73
Wall Street 162
Wanchai 95
Wangfujing Street 135
Waters, Thomas 58, 99
Wenzhou 88, 113
West Kowloon Cultural District 134, 136
West Railway Station 141, *40*
Wood, Benjamin 35, 106, *23*
Woodlands 79
World Trade Organization 21
World War II 20, 21, 23, 35, 38, 57, 65, 66, 67, 187
World Wide Web 161
Wu Liangyong 35, 141, *39*
Wuchang 87
Wuhan *10*, *16*, 86–7, 135

Xi'an 141
Xintiandi 106, *23*

Yamamoto, Riken 139
Yamanote 52, 53, 85
Yan'an central green space 133, 134
Yano, Ysuneta 120
Yi Songye, General 54
Yishun 79
Yoido Island 82
Yokohama 52, 59
Yokohama Passenger Ferry Terminal 140
Yongle, Emperor 57
Yongdongpo 82
Yoshida Deal 87
Yuan dynasty 56, 124
Yuan Liang 61, 64
Yuen Long 81

zaibatsu 23, 59, 75, 152
Zhangjiagang 73
Zhang Jinqiu 141
Zhang Xisheng 89
Zhang Yonghe 141
Zheng Shiling 134
Zhu Jialu 141, *40*
Zhu Qiqian 56, 58
Zhu Rongji 193